Undergraduate Topics in Computer Science

Undergraduate Topics in Computer Science (UTiCS) delivers high-quality instructional content for undergraduates studying in all areas of computing and information science. From core foundational and theoretical material to final-year topics and applications, UTiCS books take a fresh, concise, and modern approach and are ideal for self-study or for a one- or two-semester course. The texts are all authored by established experts in their fields, reviewed by an international advisory board, and contain numerous examples and problems. Many include fully worked solutions.

For further volumes:
http://www.springer.com/series/7592

Thomas B. Moeslund

Introduction to Video and Image Processing

Building Real Systems and Applications

 Springer

Thomas B. Moeslund
Visual Analysis of People Laboratory
Department of Architecture, Design, and
    Media Technology
Aalborg University
Aalborg
Denmark

ISSN 1863-7310   Undergraduate Topics in Computer Science
ISBN 978-1-4471-2502-0   e-ISBN 978-1-4471-2503-7
DOI 10.1007/978-1-4471-2503-7
Springer London Dordrecht Heidelberg New York

British Library Cataloguing in Publication Data
A catalogue record for this book is available from the British Library

Library of Congress Control Number: 2012930996

Springer is part of Springer Science+Business Media (www.springer.com)

Preface

One of the first times I ever encountered video and image processing was in a semester project at my fourth year of studying. The aim of the project was to design a system that automatically located the center and size of mushrooms in an image. Given this information a robot should pick the mushrooms. I was intrigued by the notion of a "seeing computer". Little did I know that this encounter would shape most parts (so far) of my professional life.

I decided to study video and image processing in depth and signed up for a master's program focusing on these topics. I soon realized that I had made a good choice, but was puzzled by the fact that the wonders of digital video and image processing often were presented in a strict mathematical manner. While this is fine for hardcore engineers (including me) and computer scientists, it makes video and image processing unnecessarily difficult for others. I really felt this was a pity and decided to do something about it—that was 15 years ago.

In this book the concepts and methods are described in a less mathematical manner and the language is in general casual. In order to assist the reader with the math that *is* used in the book Appendix B is included. In this regards this textbook is self-contained. Some of the key algorithms are exemplified in C-code. Please note that the code is neither optimal nor complete and merely serves as an additional input for comprehending the algorithms.

Another aspect that puzzled me as a student was that the textbooks were all about image processing, while we constructed systems that worked with video. Many of the methods described for image processing can obviously also be applied to video data. But video data add the temporal dimension, which is often the key to success in systems processing video. This book therefore aims at not only introducing image processing but also video processing. Moreover, the last two chapters of the book describe the process of designing and implementing real systems processing video data. On the website for the book you can find detailed descriptions of other practical systems processing video: http://www.vip.aau.dk.

I have tried to make the book as concise as possible. This has forced me to leave out details and topics that might be of interest to some readers. As a compromise each chapter is ended by a "Further Information" section wherein pointers to additional concepts, methods and details are given.

For Instructors   Each chapter is ended by a number of exercises. The first exercise after each chapter aims at assessing to what degree the students have understood the main concepts. If possible, it is recommended that these exercises are discussed within small groups. The following exercises have a more practical focus where concrete problems need to be solved using the different methods/algorithms presented in the associated chapters. Lastly one or more so-called additional exercises are present. These aim at topics not discussed directly in the chapters. The idea behind these exercises is that they can serve as self-studies where each student (or a small group of students) finds the solution by investigating other sources. They could then present their findings for other students.

Besides the exercises listed in the book I strongly recommend to combine those with examples and exercises where real images/videos are processed. Personally I start with ImageJ for image processing and EyesWeb for video processing. The main motivation for using these programs is that they are easy to learn and hence the students can focus on the video and image processing as opposed to a specific programming language, when solving the exercises. However, when it comes to building real systems I recommend using OpenCV or openFrameworks (EyesWeb or similar can of course also be used to build systems, but they do not generalize as well). To this end students of course need to have a course on procedural programming before or in parallel with the image processing course. To make the switch from ImageJ/Eyesweb to a more low-level environment like OpenCV, I normally ask each student to do an assignment where they write a program that can capture an image, make some image processing and display the result. When the student can do this he has a framework for implementing "all" other image processing methods. The time allocated for this assignment of course depends on the programming experiences of the students.

Acknowledgement   The book was written primarily at weekends and late nights, and I thank my family for being understanding and supporting during that time! I would also like to thank the following people: Hans Ebert and Volker Krüger for initial discussions on the "book project". Moritz Störring for providing Fig. 2.3. Rasmus R. Paulsen for providing Figs. 2.22(a) and 4.5. Rikke Gade for providing Fig. 2.22(b). Tobias Thyrrestrup for providing Fig. 2.22(c). David Meredith, Rasmus R. Paulsen, Lars Reng and Kamal Nasrollahi for insightful editorial comments, and finally a special thanks to Lars Knudsen and Andreas Møgelmose, who provided valuable assistance by creating many of the illustrations used throughout the book.

Enjoy!

Viborg, Denmark   Thomas B. Moeslund

Contents

Introduction

If you look at the image in Fig. 1.1 you can see three children. The two oldest children look content with life, while the youngest child looks a bit puzzled. We can detail this description further using adjectives, but we will never *ever* be able to present a textual description, which encapsulates all the details in the image. This fact is normally referred to as "*a picture is worth a thousand words*".

So, our eyes and our brain are capable of extracting detailed information far beyond what can be described in text, and it is this ability we want to replicate in the "seeing computer". To this end a camera replaces the eyes and the (video and image) processing software replaces the human brain. The purpose of this book is to present the basics within these two topics; cameras and video/image processing.

Cameras have been around for many years and were initially developed with the purpose of "freezing" a part of the world, for example to be used in newspapers. For a long time cameras were analog, meaning that the video and images were captured on film. As digital technology matured, the possibility of digital video and images arose, and video and image processing became relevant and necessary sciences.

Fig. 1.1 An image containing three children

T.B. Moeslund, *Introduction to Video and Image Processing*,
Undergraduate Topics in Computer Science,
DOI 10.1007/978-1-4471-2503-7_1, © Springer-Verlag London Limited 2012

Some of the first applications of digital video and image processing were to improve the quality of the captured images, but as the power of computers grew, so did the number of applications where video and image processing could make a difference. Today, video and image processing are used in many diverse applications, such as astronomy (to enhance the quality), medicine (to measure and understand some parameters of the human body, e.g., blood flow in fractured veins), image compression (to reduce the memory requirement when storing an image), sports (to capture the motion of an athlete in order to understand and improve the performance), rehabilitation (to assess the locomotion abilities), motion pictures (to capture actors' motion in order to produce special effects based on graphics), surveillance (detect and track individuals and vehicles), production industries (to assess the quality of products), robot control (to detect objects and their pose so a robot can pick them up), TV productions (mixing graphics and live video, e.g., weather forecast), biometrics (to measure some unique parameters of a person), photo editing (improving the quality or adding effects to photographs), etc.

Many of these applications rely on the same video and image processing methods, and it is these basic methods which are the focus of this book.

1.1   The Different Flavors of Video and Image Processing

The different video and image processing methods are often grouped into the categories listed below. There is no unique definition of the different categories and to make matters worse they also overlap significantly. Here is one set of definitions:

Video and Image Compression This is probably the most well defined category and contains the group of methods used for compressing video and image data.

Image Manipulation This category covers methods used to edit an image. For example, when rotating or scaling an image, but also when improving the quality by for example changing the contrast.

Image Processing Image processing originates from the more general field of *signal processing* and covers methods used to *segment* the object of interest. Segmentation here refers to methods which in some way enhance the object while suppressing the rest of the image (for example the edges in an image).

Video Processing Video processing covers most of the image processing methods, but also includes methods where the temporal nature of video data is exploited.

Image Analysis Here the goal is to analyze the image with the purpose of first finding objects of interest and then extracting some parameters of these objects. For example, finding an object's position and size.

Machine Vision When applying video processing, image processing or image analysis in production industries it is normally referred to as *machine vision* or simply *vision*.

Computer Vision Humans have *human vision* and similarly a computer has *computer vision*. When talking about computer vision we normally mean advanced algorithms similar to those a human can perform, e.g., face recognition. Normally computer vision also covers all methods where more than one camera is applied.

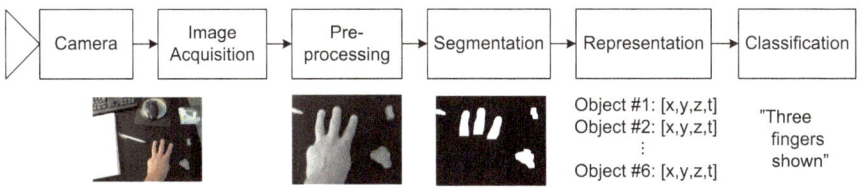

Fig. 1.2 The block diagram provides a general framework for many systems working with video and images

Even though this book is titled: "*Video and Image Processing*" it also covers basic methods from *Image Manipulation* and *Image Analysis* in order to provide the reader with a solid foundation for understanding and working with images and video.

1.2   General Framework

No matter which category you are working within (except for Video and Image Compression) you can very often apply the framework illustrated in Fig. 1.2. Sometimes not all blocks are included in a particular system, but the framework nevertheless provides a relevant guideline.

Underneath each block in the figure we have illustrated a typical output. The particular outputs are from a gesture-based human–computer-interface system that counts the number of fingers a user is showing in front of the camera.

Below we briefly describe the purpose of the different blocks:

Image Acquisition In this block everything to do with the camera and setup of your system is covered, e.g., camera type, camera settings, optics, and light sources.

Pre-processing This block does something to your image before the actual processing commences, e.g., convert the image from color to gray-scale or crop the most interesting part of the image (as seen in Fig. 1.2).

Segmentation This is where the information of interest is extracted from the image or video data. Often this block is the "heart" of a system. In the example in the figure the information is the fingers. The image below the segmentation block shows that the fingers (together with some noise) have been segmented (indicated by white objects).

Representation In this block the objects extracted in the segmentation block are represented in a concise manner, e.g., using a few representative numbers as illustrated in the figure.

Classification Finally this block examines the information produced by the previous block and classifies each object as being an object of interest or not. In the example in the figure this block determines that three finger objects are present and hence output this.

It should be noted that the different blocks might not be as clear-cut defined in reality as the figure suggests. Onc designer might place a particular method in one block while another designer will place the same method in the previous or following block. Nevertheless the framework *is* an excellent starting point for any video and image processing system.

The last two blocks are sometimes replaced by one block called *BLOB Analysis*. This is especially done when the output of the segmentation block is a black and white image as is the case in the figure. In this book we follow this idea and have therefore merged the descriptions of these two blocks into one—BLOB Analysis.

In Table 1.1 a layout of the different chapters in the book is listed together with a short overview of the contents. Please note that in Chaps. 12 and 13 the design and implementation of two systems are described. These are both based on the overall framework in Fig. 1.2 and the reader is encouraged to browse through these chapters before reading the rest of the book.

1.3   The Chapters in This Book

Table 1.1 The organization and topics of the different chapters in this book

#	Title	Topics
2	Image Acquisition	This chapter describes what light is and how a camera can capture the light and convert it into an image.
3	Color Images	This chapter describes what color images are and how they can be represented.
4	Point Processing	This chapter presents some of the basic image manipulation methods for understanding and improving the quality of an image. Moreover the chapter presents one of the basic segmentation algorithms.
5	Neighborhood Processing	This chapter presents, together with the next chapter, the basic image processing methods, i.e., how to segment or enhance certain features in an image.
6	Morphology	Similar to above, but focuses on one particular group of methods.
7	BLOB Analysis	This chapter concerns image analysis, i.e., how to detect, describe, and classify objects in an image.
8	Segmentation in Video	While most methods within image processing also apply to video, this chapter presents a particularly useful method for segmenting objects in video data.
9	Tracking	This chapter is concerned with how to following objects from image to image.
10	Geometric Transformation	This chapter deals with another aspect of image manipulation, namely how to change the geometry within an image, e.g., rotation.
11	Visual Effects	This chapters shows how video and image processing can be used to create visual effects.
12 + 13	Application Examples	In these chapters concrete examples of video processing systems are presented. The purpose of these chapters is twofold. Firstly to put some of the presented methods into a context and secondly to provide inspiration for what video and image processing can be used for.

1.4   Exercises

Exercise 1: Find additional application examples where processing of digital video and/or images is used.

Image Acquisition

Before any video or image processing can commence an image must be captured by a camera and converted into a manageable entity. This is the process known as *image acquisition*. The image acquisition process consists of three steps; *energy* reflected from the object of interest, an *optical system* which focuses the energy and finally a *sensor* which measures the amount of energy. In Fig. 2.1 the three steps are shown for the case of an ordinary camera with the sun as the energy source. In this chapter each of these three steps are described in more detail.

2.1 Energy

In order to capture an image a camera requires some sort of measurable energy. The energy of interest in this context is light or more generally *electromagnetic waves*. An electromagnetic (EM) wave can be described as massless entity, a *photon*, whose electric and magnetic fields vary sinusoidally, hence the name wave. The photon belongs to the group of fundamental particles and can be described in three different ways:

- A photon can be described by its energy E, which is measured in electronvolts [eV]
- A photon can be described by its frequency f, which is measured in Hertz [Hz]. A frequency is the number of cycles or wave-tops in one second
- A photon can be described by its wavelength λ, which is measured in meters [m]. A wavelength is the distance between two wave-tops

The three different notations are connected through the speed of light c and Planck's constant h:

$$\lambda = \frac{c}{f}, \qquad E = h \cdot f \quad \Rightarrow \quad E = \frac{h \cdot c}{\lambda} \tag{2.1}$$

An EM wave can have different wavelengths (or different energy levels or different frequencies). When we talk about all possible wavelengths we denote this as the *EM spectrum*, see Fig. 2.2.

T.B. Moeslund, *Introduction to Video and Image Processing*,
Undergraduate Topics in Computer Science,
DOI 10.1007/978-1-4471-2503-7_2, © Springer-Verlag London Limited 2012

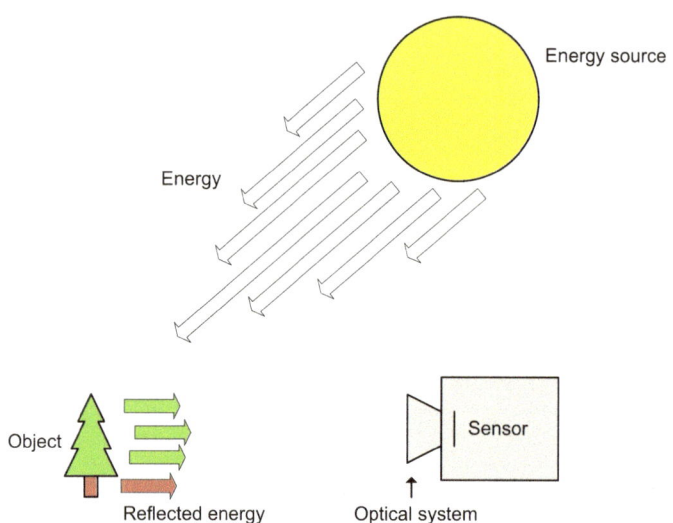

Fig. 2.1 Overview of the typical image acquisition process, with the sun as light source, a tree as object and a digital camera to capture the image. An analog camera would use a film where the digital camera uses a sensor

In order to make the definitions and equations above more understandable, the EM spectrum is often described using the names of the applications where they are used in practice. For example, when you listen to FM-radio the music is transmitted through the air using EM waves around $100 \cdot 10^6$ Hz, hence this part of the EM spectrum is often denoted "radio". Other well-known applications are also included in the figure.

The range from approximately 400–700 nm (nm = nanometer = 10^{-9}) is denoted the visual spectrum. The EM waves within this range are those your eye (and most cameras) can detect. This means that the light from the sun (or a lamp) in principle is the same as the signal used for transmitting TV, radio or for mobile phones etc. The only difference, in this context, is the fact that the human eye can sense EM waves in this range and not the waves used for e.g., radio. Or in other words, if our eyes were sensitive to EM waves with a frequency around $2 \cdot 10^9$ Hz, then your mobile phone would work as a flash light, and big antennas would be perceived as "small suns". Evolution has (of course) not made the human eye sensitive to such frequencies but rather to the frequencies of the waves coming from the sun, hence visible light.

2.1.1   Illumination

To capture an image we need some kind of energy source to illuminate the scene. In Fig. 2.1 the sun acts as the energy source. Most often we apply visual light, but other frequencies can also be applied, see Sect. 2.5.

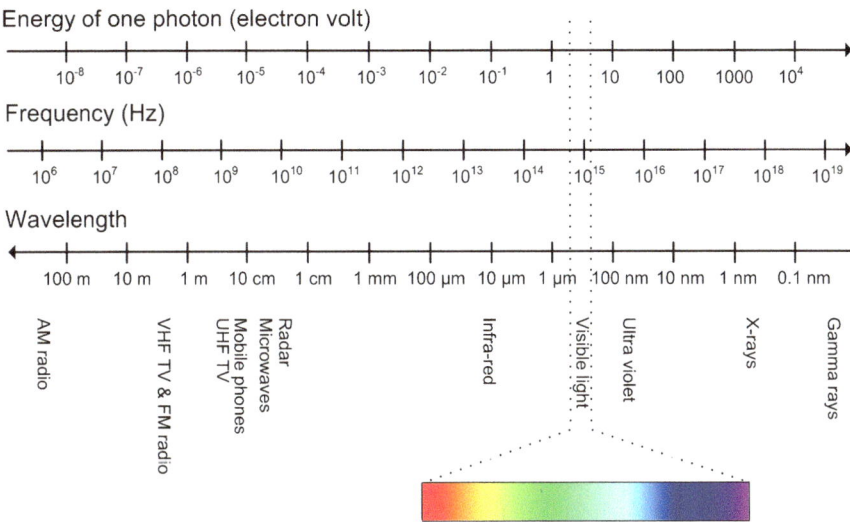

Fig. 2.2 A large part of the electromagnetic spectrum showing the energy of one photon, the frequency, wavelength and typical applications of the different areas of the spectrum

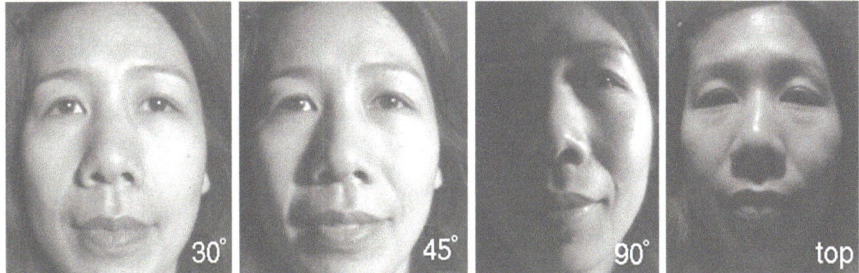

Fig. 2.3 The effect of illuminating a face from four different directions

If you are processing images captured by others there is nothing much to do about the illumination (although a few methods will be presented in later chapters) which was probably the sun and/or some artificial lighting. When you, however, are in charge of the capturing process yourselves, it is of great importance to carefully think about how the scene should be lit. In fact, for the field of Machine Vision it is a rule-of-thumb that illumination is 2/3 of the entire system design and software only 1/3. To stress this point have a look at Fig. 2.3. The figure shows four images of the same person facing the camera. The only difference between the four images is the direction of the light source (a lamp) when the images were captured!

Another issue regarding the direction of the illumination is that care must be taken when pointing the illumination directly toward the camera. The reason being that this might result in too bright an image or a nonuniform illumination, e.g., a bright circle in the image. If, however, the outline of the object is the only infor-

Fig. 2.4 Backlighting. The light source is behind the object of interest, which makes the object stand out as a black silhouette. Note that the details inside the object are lost

mation of interest, then this way of illumination—denoted *backlighting*—can be an optimal solution, see Fig. 2.4. Even when the illumination is not directed toward the camera overly bright spots in the image might still occur. These are known as *highlights* and are often a result of a shiny object surface, which reflects most of the illumination (similar to the effect of a mirror). A solution to such problems is often to use some kind of diffuse illumination either in the form of a high number of less-powerful light sources or by illuminating a rough surface which then reflects the light (randomly) toward the object.

Even though this text is about visual light as the energy form, it should be mentioned that infrared illumination is sometimes useful. For example, when tracking the movements of human body parts, e.g. for use in animations in motion pictures, infrared illumination is often applied. The idea is to add infrared reflecting markers to the human body parts, e.g., in the form of small balls. When the scene is illuminated by infrared light, these markers will stand out and can therefore easily be detected by image processing. A practical example of using infrared illumination is given in Chap. 12.

2.2   The Optical System

After having illuminated the object of interest, the light reflected from the object now has to be captured by the camera. If a material sensitive to the reflected light is placed close to the object, an image of the object will be captured. However, as illustrated in Fig. 2.5, light from different points on the object will mix—resulting in a useless image. To make matters worse, light from the surroundings will also be captured resulting in even worse results. The solution is, as illustrated in the figure, to place some kind of barrier between the object of interest and the sensing material. Note that the consequence is that the image is upside-down. The hardware and software used to capture the image normally rearranges the image so that you never notice this.

The concept of a barrier is a sound idea, but results in too little light entering the sensor. To handle this situation the hole is replaced by an *optical system*. This section describes the basics behind such an optical system. To put it into perspective, the famous space-telescope—the Hubble telescope—basically operates like a camera, i.e., an optical system directs the incoming energy toward a sensor. Imagine how many man-hours were used to design and implement the Hubble telescope. And still, NASA had to send astronauts into space in order to fix the optical system due

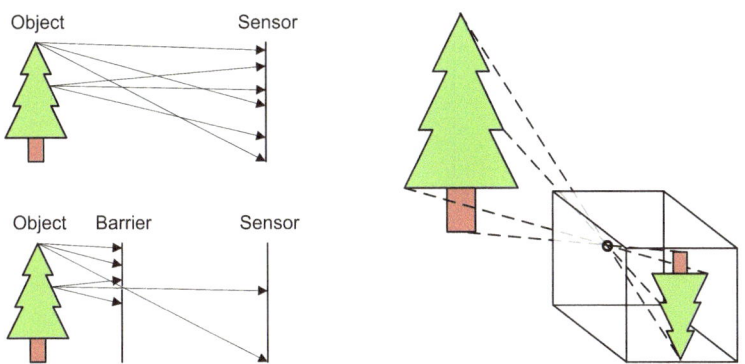

Fig. 2.5 Before introducing a barrier, the rays of light from different points on the tree hit multiple points on the sensor and in some cases even the same points. Introducing a barrier with a small hole significantly reduces these problems

to an incorrect design. Building optical systems is indeed a complex science! We shall not dwell on all the fine details and the following is therefore not accurate to the last micro-meter, but the description will suffice and be correct for most usages.

2.2.1 The Lens

One of the main ingredients in the optical system is the lens. A lens is basically a piece of glass which focuses the incoming light onto the sensor, as illustrated in Fig. 2.6. A high number of light rays with slightly different incident angles collide with each point on the object's surface and some of these are reflected toward the optics. In the figure, three light rays are illustrated for two different points. All three rays for a particular point intersect in a point to the right of the lens. Focusing such rays is exactly the purpose of the lens. This means that an image of the object is formed to the right of the lens and it is this image the camera captures by placing a sensor at exactly this position. Note that parallel rays intersect in a point, F, denoted the *Focal Point*. The distance from the center of the lens, the *optical center O*, to the plane where all parallel rays intersect is denoted the *Focal Length f*. The line on which O and F lie is *the optical axis*.

Let us define the distance from the object to the lens as, g, and the distance from the lens to where the rays intersect as, b. It can then be shown via similar triangles, see Appendix B, that

$$\frac{1}{g} + \frac{1}{b} = \frac{1}{f} \tag{2.2}$$

f and b are typically in the range [1 mm, 100 mm]. This means that when the object is a few meters away from the camera (lens), then $\frac{1}{g}$ has virtually no effect on the equation, i.e., $b = f$. What this tells us is that the image inside the camera is formed

Fig. 2.6 The figure shows how the rays from an object, here a light bulb, are focused via the lens. The real light bulb is to the *left* and the image formed by the lens is to the *right*

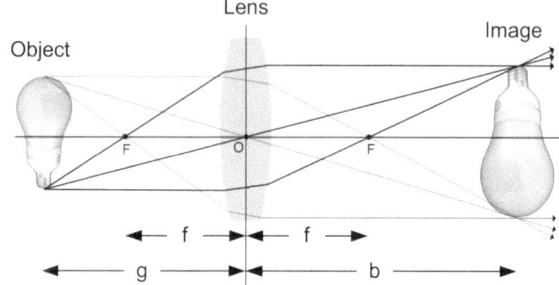

at a distance very close to the focal point. Equation 2.2 is also called the *thin lens equation*.

Another interesting aspect of the lens is that the size of the object in the image, B, increases as f increased. This is known as *optical zoom*. In practice f is changed by rearranging the optics, e.g., the distance between one or more lenses inside the optical system.[1] In Fig. 2.7 we show how optical zoom is achieved by changing the focal length. When looking at Fig. 2.7 it can be shown via similar triangles that

$$\frac{b}{B} = \frac{g}{G} \tag{2.3}$$

where G is the real height of the object. This can for example be used to compute how much a physical object will fill on the imaging censor chip, when the camera is placed at a given distance away from the object.

Let us assume that we do not have a zoom-lens, i.e., f is constant. When we change the distance from the object to the camera (lens), g, Eq. 2.2 shows us that b should also be increased, meaning that the sensor has to be moved slightly further away from the lens since the image will be formed there. In Fig. 2.8 the effect of not changing b is shown. Such an image is said to be *out of focus*. So when you adjust focus on your camera you are in fact changing b until the sensor is located at the position where the image is formed.

The reason for an *unfocused* image is illustrated in Fig. 2.9. The sensor consists of pixels, as will be described in the next section, and each pixel has a certain size. As long as the rays from one point stay inside one particular pixel, this pixel will be focused. If rays from other points also intersect the pixel in question, then the pixel will receive light from more points and the resulting pixel value will be a mixture of light from different points, i.e., it is unfocused.

Referring to Fig. 2.9 an object can be moved a distance of g_l further away from the lens or a distance of g_r closer to the lens and remain in focus. The sum of g_l and g_r defines the total range an object can be moved while remaining in focus. This range is denoted as the *depth-of-field*.

---

[1]Optical zoom should not be confused with digital zoom, which is done through software.

Fig. 2.7 Different focal
lengths results in optical
zoom

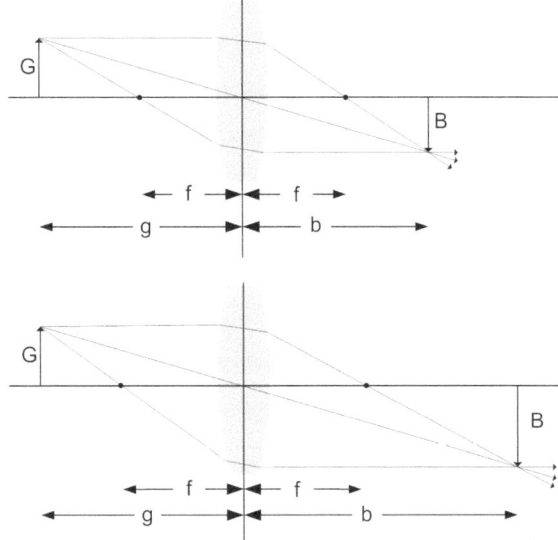

Fig. 2.8 A focused image
(*left*) and an unfocused image
(*right*). The difference
between the two images is
different values of *b*

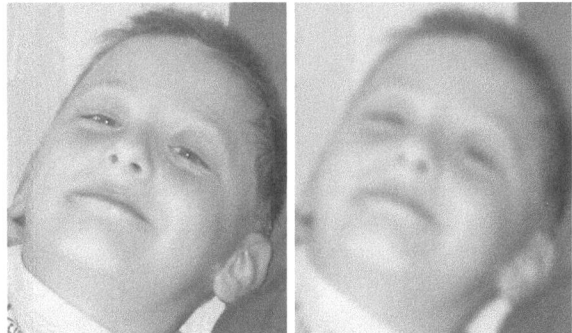

A smaller depth-of-field can be achieved by increasing the focal length. However, this has the consequence that the area of the world observable to the camera is reduced. The observable area is expressed by the angle V in Fig. 2.10 and denoted the *field-of-view* of the camera. The field-of-view depends, besides the focal length, also on the physical size of the image sensor. Often the sensor is rectangular rather than square and from this follows that a camera has a field-of-view in both the horizontal and vertical direction denoted FOV_x and FOV_y, respectively. Based on right-angled triangles, see Appendix B, these are calculated as

$$FOV_x = 2 \cdot \tan^{-1} \left(\frac{\text{width of sensor}/2}{f} \right)$$
$$FOV_y = 2 \cdot \tan^{-1} \left(\frac{\text{height of sensor}/2}{f} \right) \tag{2.4}$$

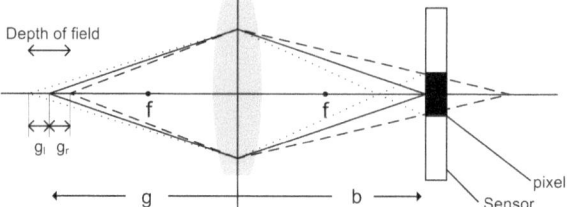

Fig. 2.9 Depth-of-field. The *solid lines* illustrate two light rays from an object (a point) on the optical axis and their paths through the lens and to the sensor where they intersect within the same pixel (illustrated as a *black rectangle*). The *dashed* and *dotted lines* illustrate light rays from two other objects (points) on the optical axis. These objects are characterized by being the most extreme locations where the light rays still enter the same pixel

Fig. 2.10 The field-of-view of two cameras with different focal lengths. The field-of-view is an angle, V, which represents the part of the world observable to the camera. As the focal length increases so does the distance from the lens to the sensor. This in turn results in a smaller field-of-view. Note that both a horizontal field-of-view and a vertical field-of-view exist. If the sensor has equal height and width these two fields-of-view are the same, otherwise they are different

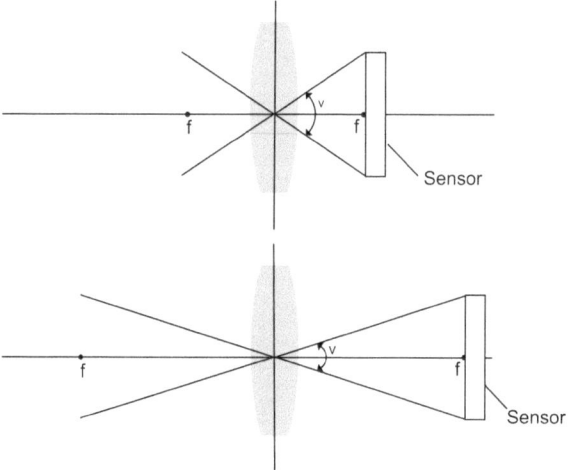

where the focal length, f, and width and height are measured in mm. So, if we have a physical sensor with width $= 14$ mm, height $= 10$ mm and a focal length $= 5$ mm, then the fields-of-view will be

$$\text{FOV}_x = 2 \cdot \tan^{-1}\left(\frac{7}{5}\right) = 108.9°, \qquad \text{FOV}_y = 2 \cdot \tan^{-1}(1) = 90° \qquad (2.5)$$

Another parameter influencing the depth-of-field is the *aperture*. The aperture corresponds to the human iris, which controls the amount of light entering the human eye. Similarly, the aperture is a flat circular object with a hole in the center with adjustable radius. The aperture is located in front of the lens and used to control the amount of incoming light. In the extreme case, the aperture only allows rays through the optical center, resulting in an infinite depth-of-field. The downside is that the more light blocked by the aperture, the lower *shutter* speed (explained below) is required in order to ensure enough light to create an image. From this it follows that objects in motion can result in blurry images.

Fig. 2.11 Three different camera settings resulting in three different depth-of-fields

To sum up, the following interconnected issues must be considered: distance to object, motion of object, zoom, focus, depth-of-field, focal length, shutter, aperture, and sensor. In Figs. 2.11 and 2.12 some of these issues are illustrated. With this knowledge you might be able to appreciate why a professional photographer can capture better images than you can!

2.3   The Image Sensor

The light reflected from the object of interest is focused by some optics and now needs to be recorded by the camera. For this purpose an image sensor is used. An image sensor consists of a 2D array of cells as seen in Fig. 2.13. Each of these cells is denoted a *pixel* and is capable of measuring the amount of incident light and convert that into a voltage, which in turn is converted into a digital number.

The more incident light the higher the voltage and the higher the digital number. Before a camera can capture an image, all cells are emptied, meaning that no charge is present. When the camera is to capture an image, light is allowed to enter and charges start accumulating in each cell. After a certain amount of time, known as the *exposure time*, and controlled by the *shutter*, the incident light is shut out again. If the exposure time is too low or too high the result is an underexposed or overexposed image, respectively, see Fig. 2.14.

Many cameras have a built-in intelligent system that tries to ensure the image is not over- or underexposed. This is done by measuring the amount of incoming light and if too low/high correct the image accordingly, either by changing the exposure time or more often by an *automatic gain control*. While the former improves the image by changing the camera settings, the latter is rather a post-processing step. Both can provide more pleasing video for the human eye to watch, but for automatic video analysis you are very often better off disabling such features. This might sound counter intuitive, but since automatic video/image processing is all about manipulating the incoming light, we need to understand and be able to foresee incoming light in different situations and this can be hard if the camera interferes beyond our control and understanding. This might be easier understood after reading the next chapter. The point is that when choosing a camera you need to remember to check if the automatic gain control is mandatory or if it can be disabled. Go for a camera where it can be disabled. It should of course be added that if you capture video

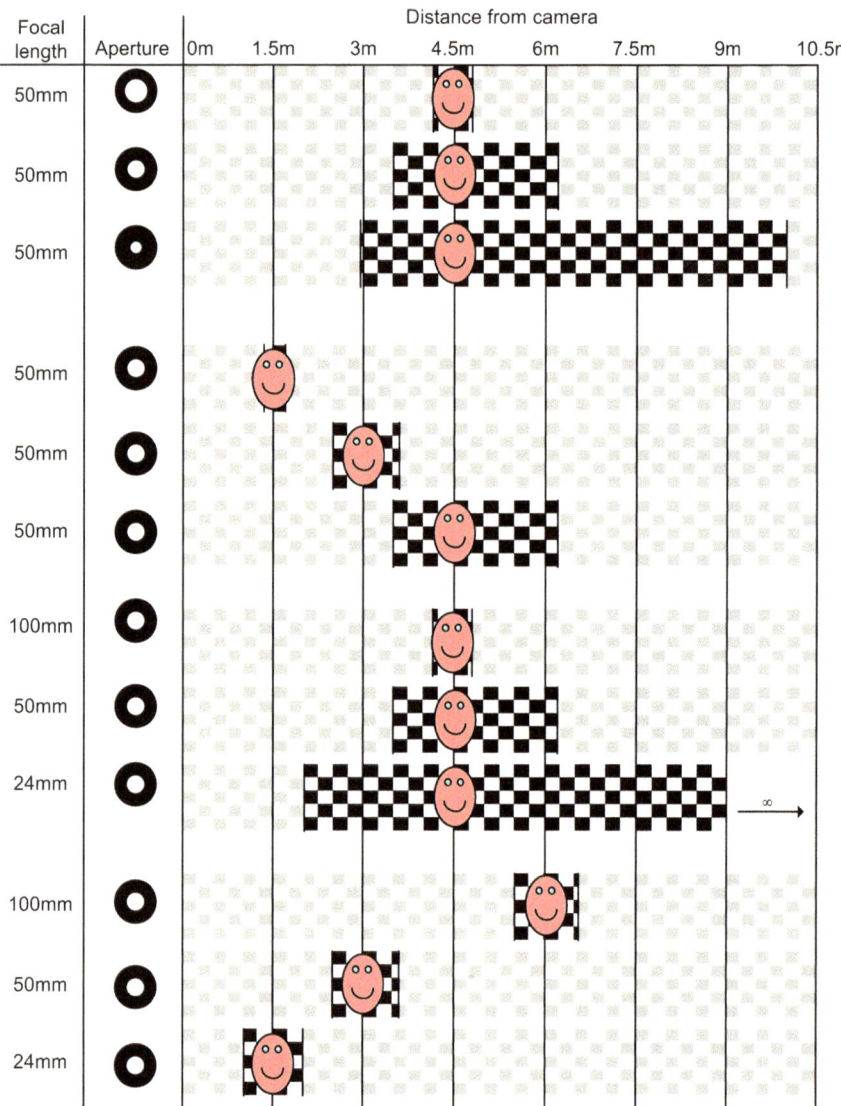

Fig. 2.12 Examples of how different settings for focal length, aperture and distance to object result in different depth-of-fields. For a given combination of the three settings the optics are focused so that the object (person) is in focus. The focused checkers then represent the depth-of-field for that particular setting, i.e., the range in which the object will be in focus. The figure is based on a Canon 400D

in situations where the amount of light can change significantly, then you *have* to enable the camera's automatic settings in order to obtain a useable image.

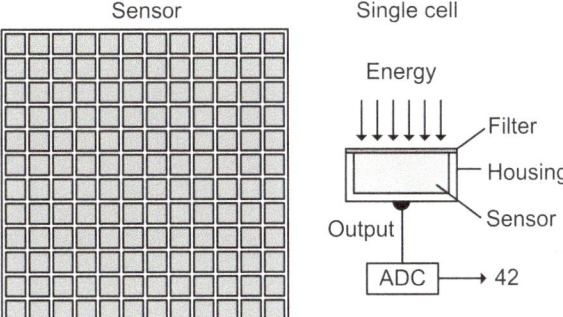

Fig. 2.13 The sensor consists of an array of interconnected cells. Each cell consists of a housing which holds a filter, a sensor and an output. The filter controls which type of energy is allowed to enter the sensor. The sensor measures the amount of energy as a voltage, which is converted into a digital number through an analog-to-digital converter (ADC)

Fig. 2.14 The input image was taken with the correct amount of exposure. The over- and underexposed images are too bright and too dark, respectively, which makes it hard to see details in them. If the object or camera is moved during the exposure time, it produces motion blur as demonstrated in the last image

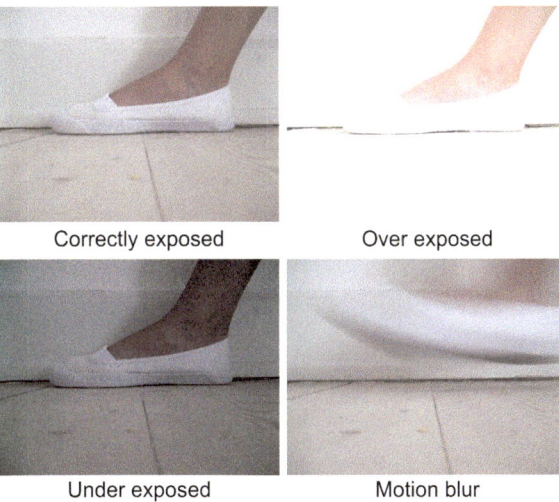

Another aspect related to the exposure time is when the object of interest is in motion. Here the exposure time in general needs to be low in order to avoid *motion blur*, where light from a certain point on the object will be spread out over more cells, see Fig. 2.14.

The accumulated charges are converted into digital form using an *analog-to-digital converter*. This process takes the continuous world outside the camera and converts it into a digital representation, which is required when stored in the computer. Or in other words, this is where the image becomes digital. To fully comprehend the difference, have a look at Fig. 2.15.

To the left we see where the incident light hits the different cells and how many times (the more times the brighter the value). This results in the shape of the object and its intensity. Let us first consider the shape of the object. A cell is sensitive to

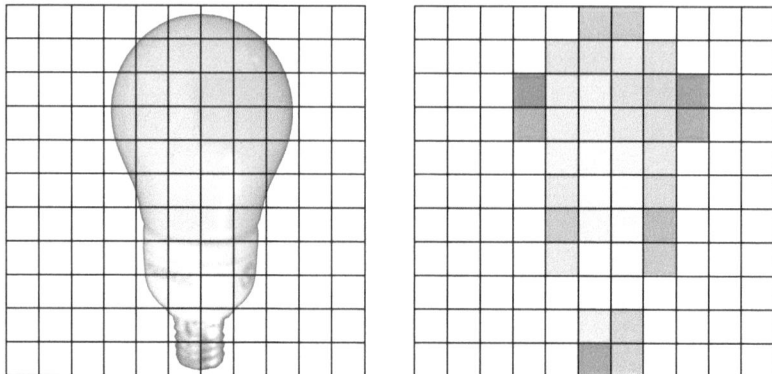

Fig. 2.15 To the *left* the amount of light which hits each cell is shown. To the *right* the resulting image of the measured light is shown

256 x 256   64 x 64   16 x 16

Fig. 2.16 The effect of spatial resolution. The spatial resolution is from *left* to *right*: 256 × 256, 64 × 64, and 16 × 16

incident light hitting the cell, but not sensitive to where exactly the light hits the cell. So if the shape should be preserved, the size of the cells should be infinitely small. From this it follows that the image will be infinitively large in both the x- and y-direction. This is not tractable and therefore a cell, of course, has a finite size. This leads to loss of data/precision and this process is termed *spatial quantization*. The effect is the blocky shape of the object in the figure to the right. The number of pixels used to represent an image is also called the *spatial resolution* of the image. A high resolution means that a large number of pixels are used, resulting in fine details in the image. A low resolution means that a relatively low number of pixels is used. Sometimes the words fine and coarse resolution are used. The visual effect of the spatial resolution can be seen in Fig. 2.16. Overall we have a trade-off between memory and shape/detail preservation. It is possible to change the resolution of an image by a process called *image-resampling*. This can be used to create a low resolution image from a high resolution image. However, it is normally not possible to create a high resolution image from a low resolution image.

| 256 gray-levels | 16 gray-levels | 4 gray-levels |

Fig. 2.17 The effect of gray-level resolution. The gray-level resolution is from *left* to *right*: 256, 16, and 4 gray levels

A similar situation is present for the representation of the amount of incident light within a cell. The number of photons hitting a cell can be tremendously high requiring an equally high digital number to represent this information. However, since the human eye is not even close to being able to distinguish the exact number of photons, we can quantify the number of photons hitting a cell. Often this quantization results in a representation of one byte (8 bits), since one byte corresponds to the way memory is organized inside a computer (see Appendix A for an introduction to bits and bytes). In the case of 8-bit quantization, a charge of 0 volt will be quantized to 0 and a high charge quantized to 255. Other gray-level quantizations are sometimes used. The effect of changing the gray-level quantization (also called the *gray-level resolution*) can be seen in Fig. 2.17. Down to 16 gray levels the image will frequently still look realistic, but with a clearly visible quantization effect. The gray-level resolution is usually specified in number of bits. While, typical gray-level resolutions are 8-, 10-, and 12-bit corresponding to 256, 1024, and 4096 gray levels, 8-bit images are the most common and are the topic of this text.

In the case of an overexposed image, a number of cells might have charges above the maximum measurable charge. These cells are all quantized to 255. There is no way of knowing just how much incident light entered such a cell and we therefore say that the cell is *saturated*. This situation should be avoided by setting the shutter (and/or aperture), and saturated cells should be handled carefully in any video and image processing system. When a cell is saturated it can affect the neighbor pixels by increasing their charges. This is known as *blooming* and is yet another argument for avoiding saturation.

2.4 The Digital Image

To transform the information from the sensor into an image, each cell content is now converted into a pixel value in the range: [0, 255]. Such a value is interpreted as the amount of light hitting a cell during the exposure time. This is denoted the *intensity* of a pixel. It is visualized as a shade of gray denoted a *gray-scale value* or *gray-level value* ranging from black (0) to white (255), see Fig. 2.18.

Fig. 2.18 The relationship between the intensity values and the different shades of gray

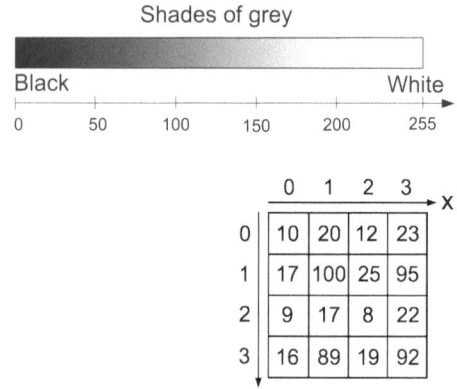

Fig. 2.19 Definition of the image coordinate system

A gray-scale image (as opposed to a color image, which is the topic of Chap. 3) is a 2D array of pixels (corresponding to the 2D array of cells in Fig. 2.13) each having a number between 0 and 255. In this text the coordinate system of the image is defined as illustrated in Fig. 2.19 and the image is represented as $f(x, y)$, where x is the horizontal position of the pixel and y the vertical position. For the small image in Fig. 2.19, $f(0, 0) = 10$, $f(3, 1) = 95$ and $f(2, 3) = 19$.

So whenever you see a gray-scale image you must remember that what you are actually seeing is a 2D array of numbers as illustrated in Fig. 2.20.

2.4.1   The Region of Interest (ROI)

As digital cameras are sold in larger and larger numbers the development within sensor technology has resulted in many new products including larger and larger numbers of pixels within one sensor. This is normally defined as the size of the image that can be captured by a sensor, i.e., the number of pixels in the vertical direction multiplied by the number of pixels in the horizontal direction. Having a large number of pixels can result in high quality images and has made, for example, digital zoom a reality.

When it comes to image processing, a larger image size is not always a benefit. Unless you are interested in tiny details or require very accurate measurements in the image, you are better off using a smaller sized image. The reason being that when we start to process images we have to process each pixel, i.e., perform some math on each pixel. And, due to the large number of pixels, that quickly adds up to quite a large number of mathematical operations, which in turn means a high computational load on your computer.

Say you have an image which is 500×500 pixels. That means that you have $500 \cdot 500 = 250{,}000$ pixels. Now say that you are processing video with 50 images per second. That means that you have to process $50 \cdot 250{,}000 = 12{,}500{,}000$ pixels per second. Say that your algorithm requires 10 mathematical operations per pixel, then in total your computer has to do $10 \cdot 12{,}500{,}000 = 125{,}000{,}000$ operations

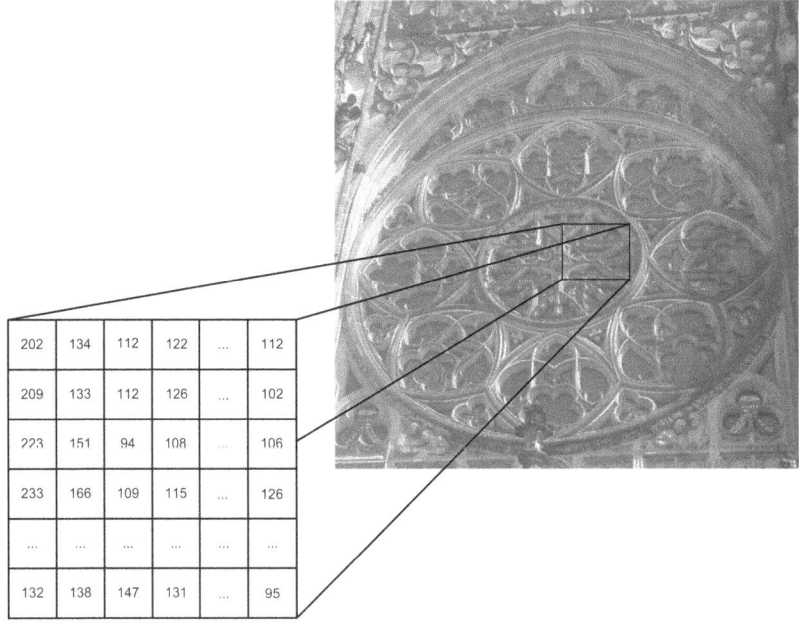

Fig. 2.20 A gray-scale image and part of the image described as a 2D array, where the cells represent pixels and the value in a cell represents the intensity of that pixel

per second. That is quite a number even for today's powerful computers. So when you choose your camera do not make the mistake of thinking that bigger is always better!

Besides picking a camera with a reasonable size you should also consider introducing a *region-of-interest* (ROI). An ROI is simply a region (normally a rectangle) within the image which defines the pixels of interest. Those pixels not included in the region are ignored altogether and less processing is therefore required. An ROI is illustrated in Fig. 2.21.

The ROI can sometimes be defined for a camera, meaning that the camera only captures those pixels within the region, but usually it is something you as a designer define in software. Say that you have put up a camera in your home in order to detect if someone comes through one of the windows while you are on holiday. You could then define an ROI for each window seen in the image and *only* process these pixels. When you start playing around with video and image processing you will soon realize the need for an ROI.

2.5   Further Information

As hinted at in this chapter the camera and especially the optics are complicated and much more information is required to comprehend those in-depth. While a full understanding of the capturing process is mainly based on electrical engineering,

Fig. 2.21 The *white rectangle* defines a region-of-interest (ROI), i.e., this part of the image is the only one being processed

understanding optics requires a study on physics and how light interacts with the physical world. A more easy way into these fields can be via the FCam [1], which is a software platform for understanding and teaching different aspects of a camera.

Another way into these fields is to pick up a book on Machine Vision. Here you will often find a practical approach to understanding the camera and guidelines on picking the right camera and optics. Such books also contain practical information on how to make your image/video analysis easier by introducing special lightning etc.

While this chapter (and the rest of the book) focused solely on images formed by visual light it should be mentioned that other wavelengths from the electromagnetic spectrum can also be converted into digital images and processed by the methods in the following chapters. Two examples are X-ray images and thermographic images, see Fig. 2.22. An X-ray image is formed by placing an object between an X-ray emitter and an X-ray receiver. The receiver measures the energy level of the X-rays at different positions. The energy level is proportional to the physical properties of the object, i.e., bones stop the X-rays while blood does not. Thermographic images capture middle- or far-infrared rays. Heat is emitted from all objects via such wavelengths meaning that the intensity in each pixel in a thermographic image corresponds directly to the temperature of the observed object, see Fig. 2.22. Other types of image not directly based on the electromagnetic spectrum can also be captured and processed and in general all 2D signals that can be measured can be represented as an image. Examples are MR and CT images known from hospitals, and 3D (or depth) images obtained by a laser scanner, a time-of-flight camera or the Kinect sensor developed for gaming, see Fig. 2.22.

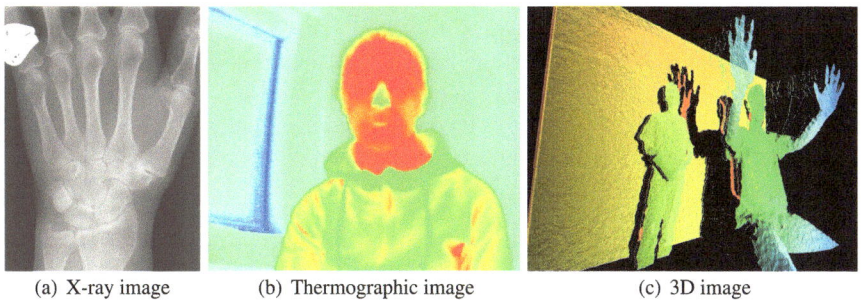

(a) X-ray image   (b) Thermographic image   (c) 3D image

Fig. 2.22 Three different types of image. (**a**) X-ray image. Note the ring on the finger. (**b**) Thermographic image. The more reddish the higher the temperature. (**c**) 3D image. The more blueish the closer to the camera

2.6 Exercises

Exercise 1: Explain the following concepts: electromagnetic spectrum, focal length, exposure time, backlighting, saturation, focus, depth-of-fields, motion blur, spatial quantization, ROI.

Exercise 2: Explain the pros and cons of backlighting.

Exercise 3: Describe the image acquisition process. That is, from light to a digital image in a computer.

Exercise 4: What is the purpose of the lens?

Exercise 5: What is the focal length and how does it relate to zoom?

Exercise 6: How many different 512×512 gray-scale (8-bit) images can be constructed?

Exercise 7: Which pixel value is represented by the following bit sequence: 00101010?

Exercise 8: What is the bit sequence of the pixel value: 150?

Exercise 9: In a 100×100 gray-scale image each pixel is represented by 256 gray levels. How much memory (bytes) is required to store this image?

Exercise 10: In a 100×100 gray-scale image each pixel is represented by 4 gray levels. How much memory (bytes) is required to store this image?

Exercise 11: You want to photograph an object, which is 1 m tall and 10 m away from the camera. The height of the object in the image should be 1 mm. It is assumed that the object is in focus at the focal point. What should the focal length be?

Exercise 12a: Mick is 2 m tall and standing 5 m away from a camera. The focal length of the camera is 5 mm. A focused image of Mick is formed on the sensor. At which distance from the lens is the sensor located?

Exercise 12b: How tall (in mm) will Mick be on the sensor?

Exercise 12c: The camera sensor contains 640×480 pixels and its physical size is 6.4 mm × 4.8 mm. How tall (in pixels) will Mick be on the sensor?

Exercise 12d: What are the horizontal field-of-view and the vertical field-of-view of the camera?

Exercise 13: Show that $\frac{1}{g} + \frac{1}{b} = \frac{1}{f}$.

Additional exercise 1: How does the human eye capture light and how does that relate to the operations in a digital camera?

Additional exercise 2: How is auto-focus obtained in a digital camera?

Additional exercise 3: How is night vision obtained in for example binoculars and riflescopes?

Color Images

3

So far we have restricted ourselves to gray-scale images, but, as you might have noticed, the real world consists of colors. Going back some years, many cameras (and displays, e.g., TV-monitors) only handled gray-scale images. As the technology matured, it became possible to capture (and visualize) color images and today most cameras capture color images.

In this chapter we turn to the topic of color images. We describe the nature of color images and how they are captured and represented.

3.1   What Is a Color?

In Chap. 2 it was explained that an image is formed by measuring the amount of energy entering the image sensor. It was also stated that only energy within a certain frequency/wavelength range is measured. This wavelength range is denoted the *visual spectrum*, see Fig. 2.2. In the human eye this is done by the so-called *rods*, which are specialized nerve-cells that act as *photoreceptors*. Besides the rods, the human eye also contains *cones*. These operate like the rods, but are not sensitive to all wavelengths in the visual spectrum. Instead, the eye contains three types of cones, each sensitive to a different wavelength range. The human brain interprets the output from these different cones as different colors as seen in Table 3.1 [4].

So, a color is defined by a certain wavelength in the electromagnetic spectrum as illustrated in Fig. 3.1.

Since the three different types of cones exist we have the notion of the *primary colors* being red, green and blue. Psycho-visual experiments have shown that the different cones have different sensitivity. This means that when you see two different colors with the same intensity, you will judge their brightness differently. On average, a human perceives red as being 2.6 times as bright as blue and green as being 5.6 times as bright as blue. Hence the eye is more sensitive to green and least sensitive to blue.

When all wavelengths (all colors) are present at the same time, the eye perceives this as a shade of gray, hence no color is seen! If the energy level increases the shade becomes brighter and ultimately becomes white. Conversely, when the energy

T.B. Moeslund, *Introduction to Video and Image Processing*,
Undergraduate Topics in Computer Science,
DOI 10.1007/978-1-4471-2503-7_3, © Springer-Verlag London Limited 2012

Table 3.1 The different types of photoreceptor in the human eye. The cones are each specialized to a certain wavelength range and peak response within the visual spectrum. The output from each of the three types of cone is interpreted as a particular color by the human brain: red, green, and blue, respectively. The rods measure the amount of energy in the visual spectrum, hence the shade of gray. The type indicators L, M, S, are short for long, medium and short, respectively, and refer to the wavelength

Photoreceptor cell	Wavelength in nanometers (nm)	Peak response in nanometer (nm)	Interpretation by the human brain
Cones (type L)	[400–680]	564	Red
Cones (type M)	[400–650]	534	Green
Cones (type S)	[370–530]	420	Blue
Rods	[400–600]	498	Shade of gray

Fig. 3.1 The relationship between colors and wavelengths

Fig. 3.2 Achromatic colors

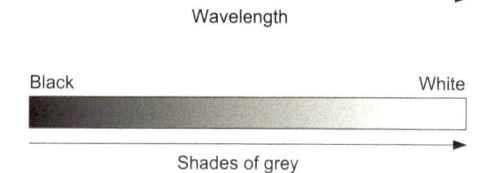

level is decreased, the shade becomes darker and ultimately becomes black. This continuum of different gray-levels (or shades of gray) is denoted the *achromatic colors* and illustrated in Fig. 3.2. Note that this is the same as Fig. 2.18.

An image is created by sampling the incoming light. The colors of the incoming light depend on the color of the light source illuminating the scene and the material the object is made of, see Fig. 3.3. Some of the light that hits the object will bounce right off and some will penetrate into the object. An amount of this light will be absorbed by the object and an amount leaves again possibly with a different color. So when you see a green car this means that the wavelengths of the main light reflected from the car are in the range of the type M cones, see Table 3.1. If we assume the car was illuminated by the sun, which emits all wavelengths, then we can reason that all wavelengths *except* the green ones are absorbed by the material the car is made of. Or in other words, if you are wearing a black shirt all wavelengths (energy) are absorbed by the shirt and this is why it becomes hotter than a white shirt.

When the resulting color is created by illuminating an object by white light and then absorbing some of the wavelengths (colors) we use the notion of *subtractive colors*. Exactly as when you mix paint to create a color. Say you start with a white piece of paper, where no light is absorbed. The resulting color will be white. If you then want the paper to become green you add green paint, which absorbs everything but the green wavelengths. If you add yet another color of paint, then more wavelengths will be absorbed, and hence the resulting light will have a new color. Keep doing this and you will in theory end up with a mixture where all wavelengths are absorbed, that is, black. In practice, however, it will probably not be black, but rather dark gray/brown.

Fig. 3.3 The different components influencing the color of the received light

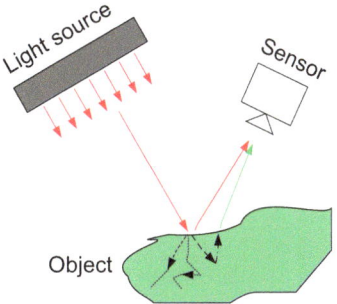

The opposite of subtractive colors is *additive colors*. This notion applies when you create the wavelengths as opposed to manipulating white light. A good example is a color monitor like a computer screen or a TV screen. Here each pixel is a combination of emitted red, green and blue light. Meaning that a black pixel is generated by not emitting anything at all. White (or rather a shade of gray) is generated by emitting the same amount of red, green, and blue. Red will be created by only emitting red light etc. All other colors are created by a combination of red, green and blue. For example yellow is created by emitting the same amount of red and green, and no blue.

3.2   Representation of an RGB Color Image

A color camera is based on the same principle as the human eye. That is, it measures the amount of incoming red light, green light and blue light, respectively. This is done in one of two ways depending on the number of sensors in the camera. In the case of three sensors, each sensor measures one of the three colors, respectively. This is done by splitting the incoming light into the three wavelength ranges using some optical filters and mirrors. So red light is only send to the "red-sensor" etc. The result is three images each describing the amount of red, green and blue light per pixel, respectively. In a color image, each pixel therefore consists of three values: red, green and blue. The actual representation might be three images—one for each color, as illustrated in Fig. 3.4, but it can also be a 3-dimensional vector for each pixel, hence an image of vectors. Such a vector looks like this:

$$\text{Color pixel} = [\text{Red, Green, Blue}] = [\text{R, G, B}] \qquad (3.1)$$

In terms of programming a color pixel is usually represented as a *struct*. Say we want to set the RGB values of the pixel at position $(2, 4)$ to: Red $= 100$, Green $= 42$, and Blue $= 10$, respectively. In C-code this can for example be written as

```
f [ 2 ] [ 4 ] . R  =  100;
f [ 2 ] [ 4 ] . G  =  42;
f [ 2 ] [ 4 ] . B  =  10;
```

Fig. 3.4 A color image
consisting of three images;
red, green and blue

respectively; or alternatively:

```
SetPixel(image, 2, 4, R, 100);
SetPixel(image, 2, 4, G, 42)};
SetPixel(image, 2, 4, B, 10)};
```

Typically each color value is represented by an 8-bit (one byte) value meaning that 256 different shades of each color can be measured. Combining different values of the three colors, each pixel can represent $256^3 = 16,777,216$ different colors.

A cheaper alternative to having three sensors including mirrors and optical filters is to only have one sensor. In this case, each cell in the sensor is made sensitive to one of the three colors (ranges of wavelength). This can be done in a number of different ways. One is using a *Bayer pattern*. Here 50% of the cells are sensitive to green, while the remaining cells are divided equally between red and blue. The reason being, as mentioned above, that the human eye is more sensitive to green. The layout of the different cells is illustrated in Fig. 3.5.

The figure shows the upper-left corner of the sensor, where the letters illustrate which color a particular pixel is sensitive to. This means that each pixel only captures one color and that the two other colors of a particular pixel must be inferred from the neighbors. Algorithms for finding the remaining colors of a pixel are known as *demosaicing* and, generally speaking, the algorithms are characterized by the required processing time (often directly proportional to the number of neighbors included) and the quality of the output. The higher the processing time the better

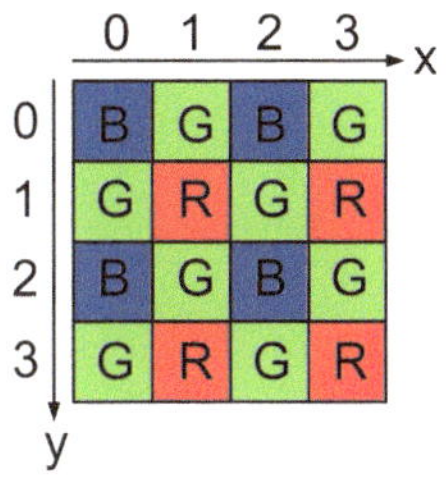

Fig. 3.5 The Bayer pattern used for capturing a color image on a single image sensor. R = red, G = green, and B = blue

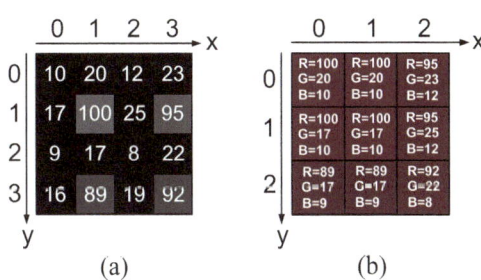

Fig. 3.6 (a) Numbers measured by the sensor. (b) Estimated RGB image using Eq. 3.2

the result. How to balance these two issues is up to the camera manufactures, and in general, the higher the quality of the camera, the higher the cost. Even very advanced algorithms are not as good as a three sensor color camera and note that when using, for example, a cheap web-camera, the quality of the colors might not be too good and care should be taken before using the colors for any processing. Regardless of the choice of demosaicing algorithm, the output is the same as when using three sensors, namely Eq. 3.1. That is, even though only one color is measured per pixel, the output for each pixel will (after demosaicing) consist of three values: R, G, and B.

An example of a simple demosaicing algorithm is to infer the missing colors from the nearest pixels, for example using the following set of equations:

$$g(x, y) \begin{cases} [R, G, B]_B = [f(x+1, y+1), f(x+1, y), f(x, y)] \\ [R, G, B]_{GB} = [f(x, y+1), f(x, y), f(x-1, y)] \\ [R, G, B]_{GR} = [f(x+1, y), f(x, y), f(x, y-1)] \\ [R, G, B]_R = [f(x, y), f(x-1, y), f(x-1, y-1)] \end{cases} \quad (3.2)$$

where $f(x, y)$ is the input image (Bayer pattern) and $g(x, y)$ is the output RGB image. The RGB values in the output image are found differently depending on which color a particular pixel is sensitive to: $[R, G, B]_B$ should be used for the pixels sensitive to blue, $[R, G, B]_R$ should be used for the pixels sensitive to red, and $[R, G, B]_{GB}$ and $[R, G, B]_{GR}$ should be used for the pixels sensitive to green followed by a blue or red pixel, respectively.

In Fig. 3.6 a concrete example of this algorithm is illustrated. In the left figure the values sampled from the sensor are shown. In the right figure the resulting RGB output image is shown using Eq. 3.2.

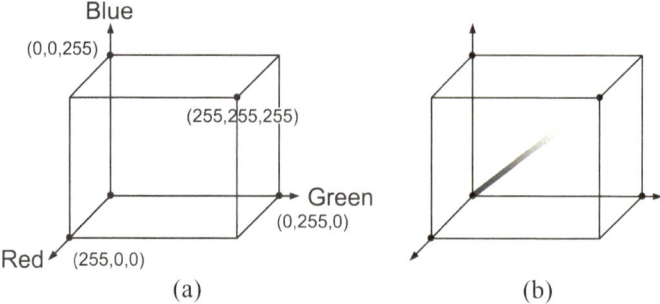

Fig. 3.7 (**a**) The RGB color cube. (**b**) The gray-vector in the RGB color cube

Table 3.2 The colors of the different corners in the RGB color cube

Corner	Color	
$(0, 0, 0)$	Black	
$(255, 0, 0)$	Red	
$(0, 255, 0)$	Green	
$(0, 0, 255)$	Blue	
$(255, 255, 0)$	Yellow	
$(255, 0, 255)$	Magenta	
$(0, 255, 255)$	Cyan	
$(255, 255, 255)$	White	

3.2.1 The RGB Color Space

According to Eq. 3.1 a color pixel has three values and can therefore be represented as one point in a 3D space spanned by the three colors. If we say that each color is represented by 8-bits, then we can construct the so-called RGB color cube, see Fig. 3.7.

In the color cube a color pixel is one point or rather a vector from $(0, 0, 0)$ to the pixel value. The different corners in the color cube represent some of the *pure colors* and are listed in Table 3.2. The vector from $(0, 0, 0)$ to $(255, 255, 255)$ passes through all the gray-scale values and is denoted the *gray-vector*. Note that the gray-vector is identical to Fig. 3.2.

3.2.2 Converting from RGB to Gray-Scale

Even though you use a color camera it might be sufficient for your algorithm to apply the intensity information in the image and you therefore need to convert the color image into a gray-scale image. Converting from RGB to gray-scale is performed as

$$I = W_R \cdot R + W_G \cdot G + W_B \cdot B \qquad (3.3)$$

Color input $W_R = 0, W_G - 0, W_B - 1$ $W_R = 1, W_G = 0, W_B = 0$ $W_R = 0.5, W_G = 0.5, W_B = 0$

Fig. 3.8 A color image and how it can be mapped to different gray-scale images depending on the weights

where I is the intensity and W_R, W_G, and W_B are weight factors for R, G, and B, respectively. To ensure the value of Eq. 3.3 is within one byte, i.e. in the range [0, 255], the weight factors must sum to one. That is $W_R + W_G + W_B = 1$. As default the three colors are equally important, hence $W_R = W_G = W_B = \frac{1}{3}$, but depending on the application one or two colors might be more important and the weight factors should be set accordingly. For example when processing images of vegetation the green color typically contains the most information or when processing images of metal objects the most information is typically located in the blue pixels. Yet another example could be when looking for human skin (face and hands) which has a reddish color. In general, the weights should be set according to your application and a good way of assessing this is by looking at the histograms of each color.[1] An example of a color image transformed into a gray-scale image can be seen in Fig. 3.8. Generally, it is not possible to convert a gray-scale image back into the original color image, since the color information is lost during the color to gray-scale transformation.

When the goal of a conversion from color to gray-scale is not to prepare the image for processing but rather for visualization purposes, then an understanding of the human visual perception can help decide the weight factors. The optimal weights vary from individual to individual, but the weights listed below are a good compromise, agreed upon by major international standardization organizations within TV and image/video coding. When the weights are optimized for the human visual system, the resulting gray-scale value is denoted *luminance* and usually represented as Y.

$$W_R = 0.299, \qquad W_G = 0.587, \qquad W_B = 0.114 \qquad (3.4)$$

---

[1] An image histogram is defined in the next chapter.

Fig. 3.9 The RGB color
cube. Each dot corresponds to
a particular pixel value.
Multiple dots on the same
line all have the same color,
but different levels of
illumination

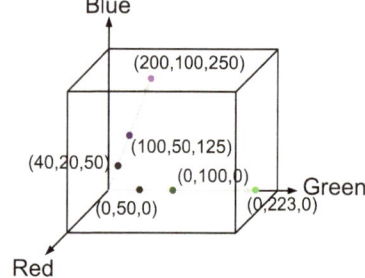

Fig. 3.10 (**a**) The triangle
where all color vectors pass
through. The value of a point
on the triangle is defined
using normalized RGB
coordinates. (**b**) The
chromaticity plane

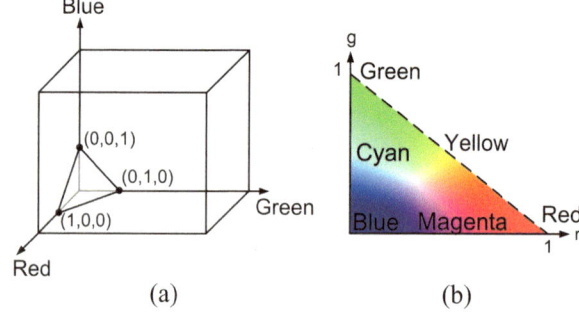

3.2.3 The Normalized RGB Color Representation

If we have the following three RGB pixel values $(0, 50, 0)$, $(0, 100, 0)$, and
$(0, 223, 0)$ in the RGB color cube, we can see that they all lie on the same vector, namely the one spanned by $(0, 0, 0)$ and $(0, 255, 0)$. We say that all values are a
shade of green and go even further and say that they all have the same color (green),
but different levels of illumination. This also applies to the rest of the color cube.
For example, the points $(40, 20, 50)$, $(100, 50, 125)$ and $(200, 100, 250)$ all lie on
the same vector and therefore have the same color, but just different illumination
levels. This is illustrated in Fig. 3.9.

   If we generalize this idea of different points on the same line having the same
color, then we can see that all possible lines pass through the triangle defined by
the points $(1, 0, 0)$, $(0, 1, 0)$ and $(0, 0, 1)$, see Fig. 3.10(a). The actual point (r, g, b)
where a line intersects the triangle is found as[2]:

$$(r, g, b) = \left(\frac{R}{R + G + B}, \frac{G}{R + G + B}, \frac{B}{R + G + B} \right) \tag{3.5}$$

   These values are named *normalized RGB* and denoted (r, g, b). In Table 3.3 the
rgb values of some RGB values are shown. Note that each value is in the interval
$[0, 1]$ and that $r + g + b = 1$. This means that if we know two of the normalized

---

[2]Note that the formula is undefined for $(R, G, B) = (0, 0, 0)$. We therefore make the following
definition: $(r, g, b) \equiv (0, 0, 0)$ when $(R, G, B) = (0, 0, 0)$.

RGB values, then we can easily find the remaining value, or in other words, we can represent a normalized RGB color using just two of the values. Say we choose r and g, then this corresponds to representing the triangle in Fig. 3.10(a) by the triangle to the right, see Fig. 3.10(b). This triangle is denoted the *chromaticity plane* and the colors along the edges of the triangle are the so-called pure colors. The further away from the edges the less pure the color and ultimately the center of the triangle has no color at all and is a shade of gray. It can be stated that the closer to the center a color is, the more "polluted" a pure color is by white light.

Summing up we can now re-represent an RGB value by its *"true"* color, r and g, and the amount of light (intensity or energy or illumination) in the pixel. That is,

$$(R, G, B) \quad \Leftrightarrow \quad (r, g, I) \tag{3.6}$$

where $I = \frac{R+G+B}{3}$. In Table 3.3 the rgI values of some RGB values are shown.[3] Separating the color and the intensity like this can be a powerful notion in many applications. In Sect. 4.4.1 one will be presented.

In terms of programming the conversion from (R, G, B) to (r, g, I) can be implemented in C-Code as illustrated below:

```
for (y = 0; y < M; y = y+1)
{
   for (x = 0; x < N; x = x+1)
   {
      temp = GetPixel(input, x, y, R) +
             GetPixel(input, x, y, G) +
             GetPixel(input, x, y, B);
      value = GetPixel(input, x, y, R) / temp;
      SetPixel(output, x, y, r, value);
      value = GetPixel(input, x, y, G) / temp;
      SetPixel(output, x, y, g, value);
      value = temp / 3;
      SetPixel(output, x, y, I, value);
   }
}
```

where M is the height of the image, N is the width of the image, *input* is the RGB image, and *output* is the rgI image. The programming example primarily consists of two *FOR-loops* which go through the image, pixel-by-pixel, and convert from an input image (RGB) to an output image (rgI). The opposite conversion from (r, g, I) to (R, G, B) can be implemented as

---

[3]If r and g need to be represented using one byte for each color we can simply multiply each with 255 and the new values will be in the interval [0, 255].

```
for  (y  =  0;  y  <  M;  y  =  y+1)
{
  for  (x  =  0;  x  <  N;  x  =  x+1)
  {
     temp  =  3  *  GetPixel(input ,x,y,I);
     value  =  GetPixel(input ,  x,  y,  r)  *  temp;
     SetPixel(output ,  x,  y,  R,  value);
     value  =  GetPixel(input ,  x,  y,  g)  *  temp;
     SetPixel(output ,  x,  y,  G,  value);
     value  =  (1  −  GetPixel(input ,  x,  y,  r)  −
              GetPixel(input ,  x,  y,  g))  *  temp;
     SetPixel(output ,  x,  y,  B,  value);
  }
}
```

where M is the height of the image, N is the width of the image, *input* is the rgI image, and *output* is the RGB image.

3.3   Other Color Representations

From a human perception point of view the triangular representation in 3.10(b) is not intuitive. Instead humans rather use the notion of *hue* and *saturation*, when perceiving colors. The hue is the dominant wavelength in the perceived light and represents the pure color, i.e., the colors located on the edges of the triangle in Fig. 3.10(b). The saturation is the purity of the color and represents the amount of white light mixed with the pure color. To understand these entities better, let us look at Fig. 3.11(a). First of all we see that the point C corresponds to the neutral point, meaning the colorless center of the triangle where $(r, g) = (1/3, 1/3)$. Let us define a random point in the triangle as P. The hue of this point is now defined as an angle, θ, between the vectors $\overrightarrow{C_{r=1}}$ and $\overrightarrow{CP}$. So hue $= 0°$ means red and hue $= 120°$ means green.

If the point P is located on the edge of the triangle then we say the saturation is 1, hence a pure color. As the point approaches C the saturation goes toward 0, and ultimately becomes 0 when $P = C$. Since the distance from C to the three edges of the triangle is not uniform, the saturation is defined as a relative distance. That is, saturation is defined as the ratio between the distance from C to P, and the distance from C to the point on the edge of the triangle in the direction of $\overrightarrow{CP}$. Mathematically we have

$$\text{Saturation} = \frac{\|\overrightarrow{CP}\|}{\|\overrightarrow{CP'}\|}, \qquad \text{Hue} = \theta \qquad (3.7)$$

where $\|\overrightarrow{CP}\|$ is the length of the vector $\overrightarrow{CP}$. The representation of colors based on hue and saturation results in a circle as opposed to the triangle in Fig. 3.10(b). In Fig. 3.11(b) the hue–saturation representation is illustrated together with some of

Table 3.3 Some different colors and their representation in the different color spaces. ND = Not Defined

Color	(R, G, B)	(r, g, b)	(r, g, I)	(H, S, I)	(H, S, V)	(Y, U, V)	(Y, C_b, C_r)
Red	(255, 0, 0)	(1, 0, 0)	(1, 0, 85)	(0, 1, 85)	(0, 1, 255)	(76, −37, 157)	(76, 85, 255)
Yellow	(255, 255, 0)	(1/2, 1/2, 0)	(1/2, 1/2, 170)	(60, 1, 170)	(60, 1, 255)	(226, −111, 26)	(226, 255, 149)
Green	(0, 255, 0)	(0, 1, 0)	(0, 1, 85)	(120, 1, 85)	(120, 1, 255)	(150, −74, −131)	(150, 100, 115)
Cyan	(0, 255, 255)	(0, 1/2, 1/2)	(0, 1/2, 170)	(180, 1, 170)	(180, 1, 255)	(179, 38, −157)	(179, 171, 0)
Blue	(0, 0, 255)	(0, 0, 1)	(0, 0, 85)	(240, 1, 85)	(240, 1, 255)	(29, 111, −26)	(29, 255, 107)
Magenta	(255, 0, 255)	(1/2, 0, 1/2)	(1/2, 0, 170)	(300, 1, 170)	(300, 1, 255)	(105, 74, 131)	(105, 212, 235)
Black	(0, 0, 0)	(0, 0, 0)	(0, 0, 0)	(ND, 0, 0)	(ND, 0, 0)	(0, 0, 0)	(0, 128, 128)
White	(255, 255, 255)	(1/3, 1/3, 1/3)	(1/3, 1/3, 255)	(ND, 0, 255)	(ND, 0, 255)	(255, 0, 0)	(255, 128, 128)
25% white	(64, 64, 64)	(1/3, 1/3, 1/3)	(1/3, 1/3, 64)	(ND, 0, 64)	(ND, 0, 64)	(64, 0, 0)	(64, 128, 128)
50% white	(128, 128, 128)	(1/3, 1/3, 1/3)	(1/3, 1/3, 128)	(ND, 0, 128)	(ND, 0, 128)	(128, 0, 0)	(128, 128, 128)
25% Blue	(0, 0, 64)	(0, 0, 1)	(0, 0, 21)	(240, 1, 21)	(240, 1, 54)	(7, 28, −6)	(7, 160, 123)
50% Blue	(0, 0, 128)	(0, 0, 1)	(0, 0, 43)	(240, 1, 43)	(240, 1, 128)	(15, 58, −13)	(15, 192, 118)
75% Blue	(0, 0, 192)	(0, 0, 1)	(0, 0, 64)	(240, 1, 64)	(240, 1, 192)	(22, 84, −19)	(22, 224, 112)
Orange	(255, 165, 0)	(0.6, 0.4, 0)	(0.6, 0.4, 140)	(40, 1, 140)	(39, 1, 255)	(173, 10, 72)	(173, 30, 186)
Pink	(255, 192, 203)	(0.4, 0.3, 0.3)	(0.4, 0.3, 217)	(351, 0.1, 217)	(350, 0.2, 255)	(212, −4, 57)	(212, 123, 157)
Brown	(165, 42, 42)	(0.6, 0.2, 0.2)	(0.6, 0.2, 83)	(0, 0.5, 83)	(0, 0.7, 165)	(79, −18, 76)	(79, 107, 190)

Fig. 3.11 (**a**) The definition
of hue and saturation. (**b**) The
hue–saturation representation.
The color of a pixel (indicated
by a dot) is represented by a
hue value and a saturation
value (denoted S in the
figure). The figure also
indicates the location of some
of the pure colors

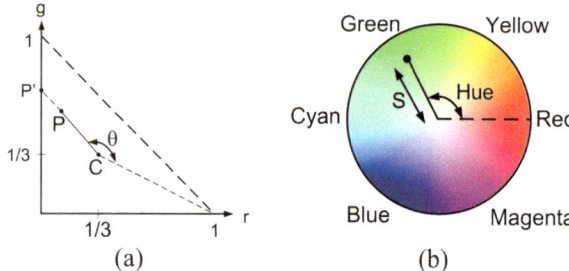

(a)   (b)

the pure colors. It is important to realize how this figure relates to Fig. 3.7, or in other words, how the hue–saturation representation relates to the RGB representation. The center of the hue–saturation circle in Fig. 3.11(b) is a shade of gray and corresponds to the gray-vector in Fig. 3.7. The circle is located so that it is perpendicular to the gray-vector. For a particular RGB value, the hue–saturation circle is therefore centered at a position on the gray-vector, so that the RGB value is included in the circle.

A number of different color representations exist, which are based on the notion of hue and saturation. Below two of these are presented.[4]

3.3.1 The HSI Color Representation

The HSI color representation is short for hue, saturation and intensity. The representation follows the exact definition mentioned above. That is, the intensity is defined as $I = \frac{R+G+B}{3}$ and hue and saturation is defined as illustrated in Fig. 3.11. When calculating the conversion from RGB to HSI we seek a way of avoiding fist converting from RGB to rg, i.e., we want to represent the conversion in terms of RGB values. In Appendix D it is shown how this is possible and the resulting conversion from RGB to HSI is defined as

$$H = \begin{cases} \cos^{-1}\left(1/2 \cdot \frac{(R-G)+(R-B)}{\sqrt{(R-G)(R-G)+(R-B)(G-B)}}\right), & \text{if } G \geq B; \\ 360° - \cos^{-1}\left(1/2 \cdot \frac{(R-G)+(R-B)}{\sqrt{(R-G)(R-G)+(R-B)(G-B)}}\right), & \text{Otherwise} \end{cases} \quad (3.8)$$

$$H \in [0, 360[$$

$$S = 1 - 3 \cdot \frac{\min\{R, G, B\}}{R+G+B} \quad S \in [0, 1] \quad\quad\quad (3.9)$$

$$I = \frac{R+G+B}{3} \quad I \in [0, 255] \quad\quad\quad (3.10)$$

---

[4]It should be noted that the naming of the different color representations based on hue and saturation is not consistent throughout the body of literature covering this subject. Please have this in mind when studying other information sources.

where $\min\{R, G, B\}$ means the smallest of the R, G, and B values, see Appendix B. Saturation is defined to be zero when $(R, G, B) = (0, 0, 0)$ and hue is undefined for gray-values, i.e., when $R = G = B$. The conversion from HSI to RGB is given as

$$H_n = \begin{cases} 0, & \text{if } 0° \leq H \leq 120°; \\ H - 120°, & \text{if } 120° < H \leq 240°; \\ H - 240°, & \text{if } 240° < H < 360° \end{cases} \qquad (3.11)$$

$$R = \begin{cases} I \cdot \left(1 + \frac{S \cdot \cos(H_n)}{\cos(60° - H_n)}\right), & \text{if } 0° \leq H \leq 120°; \\ I - I \cdot S, & \text{if } 120° < H \leq 240°; \\ 3I - G - B, & \text{if } 240° < H < 360° \end{cases} \qquad (3.12)$$

$$G = \begin{cases} 3I - R - B, & \text{if } 0° \leq H \leq 120°; \\ I \cdot \left(1 + \frac{S \cdot \cos(H_n)}{\cos(60° - H_n)}\right), & \text{if } 120° < H \leq 240°; \\ I - I \cdot S, & \text{if } 240° < H < 360° \end{cases} \qquad (3.13)$$

$$B = \begin{cases} I - I \cdot S, & \text{if } 0° \leq H \leq 120°; \\ 3I - R - G, & \text{if } 120° < H \leq 240°; \\ I \cdot \left(1 + \frac{S \cdot \cos(H_n)}{\cos(60° - H_n)}\right), & \text{if } 240° < H < 360° \end{cases} \qquad (3.14)$$

In Table 3.3 the HSI values of some RGB pixels are shown.[5]

3.3.2   The HSV Color Representation

The HSV color representation is short for *hue, saturation* and *value*. One can think of HSV as an approximation of HSI, but much simpler to calculate. This is true, but it is important to notice that HSV is not defined to be an approximation of HSI. It is rather defined from an artist's point of view. Consider the situation when an artist mixes paint. She would choose a pure color and lighten it by adding white or darkening it by adding black. In the HSV representation the actions of the artist are modeled in the following way. The pure color obviously corresponds to hue. Increasing the whiteness (by adding white) corresponds to lowing the saturation. Finally, increasing the amount of black corresponds to lowering the intensity of R, G, and B. Concretely, this is modeled by the intensity of the maximum color and denoted *value*, i.e., value $= \max\{R, G, B\}$.

Following these definitions, a very elegant geometric argument can be made leading to a computationally simpler representation of hue, saturation, and value, than HSI. The conversion from RGB to HSV is given as (see Appendix E for details):

---

[5]Note that sometimes all parameters are normalized to the interval $[0, 1]$. For example for H this is done as $H_{normalized} = \frac{H}{360}$.

$$H = \begin{cases} \frac{G-B}{V-\min\{R,G,B\}} \cdot 60°, & \text{if } V = R \text{ and } G \geq B; \\ \left(\frac{B-R}{V-\min\{R,G,B\}} + 2\right) \cdot 60°, & \text{if } G = V; \\ \left(\frac{R-G}{V-\min\{R,G,B\}} + 4\right) \cdot 60°, & \text{if } B = V; \\ \left(\frac{R-B}{V-\min\{R,G,B\}} + 5\right) \cdot 60°, & \text{if } V = R \text{ and } G < B \end{cases} \qquad H \in [0°, 360°[$$

(3.15)

$$S = \frac{V - \min\{R, G, B\}}{V} \qquad S \in [0, 1] \tag{3.16}$$

$$V = \max\{R, G, B\} \qquad V \in [0, 255] \tag{3.17}$$

where $\min\{R, G, B\}$ and $\max\{R, G, B\}$ are the smallest and biggest of the R, G, and B values, respectively, see Appendix B. As for HSI saturation is defined to be zero when $(R, G, B) = (0, 0, 0)$ and hue is undefined for gray-values, i.e., when $R = G = B$. The conversion from HSV to RGB is given as

$$K = \left\lfloor \frac{H}{60°} \right\rfloor \tag{3.18}$$

$$T = \frac{H}{60°} - K \tag{3.19}$$

$$X = V \cdot (1 - S) \tag{3.20}$$

$$Y = V \cdot (1 - S \cdot T) \tag{3.21}$$

$$Z = V \cdot \left(1 - S \cdot (1 - T)\right) \tag{3.22}$$

$$(R, G, B) = \begin{cases} (V, Z, X), & \text{if } K = 0; \\ (Y, V, X), & \text{if } K = 1; \\ (X, V, Z), & \text{if } K = 2; \\ (X, Y, V), & \text{if } K = 3; \\ (Z, X, V), & \text{if } K = 4; \\ (V, X, Y), & \text{if } K = 5 \end{cases} \tag{3.23}$$

where $\lfloor x \rfloor$ means the floor of x, see Appendix B. In Table 3.3 the HSV values of some RGB colors are shown.

3.3.3   The YUV and YC$_b$C$_r$ Color Representations

A number of other color representations exist, but those mentioned above are those most often applied in image processing. One exception, however, is the color representations used for transmission, storage, and compression of image and video. These representations all have a similar structure, which is presented in this section.

In the early days of TV only monochrome screens were available and hence only intensity information was transmitted from the TV stations. RGB cameras captured RGB signals, but converted them into luminance values, denoted Y, before transmitting them. Knowledge of human perception was taken into account when defining the weights used for the conversion, see Sect. 3.2.2:

$$Y = W_R \cdot R + W_G \cdot G + W_B \cdot B \quad Y \in [0, 255] \tag{3.24}$$

where $W_R + W_G + W_B = 1$.

As the color screen technology matured, a need for transmitting color signals arose. Two requirements were set up when defining how to transmit color signals: 1) The signal should be compatible with the already existing signals used for monochrome screens and 2) the decoding on the receiver side should be as simple as possible. From this it followed that the color information was transmitted as *weighted difference signals* with respect to Y:

$$X_1 = \frac{W_{X1}}{1 - W_B} \cdot (B - Y) \quad X_1 \in [-W_{X1} \cdot 255, W_{X1} \cdot 255] \tag{3.25}$$

$$X_2 = \frac{W_{X2}}{1 - W_R} \cdot (R - Y) \quad X_2 \in [-W_{X2} \cdot 255, W_{X2} \cdot 255] \tag{3.26}$$

where W_{X1} and W_{X2} are weight factors, W_R and W_B are from Eq. 3.24, and X_1 and X_2 encode the blue and red information, respectively. The green information can then be inferred from Y, X_1 and X_2. Note that when no color is present, i.e. $R = G = B$, we have $X_1 = 0$ and $X_2 = 0$, see Appendix F. This means that X_1 and X_2 need not be send.

So, by transmitting (Y, X_1, X_2) a monochrome receiver can simply show Y, while a color receiver can decode (R, G, B) and show a color signal using the following equations, see Appendix F for details:

$$R = Y + X_2 \cdot \frac{1 - W_R}{W_{X2}} \tag{3.27}$$

$$G = Y - X_1 \cdot \frac{W_B \cdot (1 - W_B)}{W_{X1} \cdot W_G} - X_2 \cdot \frac{W_R \cdot (1 - W_R)}{W_{X2} \cdot W_G} \tag{3.28}$$

$$B = Y + X_1 \cdot \frac{1 - W_B}{W_{X1}} \tag{3.29}$$

Note that since all the weights are known in advance the conversion becomes rather simple.

One of the most well known color spaces using this principle is the YUV color space. The YUV color space is for example used in most European TV transmission standards. YUV uses the weights: $W_R = 0.299$, $W_G = 0.587$, $W_B = 0.114$, $W_{X1} = 0.436$, and $W_{X2} = 0.615$, and has the conversion listed below, see Appendix F for details. In Table 3.3 the YUV values of some RGB values are shown.

$$\begin{bmatrix} Y \\ U \\ V \end{bmatrix} = \begin{bmatrix} 0.299 & 0.587 & 0.114 \\ -0.147 & -0.289 & 0.436 \\ 0.615 & -0.515 & -0.100 \end{bmatrix} \cdot \begin{bmatrix} R \\ G \\ B \end{bmatrix} \quad \begin{matrix} Y \in [0, 255] \\ U \in [-111, 111] \\ V \in [-157, 157] \end{matrix} \tag{3.30}$$

$$\begin{bmatrix} R \\ G \\ B \end{bmatrix} = \begin{bmatrix} 1.000 & 0.000 & 1.140 \\ 1.000 & -0.395 & -0.581 \\ 1.000 & 2.032 & 0.000 \end{bmatrix} \cdot \begin{bmatrix} Y \\ U \\ V \end{bmatrix} \quad \begin{array}{l} R \in [0, 255] \\ G \in [0, 255] \\ B \in [0, 255] \end{array} \quad (3.31)$$

Another well know color space using this principle is the YC_bC_r color space, which is used in for example JPEG and MPEG. YC_bC_r uses the weights: $W_R = 0.299$, $W_G = 0.587$, $W_B = 0.114$, $W_{X1} = 0.5$, and $W_{X2} = 0.5$, and has the conversions listed below. See Appendix F for details.

$$\begin{bmatrix} Y \\ C_b \\ C_r \end{bmatrix} = \begin{bmatrix} 0.299 & 0.587 & 0.114 \\ -0.169 & -0.331 & 0.500 \\ 0.500 & -0.419 & -0.081 \end{bmatrix} \cdot \begin{bmatrix} R \\ G \\ B \end{bmatrix} + \begin{bmatrix} 0 \\ 128 \\ 128 \end{bmatrix} \quad \begin{array}{l} Y \in [0, 255] \\ C_b \in [0, 255] \\ C_r \in [0, 255] \end{array}$$
$$(3.32)$$

$$\begin{bmatrix} R \\ G \\ B \end{bmatrix} = \begin{bmatrix} 1.000 & 0.000 & 1.403 \\ 1.000 & -0.344 & -0.714 \\ 1.000 & 1.773 & 0.000 \end{bmatrix} \cdot \begin{bmatrix} Y \\ C_b - 128 \\ C_r - 128 \end{bmatrix} \quad \begin{array}{l} R \in [0, 255] \\ G \in [0, 255] \\ B \in [0, 255] \end{array} \quad (3.33)$$

Note that 128 is added/subtracted in order to bring the values into the range [0, 255]. Note also the simplicity of the conversions compared to those for HSI and HSV. In Table 3.3 the YC_bC_r values of some RGB values are shown.

3.4   Further Information

When reading literature on color spaces and color processing it is important to realize that a number of different terms are used.[6] Unfortunately, some of these terms are used interchangeably even though they might have different physical/perceptual/technical meanings. We therefore give a guideline to some of the terms you are likely to encounter when reading literature on colors:

Chromatic Color   All colors in the RGB color cube except those lying on the gray-line spanned by $(0, 0, 0)$ and $(255, 255, 255)$.

Achromatic Color   The colorless values in the RGB cube, i.e., all those colors lying on the gray-line. The opposite of chromatic color.

Shades of gray   The same as achromatic color.

Intensity   The average amount of energy, i.e., $(R + G + B)/3$.

Brightness   The amount of light perceived by a human.

Lightness   The amount of light perceived by a human.

Luminance   The amount of light perceived by a human. Note that when you venture into the science of color understanding, the luminance defines the amount of emitted light.

Luma   Gamma-corrected luminance.

---

[6]When going into color perception and color understanding even more terms are added to the vocabulary.

| Input | Mapped to visible spectrum | Mapped to red/green spectrum |

Fig. 3.12 Examples of pseudo color mapping

Shade Darkening a color. When a subtractive color space is applied, different shades (darker nuances) of a color are obtained by mixing the color with different amounts of black.

Tint Lightening a color. When a subtractive color space is applied, different tints (lighter nuances) of a color are obtained by mixing the color with different amounts of white.

Tone A combination of shade and tint, where gray is mixed with the input color.

'(denoted prime) The primed version of a color, i.e., R', means that the value has been gamma-corrected.

Sometimes a gray-scale image is mapped to a color image in order to enhance some aspect of the image. As mentioned above a true color image cannot be reconstructed from a gray-level image. We therefore use the term *pseudo color* to underline that we are not talking about a true RGB image. How to map from gray-scale to color can be done in many different ways. In Fig. 3.12 and Fig. 2.22 examples are illustrated.

Fig. 3.13 A color image
captured by a Bayer pattern

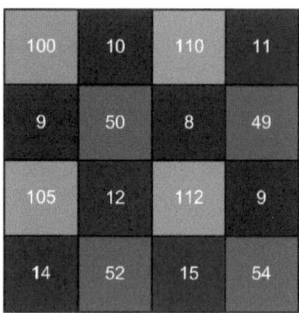

3.5   Exercises

Exercise 1: Explain the following concepts: rods, cones, achromatic, chromaticity
plane, additive colors, subtractive colors, color spaces.

Exercise 2: How many different 512×512 color (24-bit) images can be constructed?

Exercise 3: The image in Fig. 3.13 was captured by a Bayer pattern sensor. Use
demosaicing to convert the image into an RGB image.

Exercise 4: An RGB image is converted into a gray-scale image so that the cyan
color is enhanced. What are the weight factors for R, G, and B, respectively?

Exercise 5: Is the RGB pixel $(R, G, B) = (42, 42, 42)$ located on the gray-vector?

Exercise 6: An RGB image is converted into a gray-scale image. During the conversion $W_B = 0$ and the two remaining colors are weighted equally. A pixel in the
gray-scale image has the value 100. How much green was present in the corresponding RGB pixel when we know that $R = 20$?

Exercise 7: Convert the RGB pixel $(R, G, B) = (20, 40, 60)$ into (r, g, b), (r, g, I),
(H, S, I), (H, S, V), (Y, U, V), and (Y, C_b, C_r), respectively.

Exercise 8: Show that $r + g + b = 1$.

Additional exercise 1: How is color represented in HTML?

Additional exercise 2: What is the "red-eye effect" in pictures and what can be
done about it?

Additional exercise 3: What is white balance?

Additional exercise 4: What is color blindness?

Sometimes when people make a movie they lower the overall intensity in order to create a special atmosphere. Some overdo this and the result is that the viewer cannot see anything except darkness. What do you do? You pick up your remote and adjust the level of the light by pushing the brightness button. When doing so you actually perform a special type of image processing known as *point processing*.

Say we have an input image $f(x, y)$ and wish to manipulate it resulting in a different image, denoted the *output image* $g(x, y)$. In the case of changing the brightness in a movie, the input image will be the one stored on the DVD you are watching and the output image will be the one actually shown on the TV screen. Point processing is now defined as an operation which calculates the new value of a pixel in $g(x, y)$ based on the value of the pixel *in the same position* in $f(x, y)$ and some operation. That is, the values of a pixel's neighbors in $f(x, y)$ have no effect whatsoever, hence the name point processing. In the forthcoming chapters the neighbor pixels *will* play an important role. The principle of point processing is illustrated in Fig. 4.1. In this chapter some of the most fundamental point processing operations are described.

4.1 Gray-Level Mapping

When manipulating the brightness by your remote you actually change the value of b in the following equation:

$$g(x, y) = f(x, y) + b \tag{4.1}$$

Every time you push the '+' brightness button the value of b is increased and vice versa. The result of increasing b is that a higher and higher value is added to each pixel in the input image and hence it becomes brighter. If $b > 0$ the image becomes brighter and if $b < 0$ the image becomes darker. The effect of changing the brightness is illustrated in Fig. 4.2.

T.B. Moeslund, *Introduction to Video and Image Processing*,
Undergraduate Topics in Computer Science,
DOI 10.1007/978-1-4471-2503-7_4, © Springer-Verlag London Limited 2012

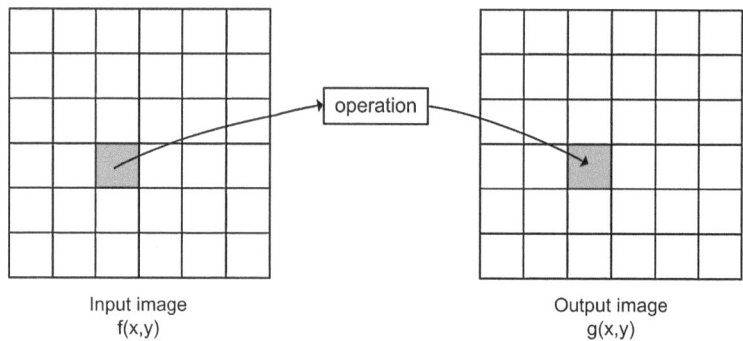

Fig. 4.1 The principle of point processing. A pixel in the input image is processed and the result is stored at the same position in the output image

Fig. 4.2 If b in Eq. 4.1 is zero, the resulting image will be equal to the input image. If b is a negative number, then the resulting image will have decreased brightness, and if b is a positive number the resulting image will have increased brightness

An often more convenient way of expressing the brightness operation is by the use of a graph, see Fig. 4.3. The graph shows how a pixel value in the input image (horizontal axis) maps to a pixel value in the output image (vertical axis). Such a graph is denoted *gray-level mapping*. In the first graph, the mapping does absolutely nothing, i.e., $g(142, 42) = f(142, 42)$. In the next graph all pixel values are increased ($b > 0$), hence the image becomes brighter. This results in two things: i) no pixel will be completely dark in the output and ii) some pixels will have a value above 255 in the output image. The latter is no good due to the upper limit of an 8-bit image and therefore all pixels above 255 are set equal to 255 as illustrated by the horizontal part of the graph. When $b < 0$ some pixels will have negative values and are therefore set equal to zero in the output as seen in the last graph.

Just like changing the brightness on your TV, you can also change the contrast. The contrast of an image is a matter of how different the gray-level values are. If we look at two pixels next to each other with values 112 and 114, then the human eye has difficulties distinguishing them and we will say there is a *low* contrast. On the other hand if the pixels are 112 and 212, respectively, then we can easily distinguish

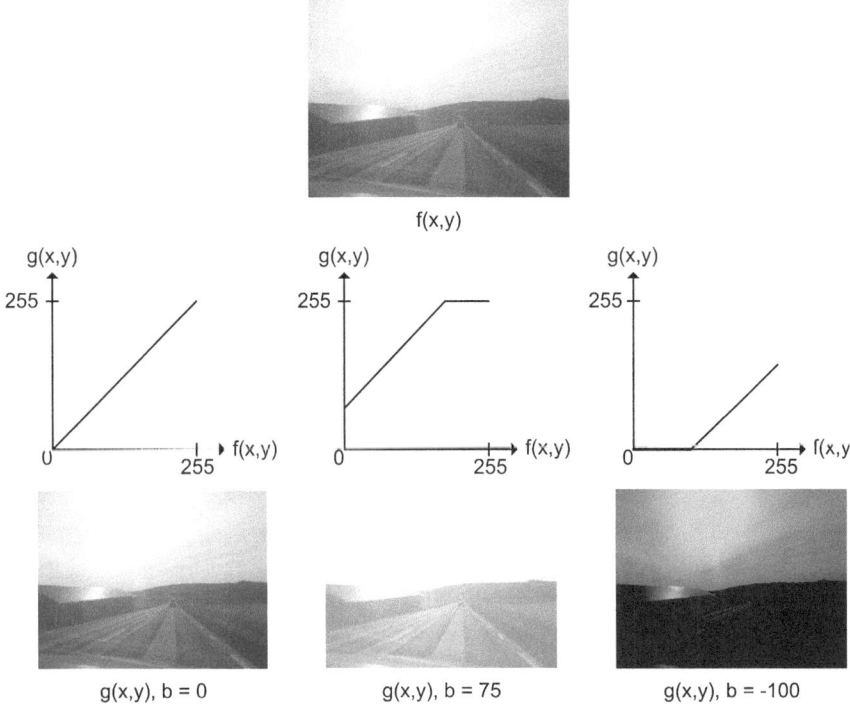

Fig. 4.3 Three examples of gray-level mapping. The top image is the input. The three other images are the result of applying the three gray-level mappings to the input. All three gray-level mappings are based on Eq. 4.1

Fig. 4.4 If a in Eq. 4.2 is one, the resulting image will be equal to the input image. If a is smaller than one then the resulting image will have decreased contrast, and if a is higher than one then the resulting image will have increased contrast

them and we will say the contrast is *high*. The contrast of an image is changed by changing the slope of the graph[1]:

---

[1] In practice the line is not rotated around $(0, 0)$ but rather around the center point $(127, 127)$, hence $b = 127(1 - a)$. However, for the discussion here it suffice to say that $b = 0$ and only look at the slope.

$$g(x, y) = a \cdot f(x, y) \tag{4.2}$$

If $a > 1$ the contrast is increased and if $a < 1$ the contrast is decreased. For example when $a = 2$ the pixels 112 and 114 will get the values 224 and 228, respectively. The difference between them is increased by a factor 2 and the contrast is therefore increased. In Fig. 4.4 the effect of changing the contrast can be seen.

If we combine the equations for brightness, Eq. 4.1, and contrast, Eq. 4.2, we have

$$g(x, y) = a \cdot f(x, y) + b \tag{4.3}$$

which is the equation of a straight line. Let us look at an example of how to apply this equation. Say we are interested in a certain part of the input image where the contrast might not be sufficient. We therefore find the range of the pixels in this part of the image and map them to the entire range, $[0, 255]$ in the output image. Say that the minimum pixel value and maximum pixel values in the input image are 100 and 150, respectively. Changing the contrast then means to say that all pixel value below 100 are set to zero in the output and all pixel values above 150 are set to 255 in the output image. The pixels in the range $[100, 150]$ are then mapped to $[0, 255]$ using Eq. 4.3 where a and b are defined as follows:

$$a = \frac{255}{f_2 - f_1}, \qquad b = -a \cdot f_1 \tag{4.4}$$

where $f_1 = 100$ and $f_2 = 150$.

4.2   Non-linear Gray-Level Mapping

Gray-level mapping is not limited to linear mappings as defined by Eq. 4.3. In fact the designer is free to define the gray-level mapping as she pleases as long as there is one and only one output value for each input value. Often the designer will utilize a well defined equation/graph as opposed to defining a new one. Below three of the most common *non-linear mapping* functions are presented.

4.2.1   Gamma Mapping

In many cameras and display devices (flat panel televisions for example) it is useful to be able to increase or decrease the contrast in the dark gray levels and the light gray levels individually since humans have a non-linear perception of contrast. A commonly used non-linear mapping is gamma mapping, which is defined for

Fig. 4.5 Gamma-mapping
curves for different gammas

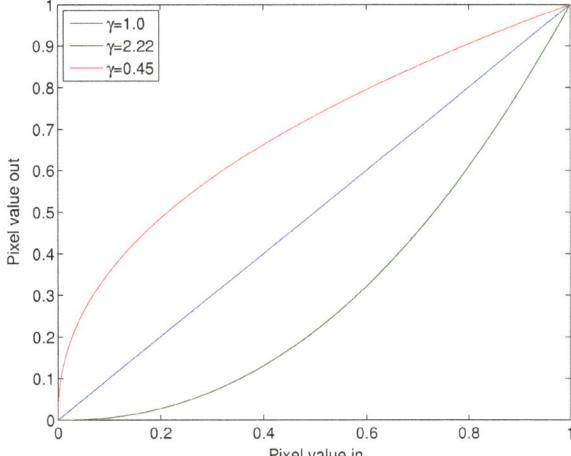

positive γ as

$$g(x, y) = f(x, y)^{\gamma} \tag{4.5}$$

Some gamma-mapping curves are illustrated in Fig. 4.5. For $\gamma = 1$ we get the identity mapping. For $0 < \gamma < 1$ we increase the dynamics in the dark areas by increasing the mid-levels. For $\gamma > 1$ we increase the dynamics in the bright areas by decreasing the mid-levels. The gamma mapping is defined so that the input and output pixel values are in the range $[0, 1]$. It is therefore necessary to first transform the input pixel values by dividing each pixel value with 255 before the gamma transformation. The output values should also be scaled from $[0, 1]$ to $[0, 255]$ after the gamma transformation.

A concrete example is given. A pixel in a gray-scale image with value $v_{in} = 120$ is gamma mapped with $\gamma = 2.22$. Initially, the pixel value is transformed into the interval $[0, 1]$ by dividing with 255, $v_1 = 120/255 = 0.4706$. Secondly, the gamma mapping is performed $v_2 = 0.4706^{2.22} = 0.1876$. Finally, it is mapped back to the interval $[0, 255]$ giving the result $v_{out} = 0.1876 \cdot 255 = 47$. Examples are illustrated in Fig. 4.6.

Gamma value: 0.45   No gamma correction   Gamma value: 2.22

Fig. 4.6 Gamma mapping to the *left* with $\gamma = 0.45$ and to the *right* with $\gamma = 2.22$. In the *middle* the original image

4.2.2 Logarithmic Mapping

An alternative non-linear mapping is based on the logarithm operator. Each pixel is replaced by the logarithm of the pixel value. This has the effect that low intensity pixel values are enhanced. It is often used in cases where the dynamic range of the image is too great to be displayed or in images where there are a few very bright spots on a darker background. Since the logarithm is not defined for 0, the mapping is defined as

$$g(x, y) = c \cdot \log\big(1 + f(x, y)\big) \qquad (4.6)$$

where c is a scaling constant that ensures that the maximum output value is 255. It is calculated as

$$c = \frac{255}{\log(1 + v_{\max})} \qquad (4.7)$$

where $v_{\max}$ is the maximum pixel value in the input image.

The behavior of the logarithmic mapping can be controlled by changing the pixel values of the input image using a linear mapping before the logarithmic mapping. The logarithmic mapping from the interval $[0, 255]$ to $[0, 255]$ is seen in Fig. 4.7. This mapping will clearly stretch the low intensity pixels while suppressing the contrast in high intensity pixels. An example is illustrated in Fig. 4.7.

4.2.3 Exponential Mapping

The exponential mapping uses a part of the exponential curve. It can be expressed as

$$g(x, y) = c \cdot \big(k^{f(x,y)} - 1\big) \qquad (4.8)$$

where k is a parameter that can be used to change of shape of the transformation curve and c is a scaling constant that ensures that the maximum output value is 255. It is calculated as

$$c = \frac{255}{k^{v_{\max}} - 1} \qquad (4.9)$$

where $v_{\max}$ is the maximum pixel value in the input image. k is normally chosen as a number just above 1. This will enhance details in the bright areas while decreasing detail in the dark areas. An example is illustrated in Fig. 4.7.

Please note that both linear and non-linear gray-level mapping can also be applied to color images. This is simply done by performing gray-level mapping on each of the three color channels.

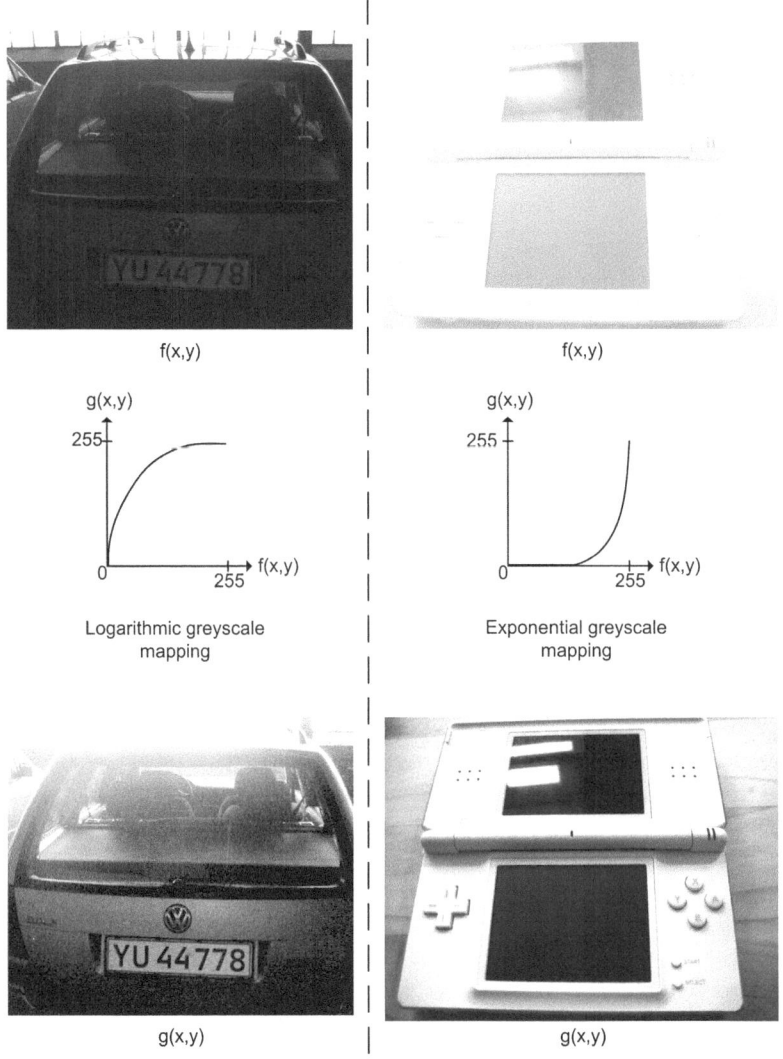

Fig. 4.7 Examples of logarithmic and exponential gray-level mappings. Logarithmic mapping is useful for bringing out details in dark images and exponential mapping is useful for bringing out details in bright images

4.3   The Image Histogram

So now we know how to correct images using gray-level mapping, but how can we tell if an image is too dark or too bright?

The obvious answer is that we can simply look at the image. But we would like a more objective way of answering this question. Moreover, we are also interested in a method enabling a computer to automatically assess whether an image is too

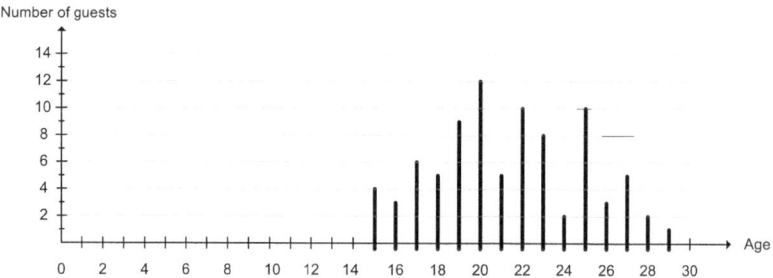

Fig. 4.8 A histogram showing the age distribution of the guests at a party. The horizontal axis represents age and the vertical axis represents the number of guests

dark, too bright or has too low a contrast, and automatically correct the image using gray-level mapping. To this end we introduce a simple but powerful tool namely *the image histogram*. Everybody processing images should always look at the histogram of an image before processing it—and so should you!

A histogram is a graphical representation of the frequency of events. Say you are at a party together with 85 other guests. You could then ask the age of each person and plot the result in a histogram, as illustrated in Fig. 4.8. The horizontal axis represents the possible ages and the vertical axis represents the number of people having a certain age. Each column is denoted a *bin* and the height of a bin corresponds to the number of guests having this particular age. This plot is the histogram of the age distribution among the guests at the party. If you divide each bin with the total number of samples (number of guests) each bin now represents the fraction of guests having a certain age—multiply by 100% and you have the numbers in percentages. We can for example see that 11.6% of the guests are 25 years old. In the rest of this book we will denote the vertical axis in a histogram by *frequency*, i.e., the number of samples.

We now do exactly the same for the pixel values of an image. That is, we go through the entire image pixel-by-pixel and count how many pixels have the value 0, how many have the value 1, and so on up to 255. This results in a histogram with 256 bins and this is the image histogram.

If the majority of the pixels in an image have low values we will see this as most high bins being to the left in the histogram and can thus conclude that the image is dark. If most high bins are to the right in the histogram, the image will be bright. If the bins are spread out equally, the image will have a good contrast and vice versa. See Fig. 4.9.

Note that when calculating an image histogram the actual position of the pixels is not used. This means i) that many images have the same histogram and ii) that an image cannot be reconstructed from the histogram. In Fig. 4.10 four images with the same histogram are shown.

We can of course also calculate the histogram of a color image. This is done separately for each color channel. An example is shown in Fig. 4.11.

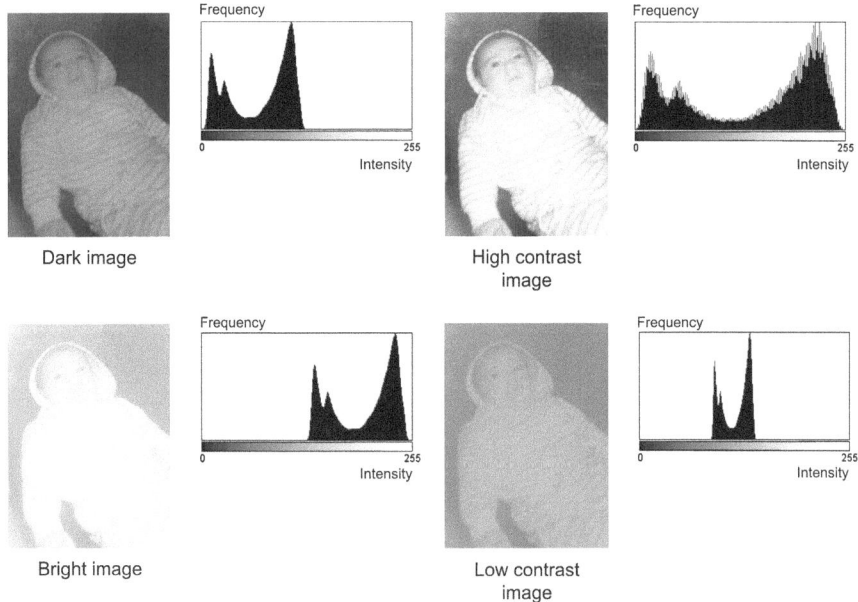

Fig. 4.9 Four images and their respective histograms

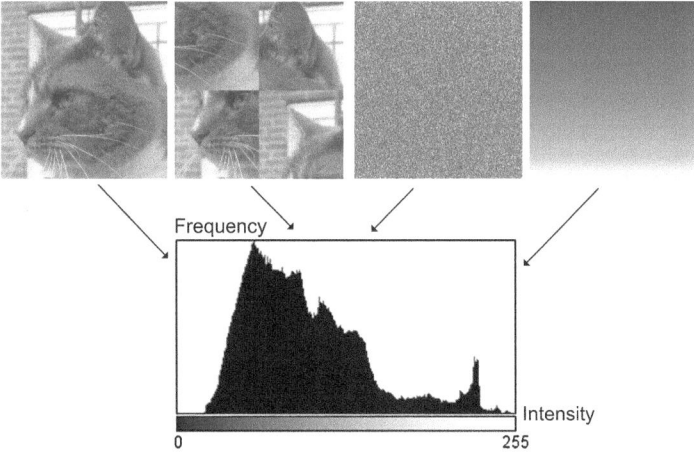

Fig. 4.10 Four images with the exact same histogram

4.3.1 Histogram Stretching

Armed with this new tool we now seek a method to automatically correct the image so that it is neither too bright nor too dark and does not have too low contrast. In terms of histograms, this means that the histogram should start at 0 and end at 255.

Fig. 4.11 The histograms of a color image

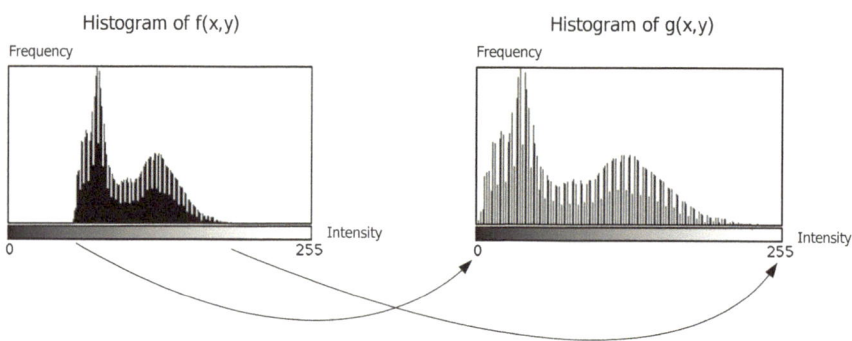

Fig. 4.12 The concept of histogram stretching

We obtain this by mapping the left-most non-zero bin in the histogram to 0 and the right-most non-zero bin to 255, see Fig. 4.12.

We can see that the histogram has been stretched so that the very dark and very bright values are now used. It should also be noted that the distance between the different bins is increased, hence the contrast is improved. This operation is denoted *histogram stretching* and the algorithm is exactly the same as Eq. 4.3 with a and b defined as in Eq. 4.4. f_1 is the left-most non-zero bin in the histogram and f_2 is the right-most non-zero bin in the histogram of the input image.

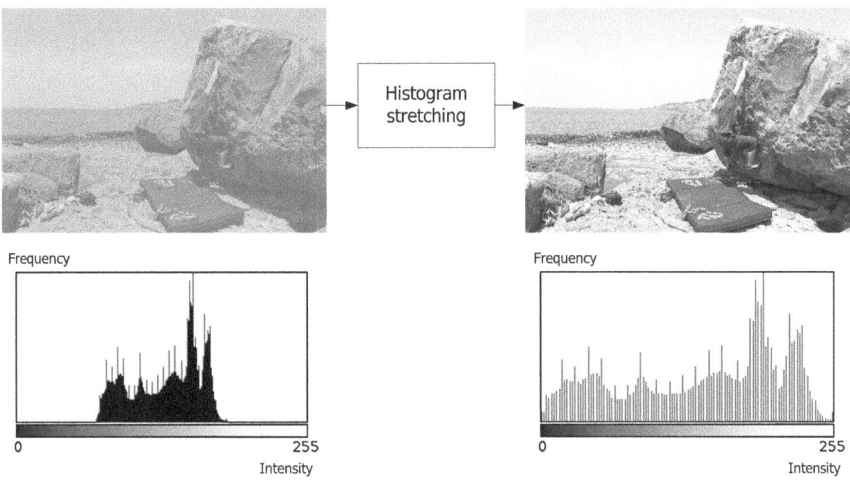

Fig. 4.13 An example of histogram stretching

Conceptually it might be easier to appreciate the equation if we rearrange Eq. 4.3:

$$g(x, y) = \frac{255}{f_2 - f_1} \cdot f(x, y) - f_1 \cdot a \quad \Leftrightarrow \quad (4.10)$$

$$g(x, y) = \frac{255}{f_2 - f_1} \cdot \left(f(x, y) - f_1 \right) \quad (4.11)$$

First the histogram is shifted left so that f_1 is located at 0. Then each value is multiplied by a factor a so that the maximum value $f_2 - f_1$ becomes equal to 255. In Fig. 4.13 an example of histogram stretching is illustrated.

If just one pixel has the value 0 and another 255, histogram stretching will not work, since $f_2 - f_1 = 255$. A solution is *modified histogram stretching* where small bins in the histogram are removed by changing their values to those of larger bins. But if a significant number of pixels with very small and very high values exit, we still have $f_2 - f_1 = 255$, and hence the histogram (and image) remains the same, see Fig. 4.15. A more robust method to improve the histogram (and image) is therefore to apply *histogram equalization*.

4.3.2   Histogram Equalization

Histogram equalization is based on non-linear gray-level mapping using a *cumulative histogram*.

Table 4.1 A small histogram and its cumulative histogram. i is the bin number, $H[i]$ the height of bin i, and $C[i]$ is the height of the ith bin in the cumulative histogram

i	0	1	2	3
$H[i]$	1	5	0	7
$C[i]$	1	6	6	13

Fig. 4.14 An example of a cumulative histogram. Notice how the tall bins in the ordinary histogram translate into steep slopes in the cumulative histogram

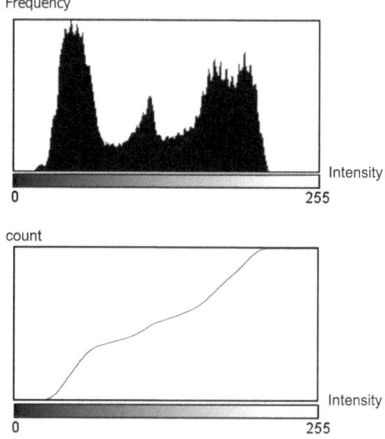

Imagine we have a histogram $H[i]$ where i is a bin number (between 0 and 255) and $H[i]$ is the height of bin i. The cumulative histogram is then defined as

$$C[j] = \sum_{i=0}^{j} H[i] \qquad (4.12)$$

In Table 4.1 a small example is provided.

In Fig. 4.14 a histogram is shown together with its cumulative histogram. Where the histogram has high bins, the cumulative histogram has a steep slope and where the histogram has low bins, the cumulative histogram has a small slope. The idea is now to use the cumulative histogram as a gray-level mapping. So the pixel values located in areas of the histogram where the bins are high and dense will be mapping to a wider interval in the output since the slope is above 1. On the other hand, the regions in the histogram where the bins are small and far apart will be mapped to a smaller interval since the slope of the gray-level mapping is below 1.

For this to work in practice we need to ensure that the y-axis of the cumulative histogram is in the range [0, 255]. This is simply done by first dividing each value on the y-axis with *count*, i.e., the total number of pixels in the image, and then multiply with 255. In Fig. 4.15 the effect of histogram equalization is illustrated.

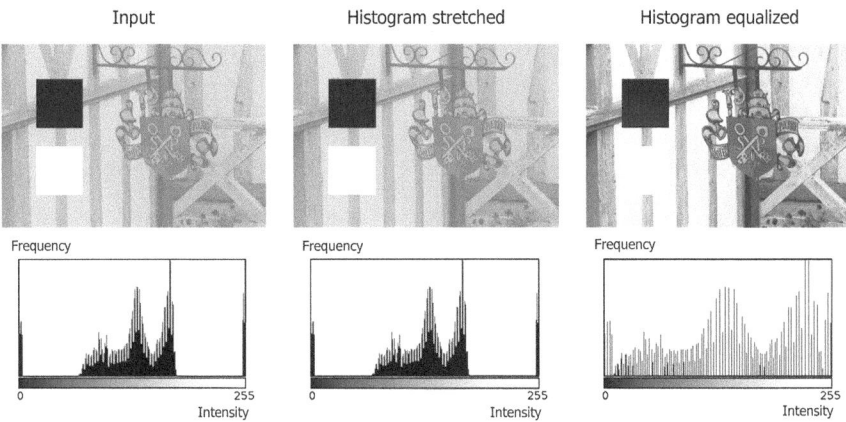

Fig. 4.15 The effect of histogram stretching and histogram equalization on an input image with both very high and very low pixel values

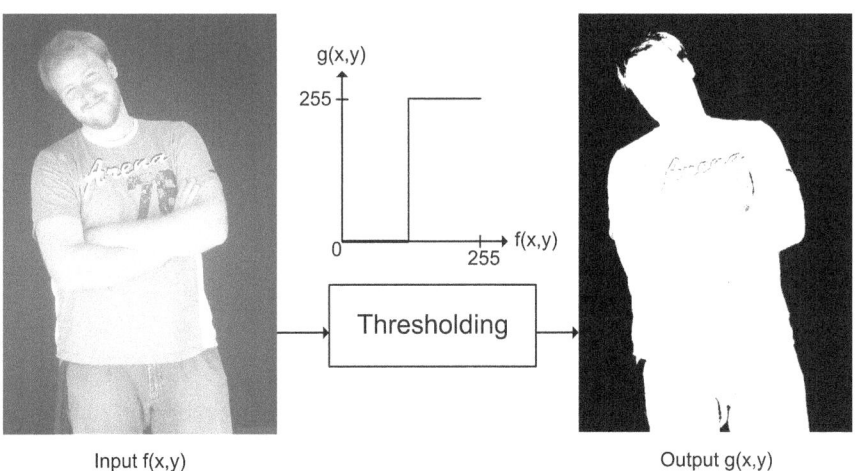

Fig. 4.16 An example of thresholding. Notice that it is impossible to define a perfect silhouette with the thresholding algorithm. This is in general the case

4.4   Thresholding

One of the most fundamental point processing operations is *thresholding*. Thresholding is the special case when $f_1 = f_2$ in Eq. 4.11. Mathematically this is undefined, but in practice it simply means that all input values below f_1 are mapped to zero in the output and all input values above f_1 are mapped to 255 in the output. This means that we will only have completely black and completely white pixel values in the output image. Such an image is denoted a *binary image*, see Fig. 4.16, and this representation of an object is denoted the *silhouette* of the object.

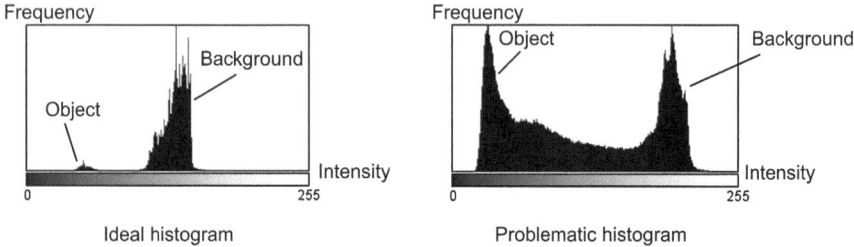

Fig. 4.17 Ideal histogram: a clear definition of object and background. Problematic histogram: the distinction between the object and the background is harder, if not impossible

One might argue that we loose information when doing this operation. However, imagine you are designing a system where the goal is to find the position of a person in a sequence of images and use that to control some parameter in a game. In such a situation all you are interested in is the position of the person and nothing more. In this case, thresholding in such a manner that the person is white and the rest is black, would be exactly what we are interested in. In fact, we can say we have removed the redundant information or eliminated noise in the image.

Thresholding is normally not described in terms of gray-level mapping, but rather as the following *segmentation* algorithm:

$$
\begin{aligned}
\text{if } f(x, y) \leq T & \quad \text{then } g(x, y) = 0 \\
\text{if } f(x, y) > T & \quad \text{then } g(x, y) = 255
\end{aligned}
\tag{4.13}
$$

where T is the threshold value. We might of course also reverse the equalities so that every pixel below the threshold value is mapped to white and every pixel above the threshold value is mapped to black.

In many image processing systems, thresholding is a key step to segmenting the foreground (information) from the background (noise). To obtain a good thresholding the image is preferred to have a histogram which is bi-modal. This means that the histogram should consist of two "mountains" where one mountain corresponds to the background pixels and the other mountain to the foreground pixels. Such a histogram is illustrated to the left in Fig. 4.17. In an ideal situation like the one shown to the right, deciding the threshold value is not critical, but in real life the two mountains are not always separated so nicely and care must therefore be taken when defining the correct threshold value.

In situations where you have influence on the image acquisition process, keep this histogram in mind. In fact, one of the sole purposes of image acquisition is often to achieve such a histogram. So it is often beneficial to develop your image processing algorithms and your setup (camera, optics, lighting, environment) in parallel.

Fig. 4.18 The box is defined by the threshold values. The box indicates the region within the RGB color cube where object pixels lie

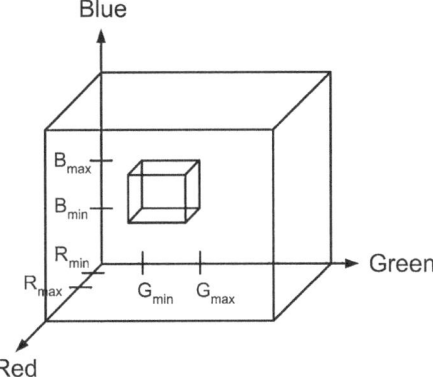

4.4.1   Color Thresholding

Color thresholding can be a powerful approach to segmenting objects in a scene. Imagine you want to detect the hands of a human for controlling some interface. This can be done in a number of ways, where the easiest might be to ask the user to wear colored gloves. If this is combined with the restriction that the particular color of the gloves is neither present in the background nor on the rest of the user, then by finding all pixels with the color of the gloves we have found the hands. This operates similarly to the thresholding operation described in Eq. 4.13. The difference is that each of the color values of a pixel is compared to two threshold values, i.e., in total six threshold values. If each color value for a pixel is within the threshold values, then the pixel is set to white (foreground pixel) otherwise black (background pixel). The algorithm looks as follows for each pixel:

$$
\textbf{If}
$$

$$
\begin{aligned}
&R > R_{\min} \quad \text{and} \quad R < R_{\max} \quad \text{and} \\
&G > G_{\min} \quad \text{and} \quad G < G_{\max} \quad \text{and} \\
&B > B_{\min} \quad \text{and} \quad B < B_{\max}
\end{aligned}
$$

$$
\textbf{Then} \quad g(x, y) = 255
$$

$$
\textbf{Else} \quad g(x, y) = 0
$$

(4.14)

where (R, G, B) are the RGB values of the pixel being processed and $R_{\min}$ and $R_{\max}$ define the range of acceptable values of red in order to accept the current pixel as belonging to an object of interest (similarly for green and blue).

The algorithm actually corresponds to defining a box in the RGB color space and classifying a pixel as belonging to an object if it is within the box and otherwise classifying it as background. This is illustrated in Fig. 4.18.

One problem with color thresholding is its sensitivity to changes in the illumination. Say you have defined your threshold values so that the system can detect the two gloved hands. If someone increases the amount of light in the room, the color

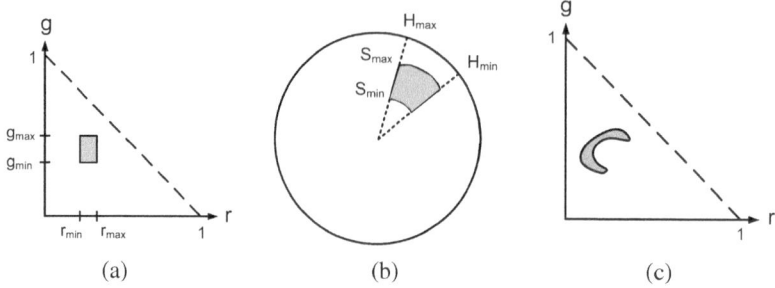

Fig. 4.19 The two gray shapes in figure (**a**) and (**b**) are defined by threshold values and indicate the regions within the two color spaces where object pixels lie. (**a**) The rg-color space. (**b**) The hs-color space. (**c**) An example of a shape that is not well defined by threshold values. Instead a LUT should be applied

will stay the same, but the intensity will change. To handle such a situation, you need to increase/decrease the threshold values accordingly. This will result in the box in Fig. 4.18 being larger and hence the risk of including non-glove pixels will increase. In the worst case, the box will be as large as the entire RGB color cube.

The solution is to convert the RGB color image into a representation where the color and intensity are separated, and then do color thresholding on only the colors, e.g., rg-values or hs-values. The thresholds can now be more tight, hence reducing the risk of false classification. In Fig. 4.19 the equivalent of Fig. 4.18 is shown for rg- and hs-representations, respectively. Regardless of which color representation is applied, the problem of choosing proper threshold values is the same. Please consult Appendix C regarding this matter.

Sometimes we can find ourselves in a situation where the colors of an object are not easily described by a few threshold values. In Fig. 4.19(c) this is illustrated by the banana-shaped region. If you fit a box to this shape (by using four thresholds values) you will clearly include non-object pixels and hence have an incorrect segmentation of the object. The solution is to define a *look-up-table* (LUT). A LUT is a table containing the color values belonging to the object of interest (in some color space). These values can be found in a training phase by manually inspecting the object of interest in a number of different images. Normally the values are considered as an image and a morphologic closing operation, see Chap. 6, is performed to obtain a smooth and coherent shape. During run-time Eq. 4.14 is replaced by a function that takes the value of a pixel and test if this value is present in the LUT. If not, the corresponding output pixel is set to black, otherwise it is set to white.

No matter which color space you use for thresholding it is often a good idea to also do some thresholding on the intensity values. If you look at the color cube you can see that all possible colors will have a vector starting in $(0,0,0)$. This means that the vectors will lie in the vicinity of $(0,0,0)$ and the practical meaning of this is that it is hard to distinguish colors when the intensity is low. Therefore it is often a good idea not to process the colors of pixels with low intensity values. Likewise, color pixels with a very high intensity might also be problematic to process. Say we have a pixel with the following RGB values $(255, 250, 250)$. This will be interpreted as very close to white and hence containing no color. But it might be that the real values are $(10000, 250, 250)$. You have no way of knowing, since the red value is saturated in the image acquisition process. So the red pixel is incorrectly classified as (close to) white. In general you should try to avoid saturated pixels in the image acquisition process, but when you do encounter them, please take great care before using the color of such a pixel. In fact, you are virtually always better off ignoring such pixels.

4.4.2 Thresholding in Video

When you need to threshold a single image you can simply try all possible threshold values and see which one provides the best result. When you built a system that operates on live input video the situation is different. Imagine you have constructed a setup with a camera and some lighting etc. You connect a monitor and look at the images being captured by the camera. If nothing is happening in the images (static scene) the images will seem to be exactly the same. But they are not. For example, if the camera is mounted on a table which moves slightly whenever someone is walking nearby, the images will change slightly. Another typical situation is the fact that most indoor lighting is powered by an alternating light source, for example 50 Hz, meaning that the level of illumination changes rapidly over time. Such changes can often not be detected by simply looking at the scene. But if you subtract two consecutive images[2] and display the result, you can experience this phenomena. If the images are in fact exactly the same, then the output image (after image subtraction) should only contain zeros, hence be black. The more non-zero pixels you have in the output image the more "noise" is present in your setup. Another way of illustrating such small changes is to calculate and visualize the histogram for each image. No matter what, it is always a good idea to use one of these methods to judge the uncertainties in your image acquisition/setup.

Due to these uncertainties you always need to *learn* the threshold values when processing video. In this context, learning means to evaluate what the right threshold value is in different situations and then select a representative value, see Appendix C. Approaching the threshold value selection like this will help in many situation. But if you have a scenario where the lighting can change significantly, then you need a different approach.

A significant change is especially observed when sunlight enters the scene, either because the system operates outside or due to windows in the room where the setup is located. When a cloud passes in front of the sun an abrupt change can be seen in the images. Even without clouds, the changing position (and intensity) of the sun during the day can also result in large changes accumulating over time. Further abrupt changes appear due to the auto gain being enabled, see

---

[2]How to subtract images is explained in Sect. 4.6. This technique plays a major role in Chap. 8.

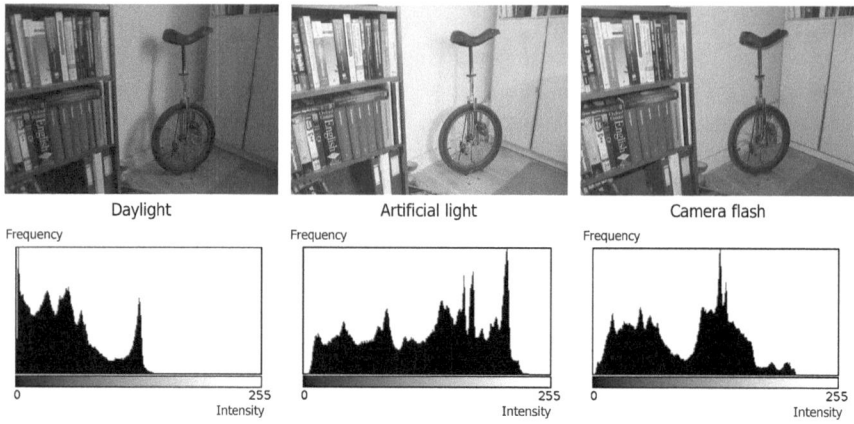

Daylight   Artificial light   Camera flash

Fig. 4.20 Three images of the same scene with different illuminations and hence different histograms

Chap. 2. Imagine a white object is entering a scene where the background is dark. As more and more of the object becomes visible in the scene the auto gain function will decrease the brightness accordingly in order to keep the overall brightness constant. This means that the threshold value needs to be changed from image to image and often rather significantly. Such significant changes can sometimes be handled by preforming a histogram stretching/equalization. This only works when the changes result in a shifted histogram (making the image brighter or darker) without changing the structure of the histogram. An example of a changed structure is when light from multiple windows illuminate the objects in the scene differently over time. In Fig. 4.20 examples of different illuminations of the same scene are shown.

Automatic Thresholding: Global Method

As mentioned above, thresholding is based on the notion that an image consists of two groups of pixels; those from the object of interest (foreground) and those from the background. In the histogram these two groups of pixels result in two "mountains" denoted modes. We want to select a threshold value somewhere between these two modes. Automatic methods for doing so exist and they are based on analyzing the histogram, i.e. all pixels are involved, and hence denoted a *global* method. The idea is to try all possible threshold values and for each, evaluate if we have two good modes. The threshold value producing the best modes is selected. Different definitions of "good modes" exits and here we describe the one suggested by Otsu [14].

The method evaluates Eq. 4.15 for each possible threshold value T and select the T where $C(T)$ is minimum. The reasoning behind the equation is that the correct threshold value will produce two narrow modes, whereas an incorrect threshold value will produce (at least one) wide mode. The narrowness of a mode can be measured by the variance σ^2, see Appendix C for a definition of σ^2. So the smaller the variances the better. To balance the measure, each variance is weighted by the

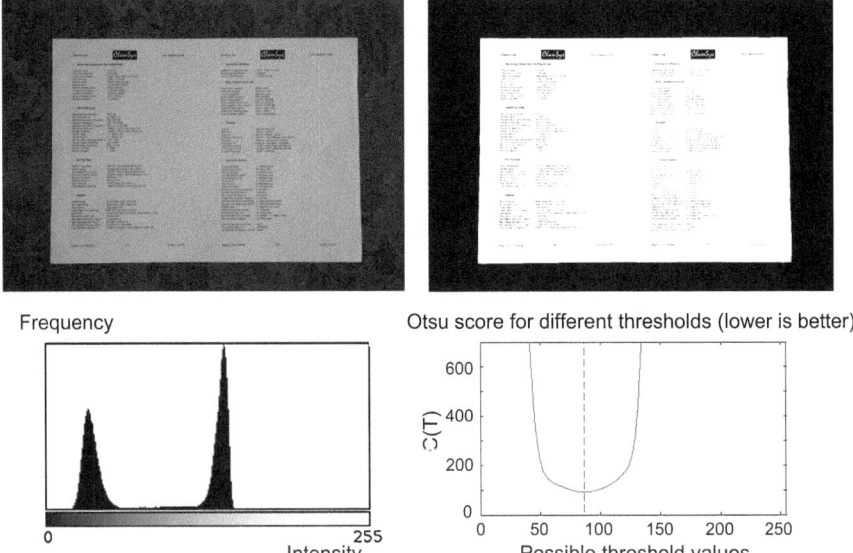

Fig. 4.21 Global automatic thresholding. *Top left*: Input image. *Top right*: Input image thresholded by the value found by Otsu's method. *Bottom left*: Histogram of input image. *Bottom right*: $C(T)$ as a function of T. See text. The *vertical dashed line* illustrates the minimum value, i.e., the selected threshold value

number of pixels used to calculate it. A very efficient implementation is described in [14]. The method works very well in situations where two distinct modes are present in the histogram, see Fig. 4.21, but it can also produce good results when the two modes are not so obvious.

$$C(T) = M_1(T) \cdot \sigma_1^2(T) + M_2(T) \cdot \sigma_2^2(T) \qquad (4.15)$$

where $M_1(T)$ is the number of pixels to the left of T and $M_2(T)$ is the rest of the pixels in the image. $\sigma_1^2(T)$ and $\sigma_2^2(T)$ are the variances of the pixels to the left and right of T, respectively.

Automatic Thresholding: Local Method

In Fig. 4.23 an image with non-even illuminating is shown. The consequence of this type of illumination is that an object pixel in one part of the image is identical to a background pixel in another part of the image. The image can therefore not be thresholded using a single (global) threshold value, see Fig. 4.23. But if we crop out a small area of the image and look at the histogram, we can see that two modes are present and that this image can easily be thresholded, see Fig. 4.22. From this follows that thresholding is possible locally, but not globally.

We can view thresholding as a matter of finding object pixels and these are per definition different from background pixels. So if we had an image of the background, we could then subtract it from the input image and the object pix-

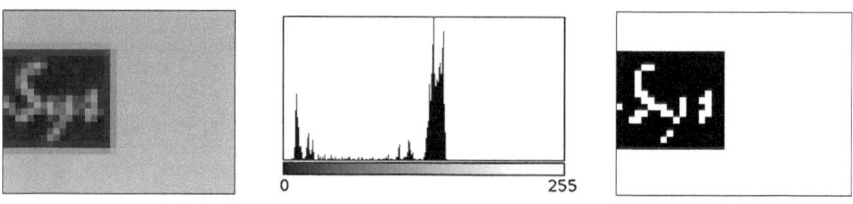

Fig. 4.22 *Left*: Cropped image. *Center*: Histogram of input. *Right*: Thresholded image

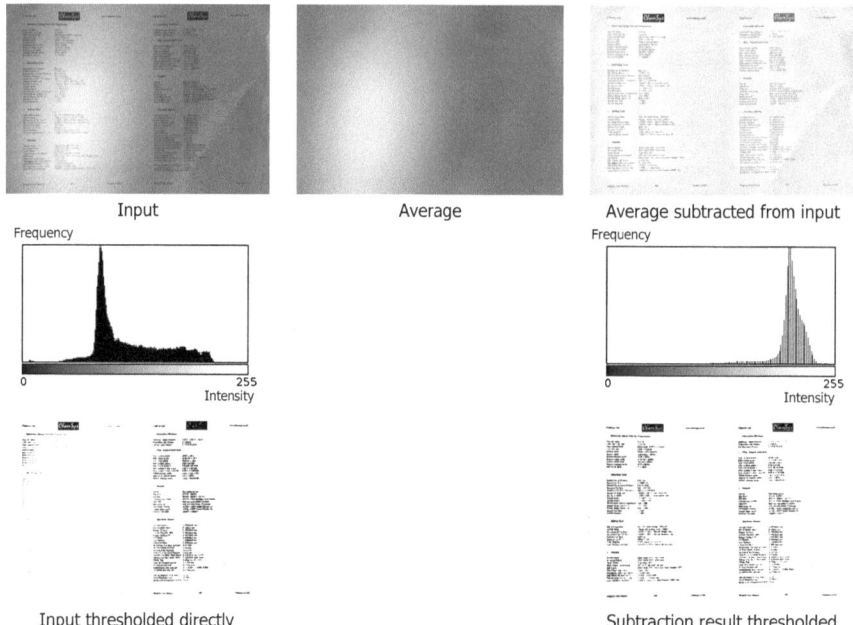

Fig. 4.23 Local automatic thresholding. *Top row*: *Left*: Input image. *Center*: Mean version of input image. *Right*: Mean image subtracted from input. *Center row*: Histograms of input and mean image subtracted from input. *Bottom row*: Thresholded images

els would stand out. We can estimate a background pixel by calculating the average of the neighboring pixels.[3] Doing this for all pixels will result in an estimate of the background image, see Fig. 4.23. We now subtract the input and the background image and the result is an image with a more even illumination where a global threshold value can be applied, see Fig. 4.23.[4] Depending on the situation this could either be a fixed threshold value or an automatic value as describe above.

---

[3] How to calculate the average is discussed in the next chapter.

[4] In the subtraction process both positive and negative values can appear. Since we are only interested in the difference we take the absolute value.

The number of neighborhood pixels to include in the calculation of the average image depends on the nature of the uneven illumination, but in general it should be a very high number. The method assumes the foreground objects of interest are small compared to the background. The more this assumption is violated, the worse the method performs.

4.5   Logic Operations on Binary Images

After thresholding we have a binary image consisting of only white pixels (255) and black pixels (0). We can combine two binary images using logic operations. The basic logic operations are NOT, AND, OR, and XOR (exclusive OR). The NOT operation do not combine two images but only works on one at a time. NOT simply means to invert the binary image. That is, if a pixel has the value 0 in the input it will have the value 255 in the output, and if the input is 255 the output will be 0. The three other basic logic operations combine two images into one output. Their operations are described using a so-called *truth table*. Below the three truth tables are listed.

(a) Truth table for AND

AND	Input 2	
	0	255
Input 1 0	0	0
Input 1 255	0	255

(b) Truth table for OR

OR	Input 2	
	0	255
Input 1 0	0	255
Input 1 255	255	255

(c) Truth table for XOR

XOR	Input 2	
	0	255
Input 1 0	0	255
Input 1 255	255	0

A truth table is interpreted in the following way. The left-most column contains the possible values a pixel in image 1 can have. The topmost row contains the possible values a pixel in image 2 can have. The four remaining values are the output values. From the truth tables we can for example see that 255 AND 0 = 0, and 0 OR 255 = 255. In Fig. 4.24 a few other examples are shown. Note that from a programming point of view white can be represented by 1 and only one byte is then required to represent each pixel. This can save memory and speed up the implementation.

4.6   Image Arithmetic

Instead of combining an image with a scalar as in Eq. 4.1, an image can also be combined with another image. Say we have two images of equal size, $f_1(x, y)$ and $f_2(x, y)$. These are combined pixel-wise in the following way:

$$g(x, y) = f_1(x, y) + f_2(x, y) \qquad (4.16)$$

Fig. 4.24 Different logic
operations

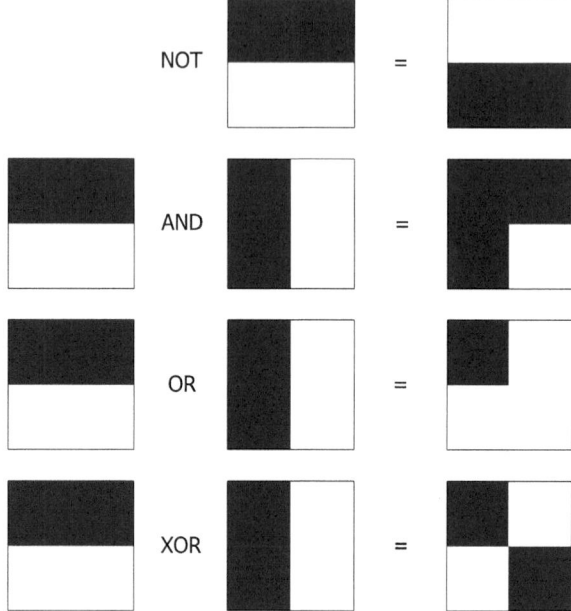

Other arithmetic operations can also be used to combine two images, but most often addition or subtraction are the ones applied. No matter the operation image arithmetic works equally well for gray-scale and color images.

When adding two images some of the pixel values in the output image might have values above 255. For example if $f_1(10, 10) = 150$ and $f_2(10, 10) = 200$, then $g(10, 10) = 350$. In principle this does not matter, but if an 8-bit image is used for the output image, then we have the problem known as *overflow*. That is, the value cannot be represented. A similar situation can occur for image subtraction where a negative number can appear in the output image. This is known as *underflow*.

One might argue that we could simply use a 16 or 32-bit image to avoid these problems. However, using more bit per pixel will take up more space in the computer memory and require more processing power from the CPU. When dealing with many images, e.g., video data, this can be a problem.

The solution is therefore to use a temporary image (16-bit or 32-bit) to store the result and then map the temporary image to a standard 8-bit image for further processing. This principle is illustrated in Fig. 4.25.

This algorithm is the same as used for histogram stretching except that the minimum value can be negative:

1. Find the minimum number in the temporary image, f_1
2. Find the maximum number in the temporary image, f_2
3. Shift all pixels so that the minimum value is 0: $g_i(x, y) = g_i(x, y) - f_1$
4. Scale all pixels so that the maximum value is 255: $g(x, y) = g_i(x, y) \cdot \frac{255}{f_2 - f_1}$

where $g_i(x, y)$ is the temporary image.

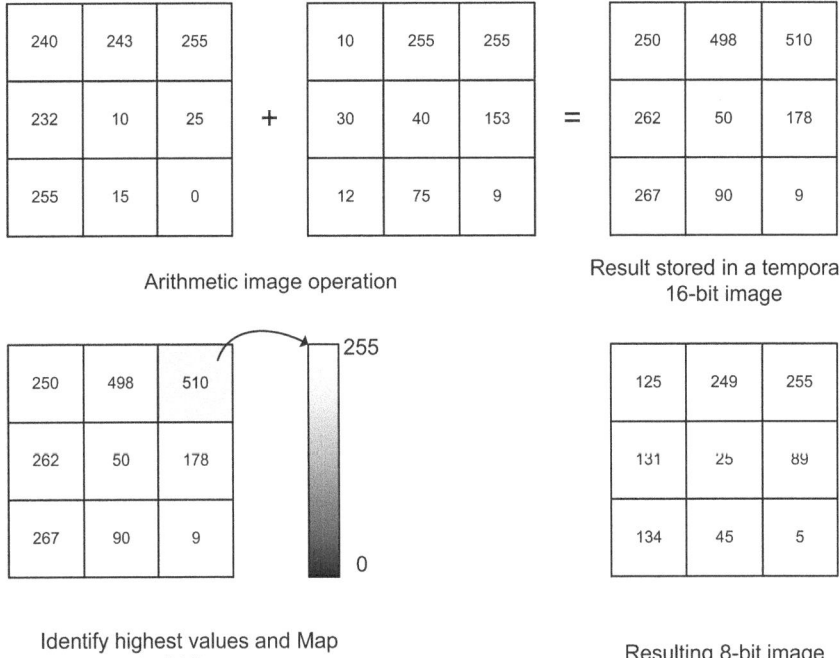

Arithmetic image operation

Result stored in a temporary 16-bit image

Identify highest values and Map onto 8-bit range

Resulting 8-bit image

Fig. 4.25 An example of overflow and how to handle it. The addition of the images produces values above the range of the 8-bit image, which is handled by storing the result in a temporary image. In this temporary image the highest value is identified, and used to scale the intensity values down into the 8-bit range. The same approach is used for underflow. This approach also works for images with both over- and underflow

Image arithmetic has a number of interesting usages and here two are presented. In Chap. 8 we present another one, which is related to video processing.

The first one is simply to invert an image. That is, a black pixel in the input becomes a white pixel in the output etc. The equation for image inversion is defined in Eq. 4.17 and an example is illustrated in Fig. 4.26.

$$g(x, y) = 255 - f(x, y) \qquad (4.17)$$

Another use of image arithmetic is *alpha blending*. Alpha blending is used when mixing two images, for example gradually changing from one image to another image. The idea is to extend Eq. 4.16 so that the two images have different importance. For example 20% of $f_1(x, y)$ and 80% of $f_2(x, y)$. Note that the sum of the two percentages should be 100%. Concretely, the equation is rewritten as

$$g(x, y) = \alpha \cdot f_1(x, y) + (1 - \alpha) \cdot f_2(x, y) \qquad (4.18)$$

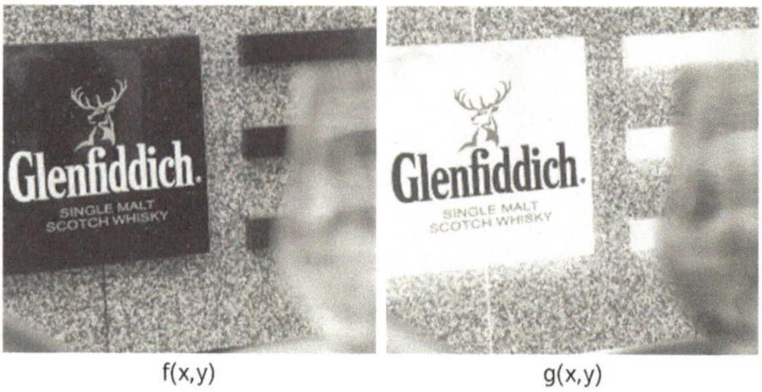

Fig. 4.26 Input image and inverted image

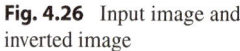

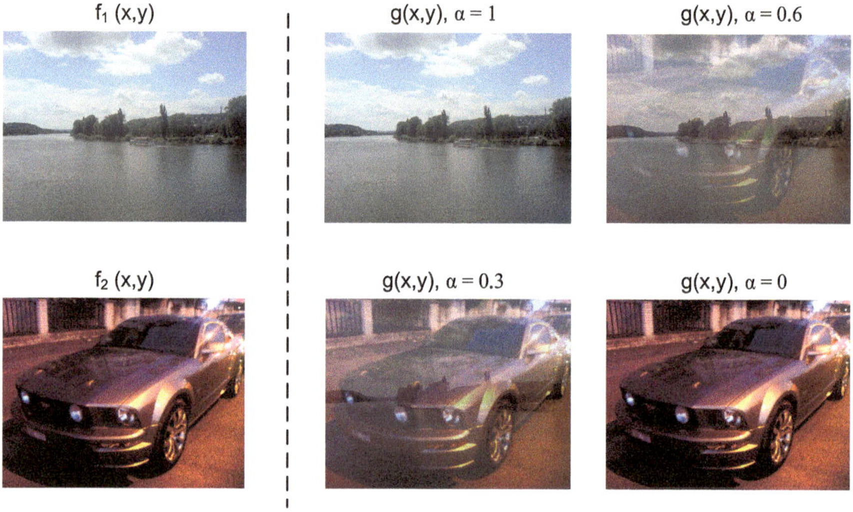

f(x,y)   g(x,y)

f₁ (x,y)   g(x,y), α = 1   g(x,y), α = 0.6

f₂ (x,y)   g(x,y), α = 0.3   g(x,y), α = 0

Fig. 4.27 Examples of alpha blending, with different alpha values

where $\alpha \in [0, 1]$ and α is the Greek letter "alpha", hence the name alpha blending. If $\alpha = 0.5$ then the two images are mixed equally and Eq. 4.18 has the same effect as Eq. 4.16. In Fig. 4.27, a mixing of two images is shown for different values of α.

In Eq. 4.18, α is the same for every pixel, but it can actually be different from pixel to pixel. This means that we have an entire image (with the same size as $f_1(x, y)$, $f_2(x, y)$ and $g(x, y)$) where we have α-values instead of pixels: $\alpha(x, y)$. Such an "α-image" is often referred to as an *alpha-channel*. This can for example be used to define the transparency of an object.

4.7 Programming Point Processing Operations

When implementing one of the point processing operations in software the following is done.

Fig. 4.28 The order in which the pixels are visited. Illustrated for a 10 × 10 image

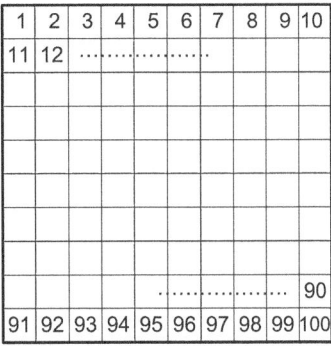

Remember that each pixel is individually processed meaning that it does not matter in which order the pixels are processed. However, we follow the order illustrated in Fig. 4.28. Starting in the upper-left corner we move from left to right and from top to bottom ending in the lower-right corner.[5]

Note that this order corresponds to the way the coordinate system is defined, see Fig. 2.19. The reason for this order is that it corresponds to the order in which the pixels from the camera are sent to the memory of the computer. Also the same order the pixels on your TV are updated. Physically the pixels are also stored in this order meaning that your algorithm is faster when you process the pixels in this order due to memory access time.

In terms of programming the point processing operations can be implemented as illustrated below—here exemplified in C-code:

```
for  (y  =  0;  y  <  M;  y  =  y  +  1)
{
   for  (x  =  0;  x  <  N;  x  =  x  +  1)
   {
      temp  =  GetPixel(input ,  x ,  y);
      value  =  Operation(temp);
      SetPixel(output ,  x ,  y ,  value);
   }
}
```

where M is the height of the image and N is the width of the image. *GetPixel* is a function, which returns the value of the pixel at position (x, y) in the image called *input*. The function *SetPixel* changes the value of the pixel at position (x, y) in the image called *output* to *value*. Note that the two functions are not built-in C-functions. That is, you either need to write them yourself or include a library where they (or similar functions) are defined.

---

[5]Note that the above order of scanning through the image and the code example is general and used for virtually all methods, operations and algorithms presented in this book.

The programming example primarily consists of two FOR-loops which go through the image, pixel-by-pixel, in the order illustrated in Fig. 4.28. For each pixel, a point processing operation is applied.

Below we show what the C-code would look like if the operation in Eq. 4.3 were implemented.

```
for (y = 0; y < M; y = y + 1)
{
    for (x = 0; x < N; x = x + 1)
    {
        value = a * GetPixel(input, x, y) + b;
        SetPixel(output, x, y, value);
    }
}
```

where a and b are defined beforehand.

Below we show what the C-code would look like if the operation in Eq. 4.13 were implemented.

```
for (y = 0; y < M; y = y + 1)
{
    for (x = 0; x < N; x = x + 1)
    {
        if (GetPixel(input, x, y) > T)
            SetPixel(output, x, y, 255);
        else
            SetPixel(output, x, y, 0);
    }
}
```

where T is defined beforehand.

4.8   Further Information

Thresholding is a key method in many video processing systems. Please remember that there is a direct relationship between your image acquisition process, your setup and your choice of threshold value. If the methods described in this chapter are not sufficient, please bear in mind that other methods for especially automatic thresholding exist.

A very popular use of color thresholding is to segment objects (especially people) by placing them in front of a unique colored background. The object pixels are then found as those pixels in the image which do *not* have this unique color. This principle is denoted *chroma-keying* and used for special effects in many movie productions as well as in TV weather-forecasts, etc. In the latter example the host appears to

Fig. 4.29 Two gray-scale images

$f_1(x,y)$ $f_2(x,y)$

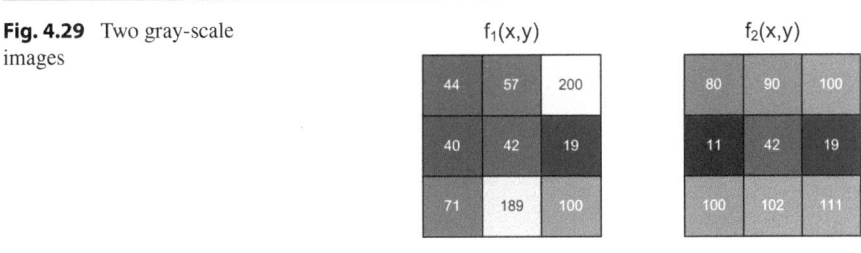

Frequency

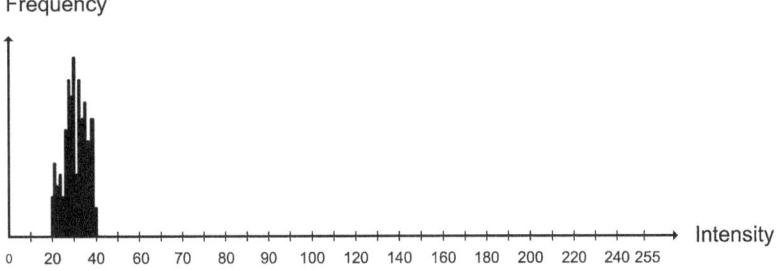

Fig. 4.30 The histogram of an image

be standing in front of a weather map. In reality the host is standing in front of a green or blue screen and the background pixels are then replaced by pixels from the weather map. Obviously, this only works when the color of the host's clothing is different from the unique color used for covering the background.

When you as a designer have the freedom of defining the colors to be recognized you can use the HSI color representation to select the most optimal colors. If you only need one color, then you are free to choose, but when more colors are to be thresholded, optimal basically means to pick colors most different and hence avoid overlap. Looking at the HS circle in Fig. 3.11 you can see that the angle between two colors should be 180° in order to minimize the risk of overlap. With three colors you need to have 120° between the colors etc. Obviously this approach assumes you can construct all possible color, which might not be realistic in a real-life situation.

4.9   Exercises

Exercise 1: Explain the following concepts: point processing, brightness, contrast, gray-level mapping, image histogram, thresholding, logic operations.

Exercise 2: A linear gray-level mapping is performed on image $f_1(x, y)$ in Fig. 4.29 where $a = 1$ and $b = 15$. What is the output value of $f_1(2, 2)$?

Exercise 3: A gamma gray-level mapping is performed on image $f_1(x, y)$ in Fig. 4.29 where $\gamma = 0.45$. What is the output value of $f_1(2, 2)$?

Exercise 4: A logarithmic gray-level mapping is performed on image $f_1(x, y)$ in Fig. 4.29. What is the output value of $f_1(2, 2)$?

Exercise 5: Given a histogram, how can the original gray-scale image be recreated?

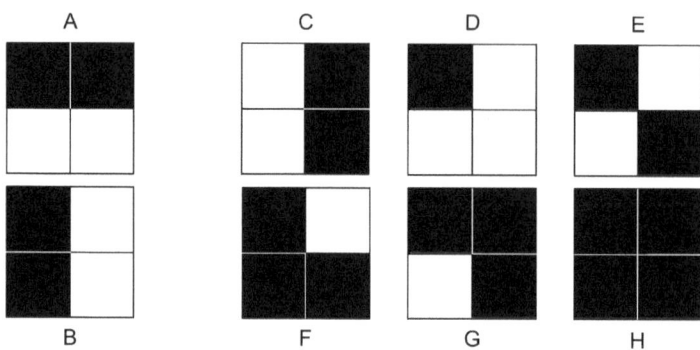

Fig. 4.31 Eight binary images

Exercise 6: Look at the histogram in Fig. 4.30. Does it come from a dark or bright image?

Exercise 7: Look at the histogram in Fig. 4.30. Does it come from an image with high or low contrast?

Exercise 8: Histogram stretching is performed on the histogram in Fig. 4.30. After histogram stretching a pixel has the value 128. What value did this pixel have before histogram stretching?

Exercise 9: Calculate the cumulative histogram of image $f_2(x, y)$ in Fig. 4.29.

Exercise 10: How will the threshold algorithm look like if two threshold values are used instead of just one?

Exercise 11: Explain the two automatic thresholding methods and discuss their differences.

Exercise 12: Given the two binary images A and B in Fig. 4.31. How can logic operations be applied to generate the binary images: C, D, E, F, G, and H?

Exercise 13: The two images $f_1(x, y)$ and $f_2(x, y)$ in Fig. 4.29 are added together. Calculate the 8-bit output image?

Exercise 14: The image $f_2(x, y)$ in Fig. 4.29 is inverted and alpha blended with $f_1(x, y)$ where $\alpha = 0.5$. Calculate the output image.

Additional exercise 1: Describe the motivation for using gamma-correction in image capturing and visualization.

Additional exercise 2: Find and describe alternative automatic thresholding methods.

Neighborhood Processing

5

In the previous chapter we saw that a pixel value in the output was set according to a pixel value in the input *at the same position* and a point processing operation. This principle has many useful applications (as we saw), but it cannot be applied to investigate the relationship between *neighboring pixels*. For example, if we look at the pixel values in the small area in Fig. 5.1, we can see that a significant change in intensity values occurs in the lower left corner. This could indicate the boundary of an object and by finding the boundary pixels we have found the object.

In this and the next chapter we present a number of methods where the neighbor pixels play a role when determining the output value of a pixel. Overall these methods are denoted *neighborhood processing* and the principle is illustrated in Fig. 5.2. The value of a pixel in the output is determined by the value of the pixel at the same position in the input *and* the neighbors together with a neighborhood processing operation. We use the same notation as in the previous chapter, i.e., $f(x, y)$ is the input image and $g(x, y)$ is the output image.[1]

5.1 The Median Filter

If we look at Fig. 5.3 we can see that it has been infected with some kind of noise (the black and white dots). Let us set out to remove this noise. First of all we zoom in on the image and look closer at particular pixel values. What we can see is that the noise is isolated pixels having a value of either 0 (black) or 255 (white), such noise is denoted *salt-and-pepper noise*. By *isolated* we mean that they have a value very different from their neighbors. We need somehow to identify such pixels and replace them by a value which is more similar to the neighbors.

One solution is to replace the noise pixel by the *mean* value of the neighbors. Say we use the eight nearest neighbors for the noise pixel at position $(1, 1)$ in the image patch in Fig. 5.3. The mean value is then

---

[1] Readers unfamiliar with vectors and matrices are advised to consult Appendix B before reading this chapter.

T.B. Moeslund, *Introduction to Video and Image Processing*,
Undergraduate Topics in Computer Science,
DOI 10.1007/978-1-4471-2503-7_5, © Springer-Verlag London Limited 2012

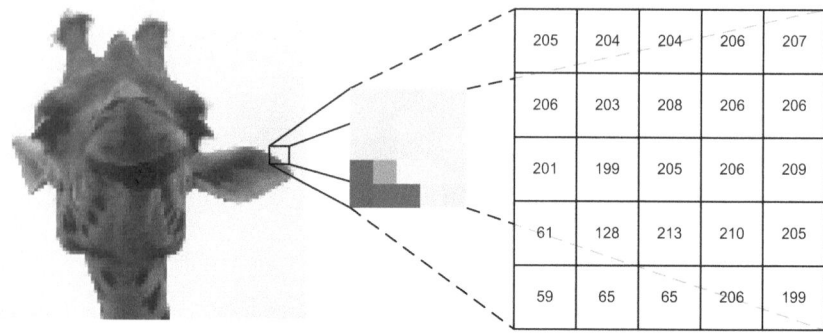

Fig. 5.1 A part of the giraffe-image has been enlarged to show the edge which humans easily perceive. Using methods described in this chapter the computer will also be able to tell where the edge is

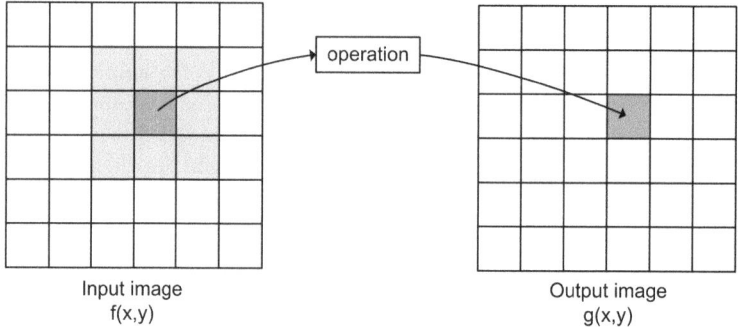

Fig. 5.2 The principle of neighborhood processing. To calculate a pixel in the output image, a pixel from the input image and its neighbors are processed

$$\text{Mean value} = \frac{205 + 204 + 204 + 206 + 0 + 208 + 201 + 199 + 205}{9}$$
$$= 181.3 \simeq 181 \tag{5.1}$$

This results in the noise pixel being replaced by 181, which is more similar to the neighbors. However, the value still stands out and therefore the *median* is often used instead. The median value of a group of numbers is found by ordering the numbers in increasing order and picking the middle value. Say we use the eight nearest neighbors for the first pixel infested by noise in Fig. 5.3. The ordering yields

$$\text{Ordering}: [0, 199, 201, 204, \underline{204}, 205, 205, 206, 208]$$
$$\text{Median} = 204 \tag{5.2}$$

and the middle value is 204, hence the median is 204. The noise pixel is now replaced by 204, which does not stand out.

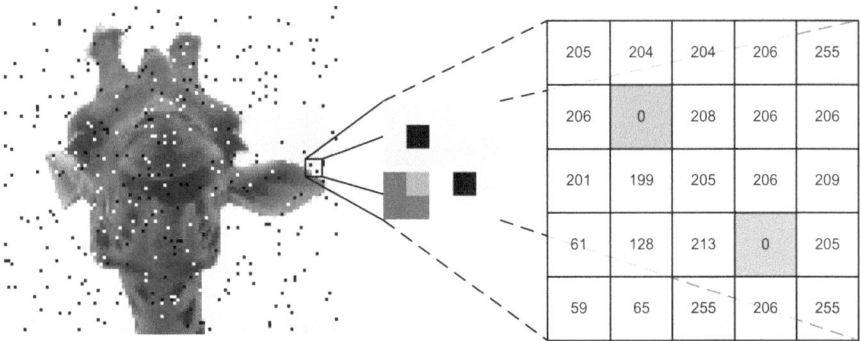

Fig. 5.3 An image infected with salt-and-pepper noise. The noise is easily recognized in both the image- and the number representations

The next question is how to find the noise pixels in order to know where to perform the median operation. For the particular example we could scan the image pixel-by-pixel and look for isolated values of 0 or 255. When encountered, the median operation could be applied. In general, however, a pixel with a value of say 234 could also be considered noise if it is isolated (stands out from its neighbors). Therefore, the median operation is applied to every single pixel in the image and we call this *filtering the image* using a *median filter*. Filtering the image refers to the process of applying a filter (here the median filter) to the entire image. It is important to note that by filtering the image we apply the filter to each and every pixel.

When filtering the image we of course need to decide which operation to apply but we also need to specify the size of the filter. The filter used in Fig. 5.2 is a 3×3 filter. Since filters are centered on a particular pixel (the center of the filter) the size of the filter is uneven, i.e., 3, 5, 7, etc. Very often filters have equal spatial dimensions, i.e., 3×3, 5×5, 7×7, etc. Sometimes a filter is described by its radius rather than its size. The radius of a 3×3 filter is 1, 2 for a 5×5 filter, 3 for a 7×7 filter etc. The radius/size of a filter controls the number of neighbors included. The more neighbors included, the more strongly the image is filtered. Whether this is desirable or not depends on the application. Note that the larger the size, the more processing power is required by the computer. Applying a filter to an image is done by scanning through the image pixel-by-pixel from the upper left corner toward the lower right corner, as described in the previous chapter. Figure 5.4 shows how the image in Fig. 5.3 is being filtered by a 3×3 (radius = 1) mean and median filter, respectively. Note the superiority of the median filter.

In terms of programming, the Median filter can be implemented as illustrated below—here exemplified in C-code:

```
for (y = Radius; y < (M - Radius); y = y + 1)
{
   for (x = Radius; x < (N - Radius); x = x + 1)
   {
```

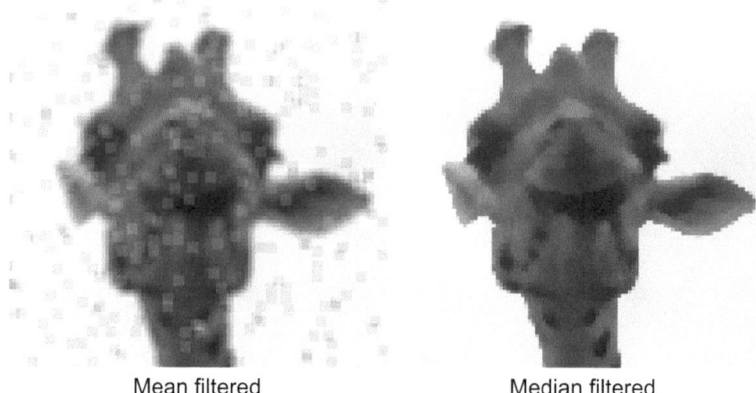

Mean filtered   Median filtered

Fig. 5.4 Resulting images of two noise filters. Notice that the mean filter does not remove all the noise and that it blurs the image. The median filter removes all the noise and only blurs the image slightly

```
    GetPixelValues(x, y);
    SortPixelValues();
    value = FindMedian();
    SetPixel(output, x, y, value);
  }
}
```

where M is the height of the image, N is the width of the image and *Radius* is the radius of the filter.

What should be noticed both in the figure and in the code is that the output image will be smaller than the input image. The reason is that the filter is defined with a center and a radius, but if the center is a pixel in for example the first row, then no neighbors are defined above. This is known as the *border problem*, see Fig. 5.5. If it is unacceptable that the output image is reduced in size (for example because it is to be added to the input image) then inspiration can be found in one of the following suggestions[2]:

Increase the output image After the output image has been generated, the pixel values in the last row (if radius = 1) is duplicated and appended to the image. The same for the first row, first column and last column.

Increase the input image Before the image is filtered the pixel values in the last row (if radius = 1) of the input image is duplicated and appended to the input image. The same for the first row, first column and last column.

Apply special filters at the rim of the image Special filters with special sizes are defined and applied accordingly, see Fig. 5.5.

---

[2]Note that this issue is common for all neighborhood processing methods.

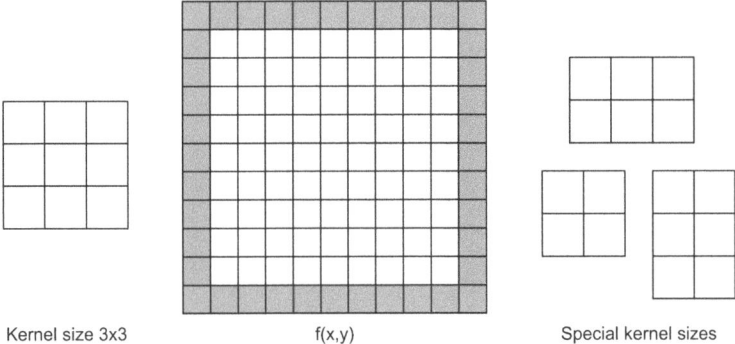

Kernel size 3x3   f(x,y)   Special kernel sizes

Fig. 5.5 An illustration of the border problem, which occurs when using neighborhood processing algorithms. If a kernel with a size of 3×3 is used, then the border illustrated in $f(x, y)$ cannot be processed. One solution to this is to apply kernels with special sizes on the borders, like the ones showed to the *right*

5.1.1 Rank Filters

The Median Filter belongs to a group of filters known as *Rank Filters*. The only difference between them is the value which is picked after the pixels have been sorted:

The minimum value This filter will make the image darker.

The maximum value This filter will make the image brighter.

The difference This filter outputs the difference between the maximum and minimum value and the result is an image where the transitions between light and dark (and opposite) are enhanced. Such a transition is often denoted an edge in an image. More on this in Sect. 5.2.2.

5.2 Correlation

Correlation is an operation which also works by scanning through the image and applying a filter to each pixel. In correlation, however, the filter is denoted a *kernel* and plays a more active role. First of all the kernel is filled by numbers—denoted *kernel coefficients*. These coefficients weight the pixel value they are covering and the output of the correlation is a sum of weighted pixel values. In Fig. 5.6 some different kernels are shown.

Similar to the median filter the kernel is centered above the pixel position whose value we are calculating. We denote this center $(0, 0)$ in the kernel coordinate system and the kernel as $h(x, y)$, see Fig. 5.7. To calculate the output value we take the value of $h(-1, -1)$ and multiply it by the pixel value beneath. Let us say that we are calculating the output value of the pixel at position $(2, 2)$. Then $h(-1, -1)$ will be above the pixel $f(1, 1)$ and the value of these two pixels are multiplied together. The result is added to the product of the next kernel element $h(0, -1)$ and the pixel

1	4	7	4	1
4	16	26	16	4
7	26	41	26	7
4	16	26	16	4
1	4	7	4	1

1	1	1
1	1	1
1	1	1

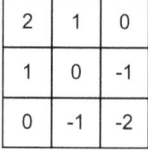

3x3 Mean kernel   5x5 Gaussian kernel   3x3 Sobel kernel

Fig. 5.6 Three different kernels

value beneath $f(2, 1)$, etc. The final value which will be written into the output image as $g(2, 2)$ is found as

$$g(2, 2) = h(-1, -1) \cdot f(1, 1) + h(0, -1) \cdot f(2, 1) + h(1, -1) \cdot f(3, 1)$$
$$+ h(-1, 0) \cdot f(1, 2) + h(0, 0) \cdot f(2, 2) + h(1, 0) \cdot f(3, 2)$$
$$+ h(-1, 1) \cdot f(1, 3) + h(0, 1) \cdot f(2, 3) + h(1, 1) \cdot f(3, 3) \qquad (5.3)$$

The principle is illustrated in Fig. 5.7. We say that we correlate the input image $f(x, y)$ with the kernel $h(x, y)$ and the result is $g(x, y)$. Mathematically this is expressed as $g(x, y) = f(x, y) \circ h(x, y)$ and written as

$$g(x, y) = \sum_{j=-R}^{R} \sum_{i=-R}^{R} h(i, j) \cdot f(x + i, y + j) \qquad (5.4)$$

where R is the radius of the kernel.[3] Below, a C-code example of how to implement correlation is shown:

```
for (y = Radius; y < (M - Radius); y = y + 1)
{
    for (x = Radius; x < (N - Radius); x = x + 1)
    {
        temp = 0;
        for (j = -Radius; j < (Radius + 1); j = j + 1)
        {
            for (i = -Radius; i < (Radius+1); i = i + 1)
            {
                temp = temp + h(i,j) * GetPixel(input,x+i,y+j);
            }
```

---

[3]The reader is encouraged to play around with this equation in order to fully comprehend it.

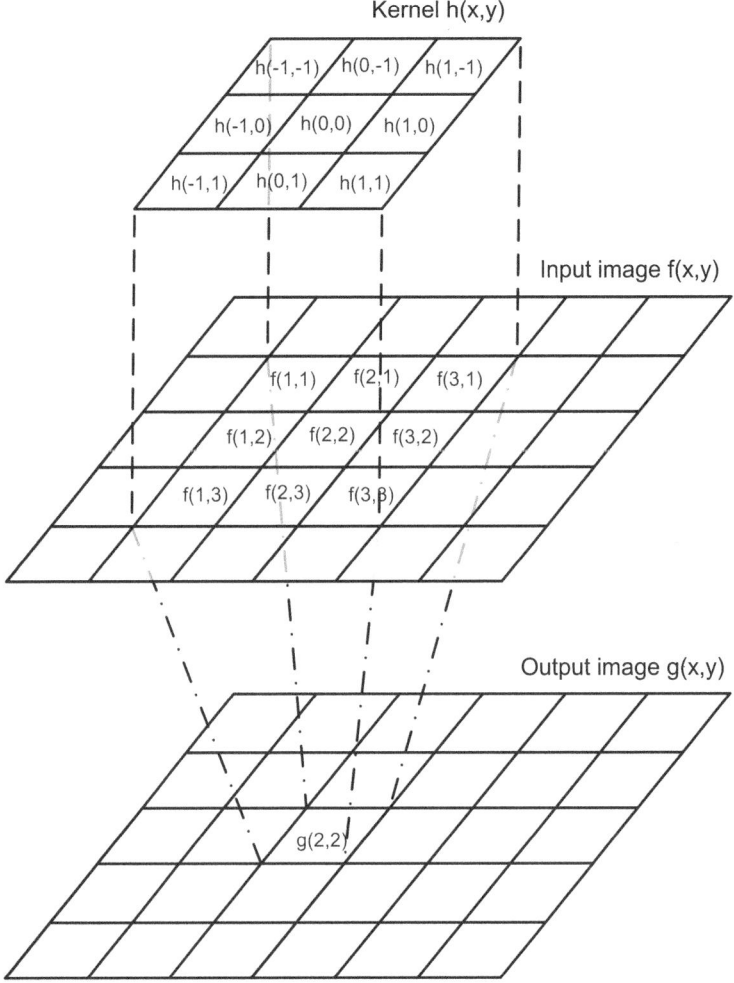

Fig. 5.7   The principle of correlation, illustrated with a 3 × 3 kernel on a 6 × 6 image

```
        }
        SetPixel(output, x, y, temp);
    }
}
```

When applying correlation, the values in the output can be above 255. If this is the case, then we normalize the kernel coefficients so that the maximum output of the correlation operation is 255. The normalization factor is found as the sum of the kernel coefficients. That is $\sum_x \sum_y h(x, y)$. For the left-most kernel in Fig. 5.6 the normalization factor becomes $1 + 1 + 1 + 1 + 1 + 1 + 1 + 1 + 1 = 9$, and the resulting kernel coefficients are $1/9$ as opposed to 1.

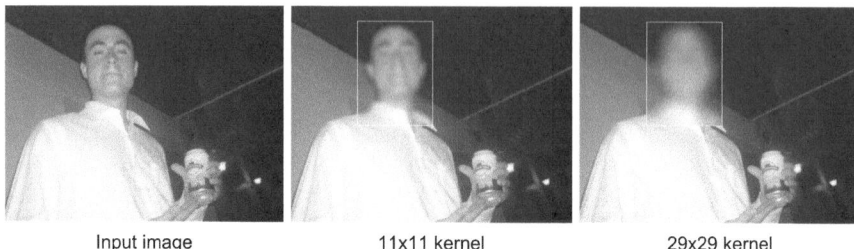

Input image   11x11 kernel   29x29 kernel

Fig. 5.8   An example of how a mean filter can be used to hide the identity of a person. The size of the mean kernel decides the strength of the filter. Actual image size: 512×384

Looking back on the previous section we can now see that the left-most kernel in Fig. 5.6 is exactly the mean filter. The mean filter smooths or blurs the image which has different applications. In Fig. 5.8 one application is shown where the mean filter is applied within the white box in order to hide the identity of a person. The bigger the kernel, the more the smoothing. Another type of mean filter is when a kernel like the middle one in Fig. 5.6 is applied. This provides higher weights to pixels close to the center of the kernel. This mean filter is known as a *Gaussian filter*, since the kernel coefficients are calculated from the Gaussian distribution (a bell-shaped curve).

5.2.1   Template Matching

An important application of correlation is *template matching*. Template matching is used to locate an object in an image. When applying template matching the kernel is denoted a *template*. It operates by defining an image of the object we are looking for. This object is now the template (kernel) and by correlating an image with this template, the output image indicates where the object is. Each pixel in the output image now holds a value, which states the similarity between the template and an image patch (with the same size as the template) centered at this particular pixel position. The brighter a value, the higher the similarity.

In Fig. 5.9 the correlation-based template matching is illustrated.[4] We can see a bright spot in the center of the upper part of the output corresponding to where the template matches best. Note also that as the template is shifted left and right with respect to this position, a number of bright spots appear. The distances between these spots correspond to the distance between the letters in the text.

Since correlation is based on multiplying the template and the input image, bright areas in the input image tend to produce high values in the output. This is illustrated in Fig. 5.10 where the large white section in the clothing of the child in the middle produces the highest values in the output. This problem in general makes it difficult,

---

[4]For binary images, template matching is normally performed using XOR.

Fig. 5.9 Template matching performed by correlating the input image with a template. The result of template matching is seen to the *right*. The *gray outer* region illustrates the pixels that cannot be processed due to the border problem

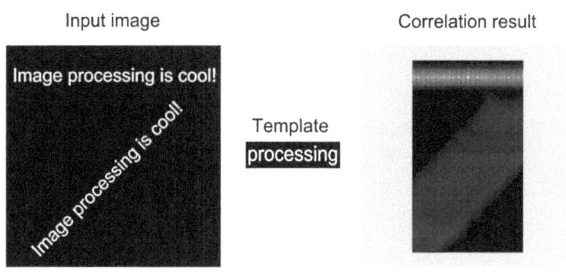

Fig. 5.10 Template matching using correlation and normalized cross-correlation. The *gray regions* illustrate the pixels that cannot be processed due to the border problem

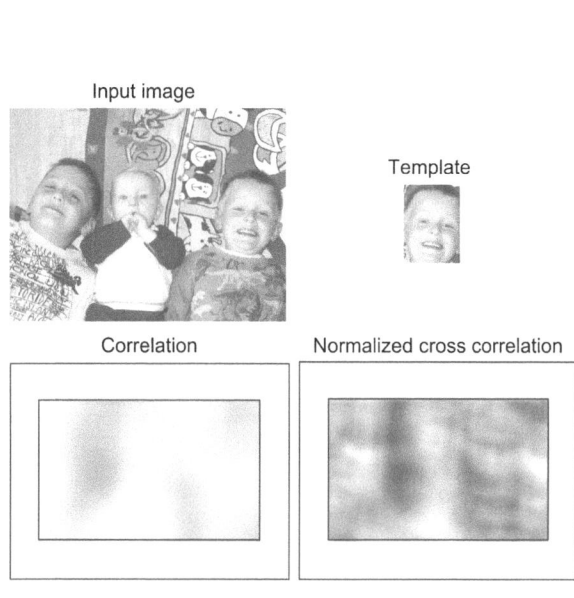

and in this particular case impossible, to actually find the position of the object by looking at the values in the output image.

To avoid this problem we need to normalize the values in the output so they are independent of the overall level of light in the image. To assist us in doing so we use a small trick. Let us denote the template H and the image patch F. These are both matrices, but by rearranging we can easily convert each matrix into a vector by concatenating each row (or column) in the matrix, i.e., $\vec{H}$ and $\vec{F}$.

If we now look at correlation in terms of this vector representation, we can see that Eq. 5.4 is actually the dot product between the two vectors, see Appendix B. From geometry we know that the dot product between two vectors can be normalized to the interval $[-1, 1]$ using the following equation:

$$\cos\theta = \frac{\vec{H} \bullet \vec{F}}{|\vec{H}| \cdot |\vec{F}|} \tag{5.5}$$

where θ is the angle between the two vectors, and $|\vec{H}|$ and $|\vec{F}|$ are the lengths of the two vectors. The normalization of the dot product between the vectors is a fact because $\cos\theta \in [-1, 1]$. The length of $|\vec{H}|$, which is also the "length" of the template, is calculated as

$$\text{Length of template} = \sqrt{\sum_{j=-R}^{R} \sum_{i=-R}^{R} h(i, j) \cdot h(i, j)} \tag{5.6}$$

where R is the radius of the template and $h(i, j)$ is the coefficient in the template at position (i, j). The length of the image patch is calculated in the same manner.

When using this normalization the bright spots in the output no longer depend on whether the image is bright or not but only on how similar the template and the underlying image patch are. This version of template matching is denoted *normalized cross-correlation* (NCC) and calculated for each pixel (x, y) using the following equation:

$$\text{NCC}(x, y) = \frac{\text{Correlation}}{\text{Length of image patch} \cdot \text{Length of template}} \Rightarrow$$

$$\text{NCC}(x, y) = \frac{\sum_{j=-R}^{R} \sum_{i=-R}^{R} (H \cdot F)}{\sqrt{\sum_{j=-R}^{R} \sum_{i=-R}^{R} (F \cdot F)} \cdot \sqrt{\sum_{j=-R}^{R} \sum_{i=-R}^{R} (H \cdot H)}} \tag{5.7}$$

where R is the radius of the template, $H = h(i, j)$ is the template and $F = f(x + i, y + j)$ is the image patch. $\cos\theta \in [-1, 1]$ but since the image patch and the template always contain positive numbers, $\cos\theta \in [0, 1]$, i.e., the output of normalized cross-correlation is normalized to the interval $[0, 1]$, where 0 means no similarity and 1 means a complete similarity. In Fig. 5.10 the benefit of applying normalized cross-correlation can be seen.

An even more advanced version of template matching exist. Here the mean values of the template and image patch are subtracted from H and F, respectively. This is known as the *zero-mean normalized cross-correlation* or the *correlation coefficient*. The output is in the interval $[-1, 1]$ where 1 indicates a maximum similarity (as for NCC) and -1 indicates a maximum *negative* similarity, meaning the same pattern but opposite gray-scale values: 255 instead of 0, 254 instead of 1, etc.

Independent of the type of template matching, the kernel (template) is usually much bigger than the kernels/filters used in other neighborhood operations. Template matching is therefore a time consuming method and can benefit from introducing a region-of-interest, see Sect. 2.4.1.

A general assumption in template matching is that the object we are looking for has roughly the same size and rotation in both the template and the image. If this cannot be ensured, then we need to have multiple scaled and rotated versions of the template and perform template matching using each of these templates. This requires significant resources and the speed of the system is likely to drop.

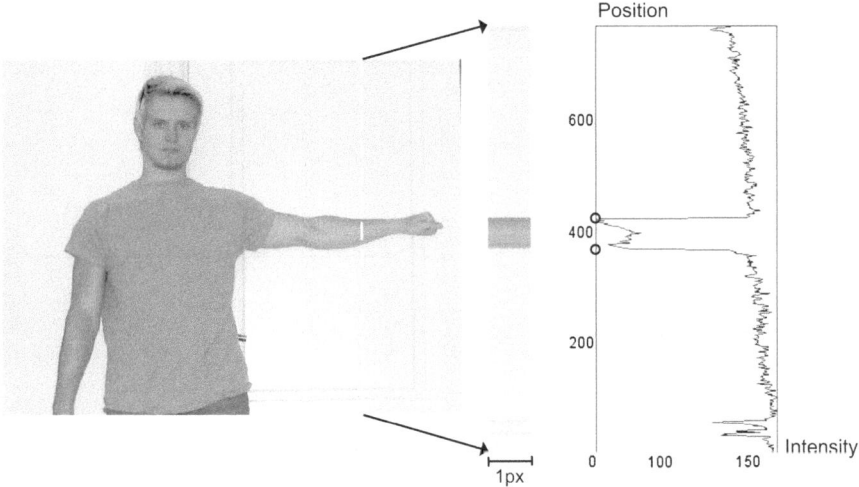

Fig. 5.11 A single column of the image is enlarged and presented in a graph. This graph contains two very significant changes in height, the position of which is marked with *circles* on the graph. This is how edges are defined in an image

5.2.2 Edge Detection

Another important application of correlation is *edge detection*. An edge in an image is defined as a position where a significant change in gray-level values occur. In Fig. 5.11 an image is shown to the left. We now take an image slice defined by the vertical line between the two arrows. This new image will have the same height as the input image, but only be one pixel wide. In the figure this is illustrated. Note that we have made it wider in order to be able to actually see it. Imagine now that we interpret the intensity values as height values. This gives us a different representation of the image, which is shown in the graph to the right.

What can be seen in the graph is that locations in the original image where we have a significant change in gray-scale value appear as significant changes in height. Such positions are illustrated by circles in the figure. It is these positions where we say we have an edge in an image.

Edges are useful in many applications since they define the contour of an object and are less sensitive to changes in the illumination compared to for example thresholding. Moreover, in many industrial applications image processing (or rather machine vision) is used to measure some dimensions of objects. It is therefore of great importance to have a clear definition of where an object starts and ends. Edges are often used for this purpose.

Gradients

To enable edge detection we utilize the concept of gradients. We first present gradients for a general curve and then turn to gradients in images. In the 1D case we can define the gradient of a point as the slope of the curve at this point. Concretely

Fig. 5.12 A curve and the
tangent at four points

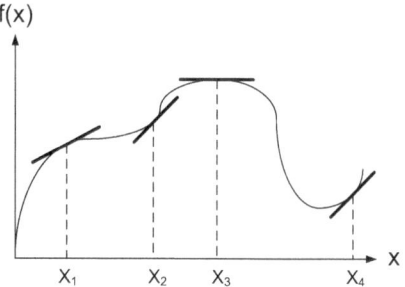

this corresponds to the slope of the tangent at this point. In Fig. 5.12 the tangents of several different points are shown.

If we represent an image by height as opposed to intensity, see Fig. 5.13, then edges correspond to places where we have steep hills. For each point in this image landscape we have two gradients: one in the x-direction and one in the y-direction. Together these two gradients span a plane, known as the *tangent plane*, which intersects the point. The resulting gradient is defined as a vector $\vec{G}(g_x, g_y)$, where g_x is the gradient in the x-direction and g_y is the gradient in the y-direction. This resulting gradient lies in the tangent plane, see Fig. 5.14.

We can consider $\vec{G}(g_x, g_y)$ as the direction with the steepest slope (or least steepest slope depending on how we calculate it), or in other words, if you are standing at this position in the landscape you need to follow the opposite direction of the gradient in order to get down fastest. Or in yet another way, when water falls at this point it will run in the opposite direction of the gradient.

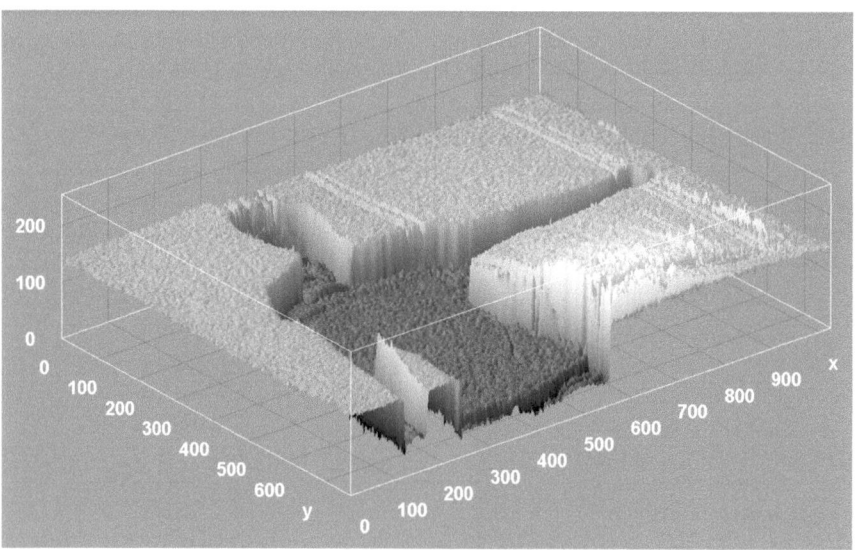

Fig. 5.13 A 3D representation of the image from Fig. 5.11, where the intensity of each pixel is interpreted as a height

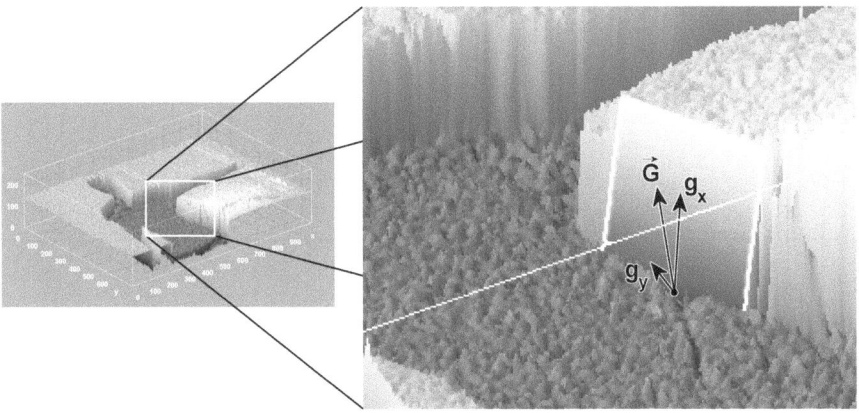

Fig. 5.14 In a 3D representation of an image, a tangent plane is present for each point. Such a plane is defined by two gradient vectors in x- and y-direction, respectively. Here the tangent plane is shown for one pixel

Besides a direction the gradient also has a *magnitude*. The magnitude expresses how steep the landscape is in the direction of the gradient, or how fast the water will run away (if you go skiing you will know that the magnitude of the gradient usually defines the difficulty of the piste). The magnitude is the length of the gradient vector and calculated as

$$\text{Magnitude} = \sqrt{g_x^2 + g_y^2} \qquad (5.8)$$

$$\text{Approximated magnitude} = |g_x| + |g_y| \qquad (5.9)$$

where the approximation is introduced to achieve a faster implementation.

Image Edges

For the curves shown above, the gradients are found as the first order derivatives denoted $f'(x)$. This can only be calculated for continuous curves and since an image has a discrete representation (we only have pixel values at discrete positions: $0, 1, 2, 3, 4$ etc.) we need an approximation. Recalling that the gradient is the slope at a point we can define the gradient as the difference between the previous and next value. Concretely we have the following image gradient approximations:

$$g_x(x, y) \approx f(x + 1, y) - f(x - 1, y) \qquad (5.10)$$

$$g_y(x, y) \approx f(x, y + 1) - f(x, y - 1) \qquad (5.11)$$

We have included (x, y) in the definition of the gradients to indicate that the gradient values depend on their spatial position. This approximation will produce positive gradient values when the pixels change from dark to bright and negative values when a reversed edge is present. This will of course be opposite if the signs

Prewitt											
Vertical			Horizontal			Vertical			Horizontal		
-1	0	1	-1	-1	-1	-1	0	1	-1	-2	-1
-1	0	1	0	0	0	-2	0	2	0	0	0
-1	0	1	1	1	1	-1	0	1	1	2	1

Fig. 5.15 Prewitt and Sobel kernels

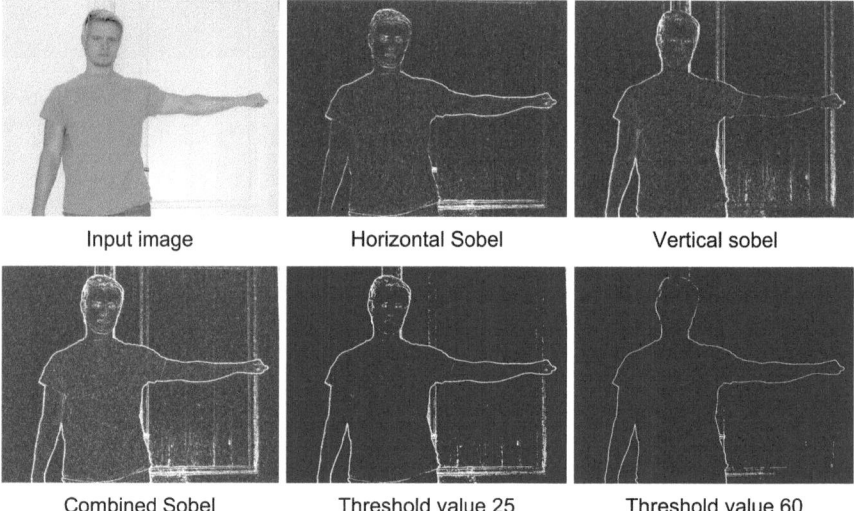

| Input image | Horizontal Sobel | Vertical sobel |
| Combined Sobel | Threshold value 25 | Threshold value 60 |

Fig. 5.16 Sobel kernels applied to an image. Each individual kernel finds edges that the other does not find. When they are combined a very nice resulting edge is created. Depending on the application, the threshold value can be manipulated to include or exclude the vaguely defined edges

are switched, i.e., $g_x(x, y) \approx f(x - 1, y) - f(x + 1, y)$ and $g_y(x, y) \approx f(x, y - 1) - f(x, y + 1)$. Normally the order does not matter as we will see below.

Equation 5.10 is applied to each pixel in the input image. Concretely this is done using correlation. We correlate the image with a 1×3 kernel containing the following coefficients: $-1, 0, 1$. Calculating the gradient using this kernel is often too sensitive to noise in the image and the neighbors are therefore often also included into the kernel. The most well know kernels for edge detection are illustrated in Fig. 5.15: the *Prewitt kernels* and the *Sobel kernels*. The difference is that the Sobel kernels weight the row and column pixels of the center pixel more than the rest.

Correlating the two Sobel kernels with the image in Fig. 5.11 yields the edge images in Fig. 5.16. The image to the left enhances horizontal edges, while the image to the right enhances vertical edges. To produce the final edge image we use

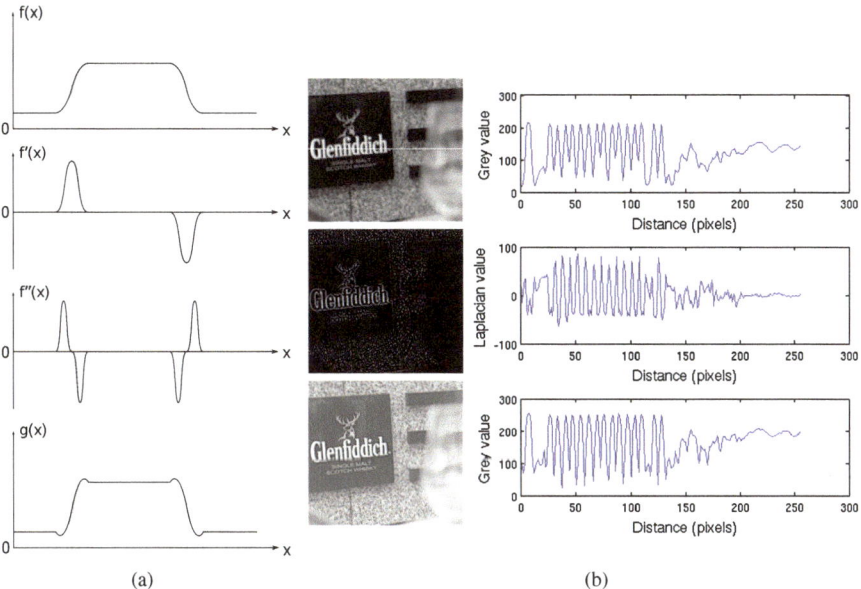

Fig. 5.17 (**a**) The principal behind image sharpening. (**b**) An example of image sharpening with $c = 0.6$. The pixel values of a horizontal line (the location is indicated by the *white line* in the *top image*) are shown to the *right*

Eq. 5.9. That is, we first calculate the absolute value of each pixel in the two images and then add them together. The result is the final edge enhanced image. After this, the final task is often to binarize the image, so that edges are white and the rest is black. This is done by a standard thresholding algorithm. In Fig. 5.16 the final edge enhanced image is shown together with binary edge images obtained using different thresholds. The choice of threshold depends on the application.

5.2.3 Image Sharpening

The method presented in Sect. 4.4.2 and illustrated in Fig. 4.23 is not only applicable to thresholding, but can also be used to increase the overall contrast of the image. The method is expressed as follows in terms of correlation:

$$g(x, y) = f(x, y) - \big(f(x, y) \circ h(x, y)\big) \qquad (5.12)$$

where $h(x, y)$ is a large mean filter kernel. The method belongs to the class of methods aimed at sharpening or enhancing the image. Another method for this purpose is based on image edges and is explained in the following.

What makes it possible to see an object in a scene, is the fact that the object is different from the background. From this follows that the transition between object and background is of great importance and this is of course exactly why we measure

Fig. 5.18 *Left*: Kernels for approximating the second order derivatives. *Right*: Laplacian kernel

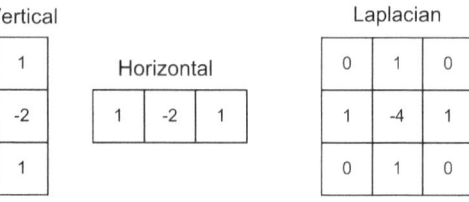

edges in an image. If we could somehow make the edges steeper the difference between object and background would be even more profound and hence the image sharper to look at. A way of doing this is shown in Fig. 5.17(a). The first figure shows the pixel values of an image row. x denotes the position in the row and $f(x)$ is the gray-level value. The next figure shows the gradient value, or the first derivative $f'(x)$, of $f(x)$. The third figure is the second order derivative of $f(x)$, denoted $f''(x)$. It expresses the gradient of the gradient. What we can see is that $g(x) = f(x) - c \cdot f''(x)$ does exactly what we are interested in, namely to make the edges steeper. The constant c can be used to weight the amount of sharpness that is desired. For an image the second order derivatives can be approximated as

$$g_{xx}(x, y) \approx f(x - 1, y) - 2 \cdot f(x, y) + f(x + 1, y) \qquad (5.13)$$

$$g_{yy}(x, y) \approx f(x, y - 1) - 2 \cdot f(x, y) + f(x, y + 1) \qquad (5.14)$$

where $g_{xx}(x, y)$ and $g_{yy}(x, y)$ are the second order derivatives in the x- and y-direction, respectively. These two expressions can easily be expressed as kernels, see Fig. 5.18, and correlated with the image. However, instead of correlating with both kernels and combining the results, we can combine them into the joint kernel, $h(x, y)$, and only do one correlation. This joint kernel is denoted the *Laplacian kernel* and shown below. Mathematically this image sharpening method is expressed as follows and illustrated in Fig. 5.17(b):

$$g(x, y) = f(x, y) - c\big(f(x, y) \circ h(x, y)\big) \qquad (5.15)$$

where c is a constant and $h(x, y)$ is the Laplacian kernel. Note that for both Eqs. 5.12 and 5.15 an implementation needs to make sure the output image is mapped to $[0, 255]$. This can be done by the method in Sect. 4.6.

5.3   Further Information

Correlation is related to the term *convolution* and both are used throughout the video and image processing literature. Convolution only differs by the way the kernel is applied to the image beneath it. Mathematically convolution is defined as:

$$g(x, y) = \sum_{j=-R}^{R} \sum_{i=-R}^{R} h(i, j) \cdot f(x - i, y - j) \qquad (5.16)$$

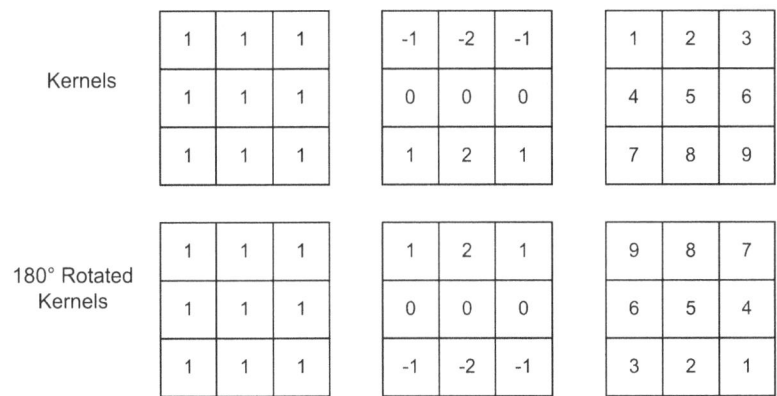

Fig. 5.19 Three kernels and their rotated counterparts

Comparing this to the equation for correlation in Eq. 5.4 we can see that the only differences are the two minus signs. The interpretation of these is that the kernel is rotated 180° before doing a correlation. In Fig. 5.19 examples of rotated kernels are shown. What we can see is that symmetric kernels are equal before and after rotation, and hence convolution and correlation produce the same result. Edge detection kernels are not symmetric. However, since we often only are interested in the absolute value of an edge the correlation and convolution again yield the same result.

When applying smoothing filters, finding edges etc. the process is often denoted convolution even though it is often implemented as correlation! When doing template matching it is virtually always denoted correlation.

One might rightfully ask why convolution is used in the first place. The answer is that from a general signal processing[5] point of view we actually do convolution, and correlation is convolution done with a rotated kernel. However, since correlation is easier to explain and since it is most often what is done in practice, it has been presented as though it were the other way around in this (and many other) texts. The technical reasons for the definition of convolution are beyond the scope of this text and the interested reader is referred to a general signal processing textbook.

Edge detection is a key method in many image processing systems and a number of different methods have therefore been suggested over the years. Using the Sobel kernels works well, but results in wide edges as can bee seen in Fig. 5.17. If we are interested in knowing the exact edge, i.e., a 1-pixel thin edge, then the same figure suggests to use the second order derivatives and look for the places where the values change from positive to negative or vise versa. These places are denoted *zero-crossings*. As mentioned above the first order derivatives are sensitive to noise in the images. This problem is even more profound for the second order derivatives. The

---

[5]Image processing is a subset of signal processing.

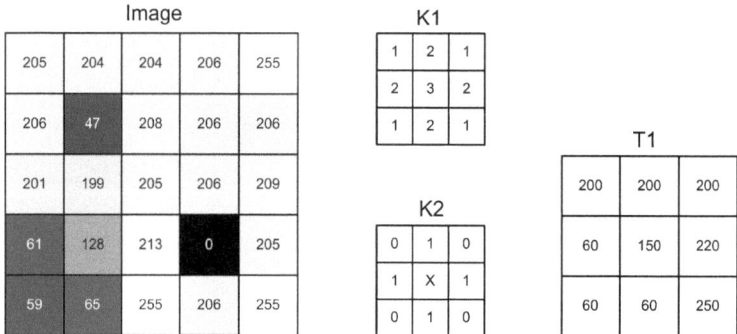

Fig. 5.20 K1 and K2 are kernels, while T1 is a template

image is therefore smoothed using a Gaussian filter before the Laplacian is applied to approximate the second order derivatives and looking for zero-crossings.

Another approach to finding 1-pixel thin edges is the Canny edge detector [5]. It first smooths the image using a Gaussian filter before applying the Sobel kernels. From the Sobel kernels the direction of the gradient in each point is estimated. Next, the principle of *non-maximum suppression* is applied. For each pixel the magnitude of the gradient is compared with the magnitudes of the two nearest neighbors in the gradient direction. The two smallest are deleted. Applying this to all pixels results in 1-pixel thin edges. Finally a threshold is applied to prune edges with too small magnitudes. If, however, an edge with a too small magnitude is connected[6] to a pixel with a magnitude above another threshold value, then the edge is not pruned. This allows for an adaptive pruning and is known as the principle of *hysteresis thresholding*.

Sometimes template matching is preformed on binary edge images. If the shape of the object in the image is slightly different from the input image, the template matching will output a very low similarity even though the two objects might look very similar. Therefore Chamfer matching [2] can be applied instead. Here the template image is converted into an image where each pixel contains a value indicating the distance to the nearest edge, see Sect. 6.4. Using such a distance-image as the template will provide a much more stable result.

5.4   Exercises

Exercise 1: Explain the following concepts: neighborhood processing, kernel, correlation, border problem, image edge.

Exercise 2: What is the role of the kernel size?

Exercise 3: What is the normalization factor of the kernel K1 in Fig. 5.20?

Exercise 4: Apply a 3×3 median filter to the image in Fig. 5.20.

---

[6]Connectivity among pixels is discussed in Chap. 7.

Exercise 5: Apply a 3 × 3 mean filter to the image in Fig. 5.20.

Exercise 6: Discuss the difference between the median filter and mean filter.

Exercise 7: Apply a 5 × 5 difference filter to the image in Fig. 5.20.

Exercise 8: The image in Fig. 5.20 is correlated with the kernel K2. No kernel normalization is performed. At the position $(1, 1)$ the output value is 911. What is the value of x?

Exercise 9: Template matching is performed on the image in Fig. 5.20 with the template T1. Normalized cross-correlation is used. What is the output value at position $(1, 3)$?

Exercise 10: Why are the Sobel kernels 3 × 3 and not 1 × 3 and 3 × 1?

Exercise 11: The Prewitt kernels are applied to the image in Fig. 5.20. What is the approximated magnitude at position $(1, 3)$?

Additional exercise: Describe the principle behind the Canny edge detector.

Morphology

One important branch of neighborhood processing is *mathematical morphology*—
or simply *morphology*. It is applicable to both gray-scale images as well as binary
images, but in this text only operations related to binary images are covered. Morphology on binary images has a number of applications and in Fig. 6.1 three typical
ones are illustrated. The first two illustrate how to remove the noise that very often
is a side effect of thresholding. It is next to impossible to achieve a perfect
binary image using thresholding. We are very likely to under-segmentation in some
regions and over-segmentation in other regions. The leftmost figure illustrates oversegmentation in the form of the small objects in the image. Under-segmentation is
illustrated in the middle figure as holes inside the object. The problems associated
with thresholding were also mentioned in Chap. 4 where it could be seen as the
problematic histogram in Fig. 4.17.

The rightmost example in Fig. 6.1 illustrates a problem which is related to the
next chapter, where we will start to analyze individual objects. To this end we need
to ensure that the objects are separated from each other.

Morphology operates like the other neighborhood processing methods by applying a kernel to each pixel in the input. In morphology, the kernel is denoted a
structuring element and contains '0's and '1's. You can design the structuring element as you please, but normally the pattern of '1's form a box or a disk. In Fig. 6.2
different sized structuring elements are visualized. Which type and size to use is up
to the designer, but in general a box-shaped structuring element tends to preserve
sharp object corners, whereas a disk-shaped structuring element tends to round the
corners of the objects.

A structuring element is *not* applied in the same way as we saw in the previous
chapter for the kernels. Instead of using multiplications and additions in the calculations, a structuring element is applied using either a *Hit* or a *Fit* operation. Applying
one of these operations to each pixel in an image is denoted *Dilation* and *Erosion*,
respectively. Combining these two methods can result in powerful image processing
tools known as *Compound Operations*. We can say that there exist three levels of
operation, see Fig. 6.3, and in the following, these three levels will be described one
at a time. Note that for simplicity, we will in this chapter represent white as 1 instead
of 255.

T.B. Moeslund, *Introduction to Video and Image Processing*,
Undergraduate Topics in Computer Science,
DOI 10.1007/978-1-4471-2503-7_6, © Springer-Verlag London Limited 2012

91

Fig. 6.1 Three examples of
the uses of morphology.
(**a**) Removing small objects.
(**b**) Filling holes. (**c**) Isolating
objects

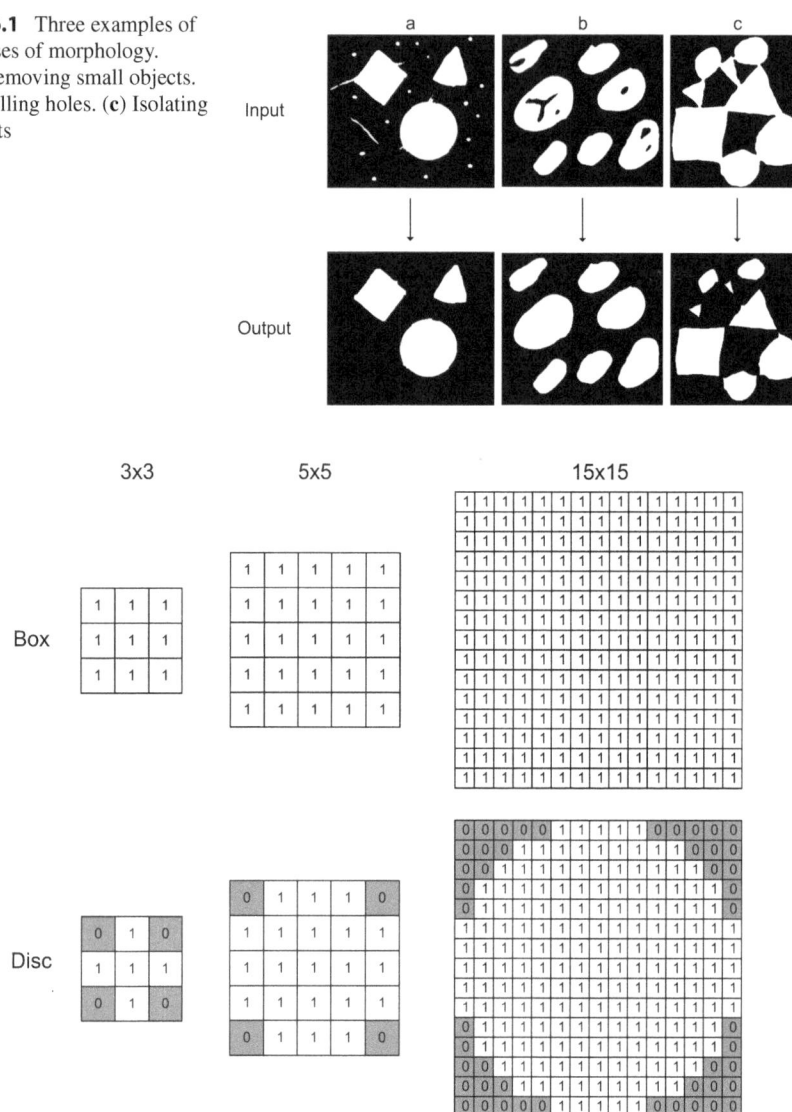

Fig. 6.2 Two types of structuring elements at different sizes

6.1   Level 1: Hit and Fit

The structuring element is placed on top of the image as was the case for the kernels
in the previous chapter. The center of the structuring element is placed at the position
of the pixel in focus and it is the value of this pixel that will be calculated by applying
the structuring element. After having placed the structuring element we can apply
one of two methods: Hit or Fit.

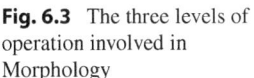**Fig. 6.3** The three levels of
operation involved in
Morphology

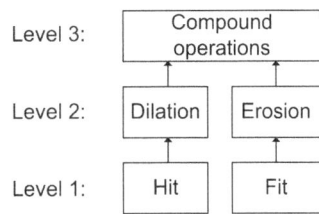

6.1.1 Hit

For each '1' in the structuring element we investigate whether the pixel at the same
position in the image is also a '1'. If this is the case for just one of the '1's in the
structuring element we say that the structuring element *hits* the image at the pixel
position in question (the one on which the structuring element is centered). This
pixel is therefore set to '1' in the output image. Otherwise it is set to '0'. In Fig. 6.4
and Table 6.1 the hit operation is illustrated with two different structuring elements.

6.1.2 Fit

For each '1' in the structuring element we investigate whether the pixel at the same
position in the image is also a '1'. If this is the case for *all* the '1's in the structuring
element we say that the structuring element *fits* the image at the pixel position in
question (the one on which the structuring element is centered). This pixel is therefore set to '1' in the output image. Otherwise it is set to '0'. In Fig. 6.4 and Table 6.1
the fit operation is illustrated with two different structuring elements. Below we
show C-code for the fit operation using a 3×3 box-shaped structuring element:

```
Temp = 0;
for (j = y-1; j < (y+2); j = j+1)
{
   for (i = x-1; i< (x+2); i = i+1)
   {
      if (GetPixel(input, i, j) == 1)
         Temp = Temp + 1;
   }
}
if (Temp == 9)
   SetPixel(output, x, y, 1);
else
   SetPixel(output, x, y, 0);
```

where (x, y) is the position of the pixel being processed.

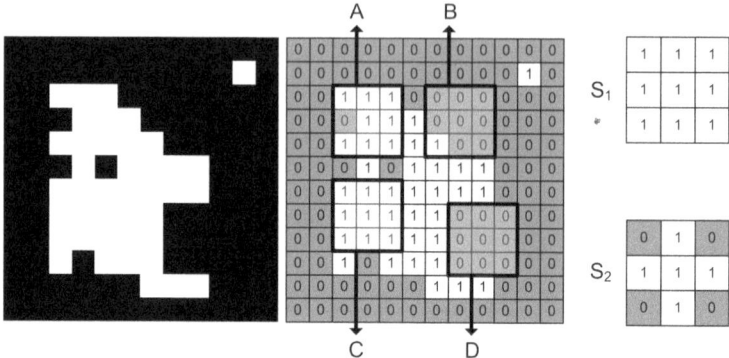

Fig. 6.4 A binary image illustrated both by colors (black and white) and numbers (0 and 1). A, B, C and D illustrate four 3×3 image regions centered at: A: $f(3, 3)$, B: $f(7, 3)$, C: $f(3, 7)$ and D: $f(8, 8)$. Lastly two different 3×3 structuring elements are illustrated

Table 6.1 Results of applying the two structuring elements (*SE*) in Fig. 6.4 to the input image in Fig. 6.4 at four positions: A, B, C, and D

Position	SE	Fit	Hit
A	S_1	No	Yes
A	S_2	No	Yes
B	S_1	No	Yes
B	S_2	No	No
C	S_1	Yes	Yes
C	S_2	Yes	Yes
D	S_1	No	No
D	S_2	No	No

6.2 Level 2: Dilation and Erosion

At the next level Hit or Fit is applied to every single pixel by scanning through the image as shown in Fig. 4.28. The size of the structuring element in these operations has the same importance as the kernel size did in the previous chapter. The bigger the structuring element, the bigger the effect in the image. As described in the previous chapter we also have the border problem present here and solution strategies similar to those listed in Sect. 5.1 can be followed. For simplicity we will ignore the border problem in this chapter.

6.2.1 Dilation

Applying Hit to an entire image is denoted *Dilation* and is written as

$$g(x, y) = f(x, y) \oplus SE \qquad (6.1)$$

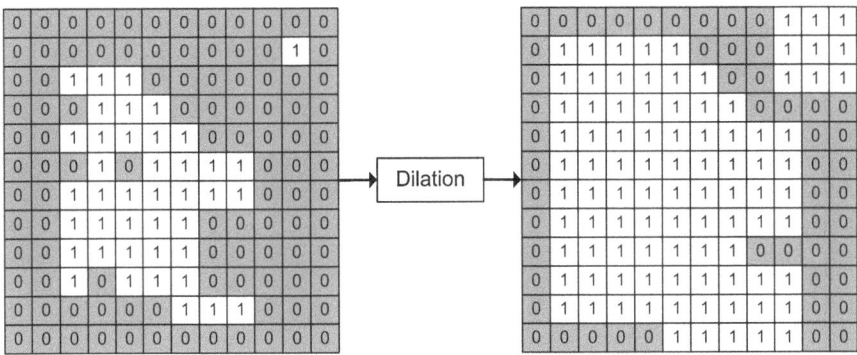

Fig. 6.5 Dilation of the binary image in Fig. 6.4 using S_1

The term *dilation* refers to the fact that the object in the binary image is increased in size. In general, dilating an image results in objects becoming bigger, small holes being filled, and objects being merged. How big the effect is depends on the size of the structuring element. It should be noticed that a large structuring element can be implemented by iteratively applying a smaller structuring element. This makes sense since Eq. 6.2 holds. The equation states that dilating twice with SE_1 is similar to dilating one time with SE_2, where SE_2 is the same type but has twice the radius of SE_1. For example, if SE_2 is a 5×5 structuring element, then SE_1 is a 3×3, etc.

$$f(x, y) \oplus SE_2 \approx \left(f(x, y) \oplus SE_1 \right) \oplus SE_1 \qquad (6.2)$$

In Fig. 6.5 the binary image in Fig. 6.4 is dilated using the structuring element S_1. First of all we can see that the object gets bigger. Secondly we can observe that the hole and the convex parts of the object are filled, which makes the object more compact.

In Fig. 6.6 a real image is dilated with different sized box-shaped structuring elements. Again we can see that the object is becoming bigger and that holes inside the person are filled. What is, however, also apparent is that the noisy small objects are also enlarged. Below we will return to this problem.

6.2.2 Erosion

Applying Fit to an entire image is denoted Erosion and is written as

$$g(x, y) = f(x, y) \ominus SE \qquad (6.3)$$

The term *erosion* refers to the fact that the object in the binary image is decreased in size. In general, erosion of an image results in objects becoming smaller, small objects disappearing, and larger objects splitting into smaller objects. As for dilation the effect depends on the size of the structuring element and large structuring elements can be implemented using an equation similar to Eq. 6.2.

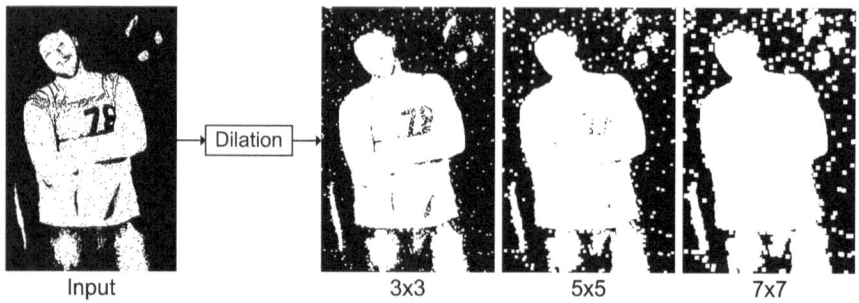

Fig. 6.6 Dilation with different sized structuring elements

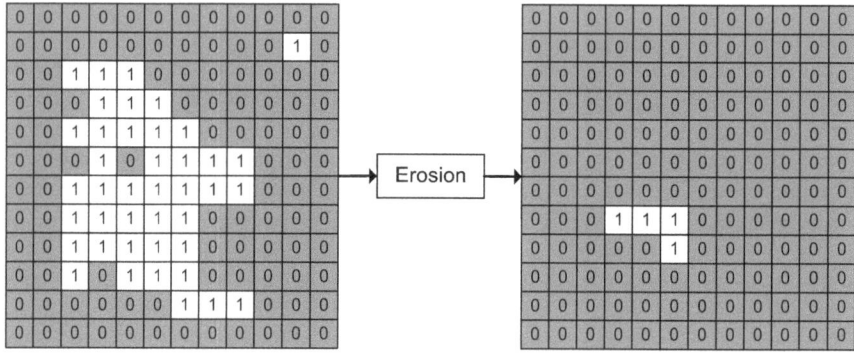

Fig. 6.7 Erosion of the binary image in Fig. 6.4 using S_1

In Fig. 6.7 the binary image in Fig. 6.4 is eroded using the structuring element S_1. First of all we can see that the main object gets smaller and the small objects disappear. Secondly we can observe that the fractured parts of the main object are removed and only the "core" of the object remains. The size of this core obviously depends on the size (and shape) of the structuring element.

In Fig. 6.8 a real image is eroded with different sized box-shaped structuring elements. Again we can see that the object becomes smaller and the small (noisy) objects disappear. So the price we pay for deleting the small noisy objects is that the object of interest becomes smaller and fractured. Below we will return to this problem.

6.3   Level 3: Compound Operations

Combining dilation and erosion in different ways results in a number of different image processing tools. These are denoted *compound operations*. Here we present three of the most common compound operations, namely *Opening*, *Closing*, and *Boundary Detection*.

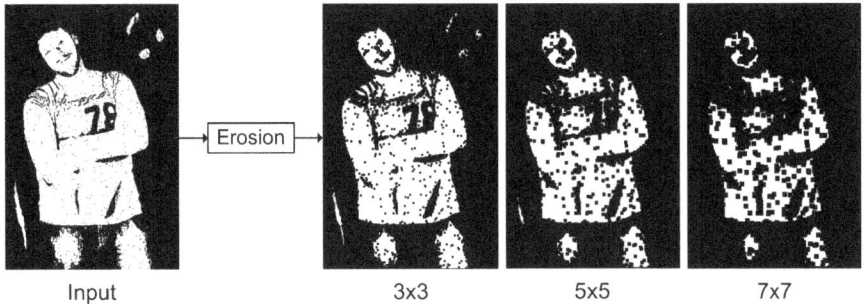

Fig. 6.8 Erosion with different sized structuring elements

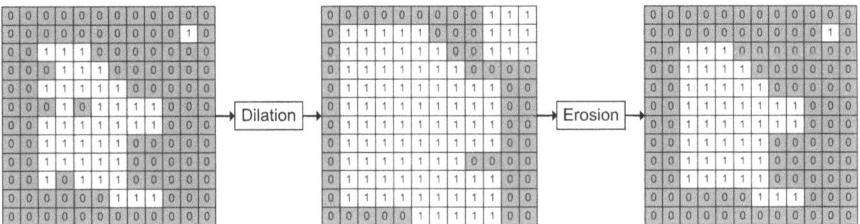

Fig. 6.9 Closing of the binary image in Fig. 6.4 using S_1

6.3.1   Closing

Closing deals with the problem associated with dilation, namely that the objects increase in size when we use dilation to fill the holes in objects. This is a problem in situations where, for example, the size of the object (number of pixels) matters. The solution to this problem is luckily straightforward: we simply shrink the object by following the Dilation by an Erosion. This operation is denoted *Closing* and is written as

$$g(x, y) = f(x, y) \bullet SE = \left(f(x, y) \oplus SE \right) \ominus SE \qquad (6.4)$$

where *SE* is the structuring element. It is essential that the structuring elements applied are exactly the same in terms of size and shape. The closing operation is said to be *idempotent*, meaning that it can only be applied one time (with the same structuring element). If applied again it has no effect whatsoever except for of course a reduced size of $g(x, y)$ due to the border problem. In Fig. 6.9, closing is illustrated for the binary image in Fig. 6.4. Closing is done with structuring element S_1. We can see that the holes and convex structures are filled, hence the object is more compact. Moreover, the object preserves its original size.

In Fig. 6.10 the closing operation is applied to a real image. We can see that most internal holes are filled while the human object preserves its original size. The noisy objects in the background have not been deleted. This can be done either by the

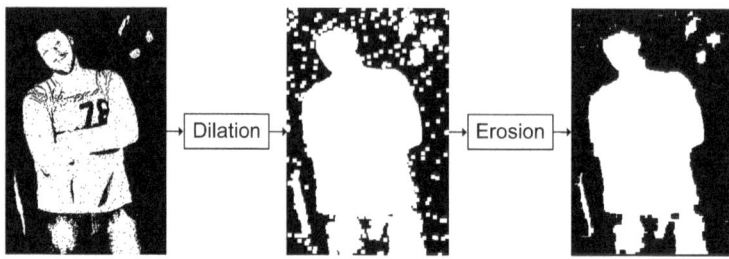

Fig. 6.10 Closing performed using 7×7 box-shaped structuring elements

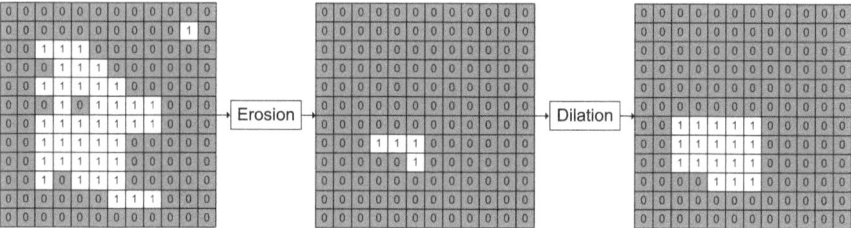

Fig. 6.11 Opening of the binary image in Fig. 6.4 using S_1

operation described just below or by finding and deleting small objects, which will be described in the next chapter.

6.3.2   Opening

Opening deals with the problem associated with erosion, namely that the objects decrease when we use erosion to erase small noisy objects or fractured parts of bigger objects. The decreasing object size is a problem in situations where for example the size of the object (number of pixels) matters. The solution to this problem is luckily straight forward, we simply enlarge the object by following the erosion by a dilation. This operation is denoted *Opening* and is written as

$$g(x, y) = f(x, y) \circ SE = \big(f(x, y) \ominus SE\big) \oplus SE \qquad (6.5)$$

where *SE* is the same structuring element. This operation is also idempotent as is the case for the closing operation. In Fig. 6.11 opening is illustrated for the binary image in Fig. 6.4. Opening is done with structuring element S_1. We can see that only a compact version of the object remains.

In Fig. 6.12 opening is applied to a real image using a 7×7 box-shaped structuring element. We can see that most noisy objects are removed while the object preserves its original size.

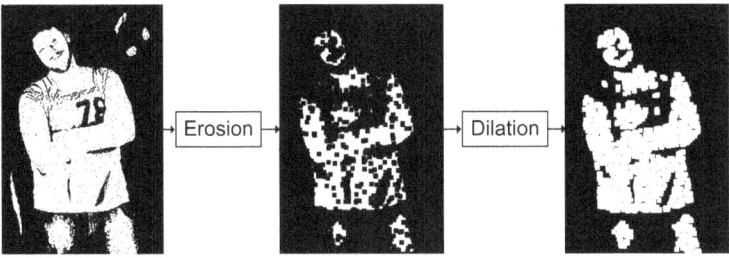

Fig. 6.12 Opening performed using a 7 × 7 box-shaped structuring element

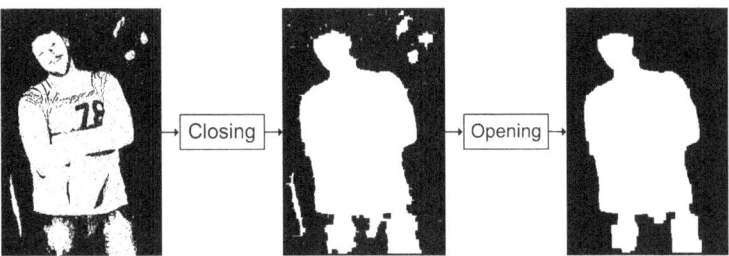

Fig. 6.13 Filtering a binary image where both holes and small noisy objects are present

6.3.3   Combining Opening and Closing

In some situations we need to apply both opening and closing to an image. For example in cases where we both have holes inside the main object *and* small noisy objects. An example is provided in Fig. 6.13. Note that the structuring elements used in the opening and the closing operations need not be the same. In Fig. 6.13 the closing was performed using a 7 × 7 box-shaped structuring element while the opening was performed using a 15 × 15 box-shaped structuring element.

6.3.4   Boundary Detection

Doing edge detection in binary images is normally referred to as *boundary detection* and can be performed as described in the previous chapter. Morphology offers an alternative approach for binary images. The idea is to use erosion to make a smaller version of the object. By subtracting this from the input image only the difference stands out, namely the boundary:

$$g(x, y) = f(x, y) - \left(f(x, y) \ominus SE \right) \tag{6.6}$$

If the task is only to locate the outer boundary, then the internal holes should first be filled using dilation or closing. In Fig. 6.14 examples of boundary detection are shown.

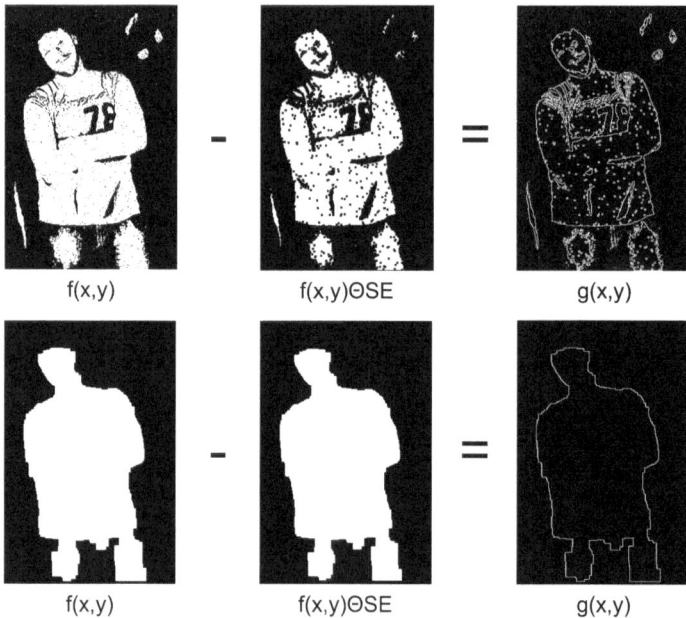

Fig. 6.14 Boundary detection

6.4   Further Information

It has been assumed in this chapter that the center of the structuring element is always located on top of the pixel being processed. This need not be the case and the position of the structuring element can be off-set in any direction if need may be. When doing so, please remember to include a procedure in you code that handles the situation when the structuring element or parts hereof is outside the image.

There exit others and more advanced morphologic operations, including gray-level morphology, than those presented in this chapter. For inspiration please pick up a book focusing on these topics, e.g., [7]. In Fig. 6.15 a few examples are provided. The first example illustrates the process of *skeletonization*, which is closely related to *thinning*. The latter can produce 1-pixel thin edges as discussed in the previous chapter. The other example illustrates the distance transform where the value of a pixel is the distance to the nearest white pixel in the image.

6.5   Exercises

Exercise 1: Explain the following concepts: structuring element, hit, fit, erosion, dilation, opening, closing.

Exercise 2: How can morphology be used to find the outline (edge) of an object?

Exercise 3: Find $g(x, y) = f(x, y) \oplus SE1$. $f(x, y)$ and $SE1$ are defined in Fig. 6.16.

Fig. 6.15 Examples of advanced morphology. *Top*: Skeletonization. *Bottom*: Distance image. White means zero and the darker the shade the further the distance

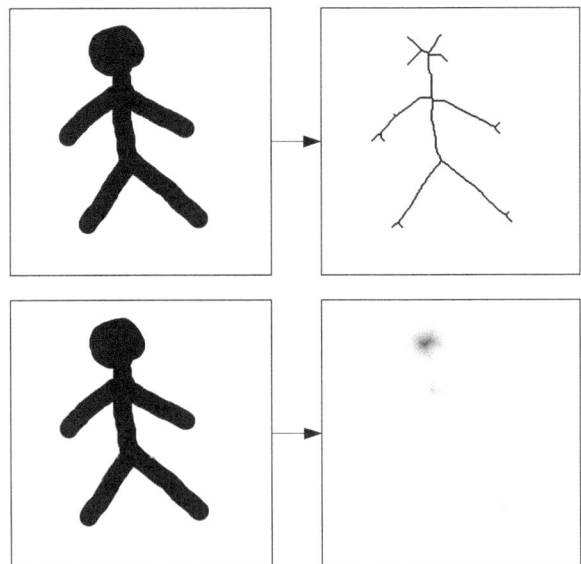

Fig. 6.16 *Left*: Input image $f(x, y)$. Object pixels are white (1) and background pixels are gray (0). *Right*: Structuring elements SE1 and SE2

f(x,y)

0	0	0	0	0	0	0	0	0	0	0	0
0	0	0	0	0	0	0	0	0	0	0	0
0	0	1	1	1	1	0	0	1	0	0	0
0	0	0	1	1	1	1	1	1	1	0	0
0	0	1	1	1	1	1	1	1	1	0	0
0	0	1	1	1	1	1	0	1	1	0	0
0	0	1	1	1	1	1	1	0	0	0	0
0	0	0	1	1	0	1	1	1	0	0	0
0	0	1	1	1	1	1	0	1	1	0	0
0	0	1	1	1	0	1	1	1	1	0	0
0	0	0	0	0	0	0	0	0	0	0	0
0	0	0	0	0	0	0	0	0	0	0	0

SE1

1	1	1
1	1	1
1	1	1

SE2

1	1	0
1	1	0
0	0	0

Exercise 4: Find $g(x, y) = f(x, y) \ominus SE1$. $f(x, y)$ and $SE1$ are defined in Fig. 6.16.

Exercise 5: Find $g(x, y) = f(x, y) \bullet SE1$. $f(x, y)$ and $SE1$ are defined in Fig. 6.16.

Exercise 6: Find $g(x, y) = f(x, y) \circ SE1$. $f(x, y)$ and $SE1$ are defined in Fig. 6.16.

Exercise 7: Find $g(x, y) = (f(x, y) \ominus SE2)$ AND (NOT $f(x, y) \ominus$ NOT $SE2$). $f(x, y)$ and $SE2$ are defined in Fig. 6.16.

Additional exercise: What is skeletonization and how does it work?

BLOB Analysis

7

Before describing what is meant by the somewhat strange title of this chapter, let us look at a few examples. In the first example the task is to design an algorithm which can figure out how many circles are present in the image to the left (see Fig. 7.1). Obviously the answer is three, but how will we make the computer figure this out? Another example could be to find the position of the person in the image to the right. How can we make the computer calculate this? The answer to both questions is twofold. First we have to separate the different objects in the image and then we have to evaluate which object is the one we are looking for, i.e., circles and humans, respectively. The former process is known as BLOB extraction and the latter as BLOB classification. BLOB stands for Binary Large OBject and refers to a group of connected pixels in a binary image. The term "Large" indicates that only objects of a certain size are of interest and that "small" binary objects are usually noise.

The title of the chapter refers to analyzing binary images by first *extracting* the BLOBs, then *representing* them compactly, and finally *classifying* the type of each BLOB. These three topics are described in more detail below.

7.1   BLOB Extraction

The purpose of BLOB extraction is to isolate the BLOBs (objects) in a binary image. As mentioned above, a BLOB consists of a group of connected pixels. Whether or not two pixels are connected is defined by the *connectivity*, that is, which pixels are neighbors and which are not. The two most often applied types of connectivity are illustrated in Fig. 7.2. The 8-connectivity is more accurate than the 4-connectivity, but the 4-connectivity is often applied since it requires fewer computations, hence it can process the image faster. The effect of the two different types of connectivity is illustrated in Fig. 7.2 where the binary images contain either one or two BLOBs depending on the connectivity.

A number of different algorithms exist for finding the BLOBs and such algorithms are usually referred to as *connected component analysis* or *connected component labeling*. In the following we describe one of these algorithms known as the *Grass-fire algorithm*. We use 4-connectivity for simplicity.

T.B. Moeslund, *Introduction to Video and Image Processing*,
Undergraduate Topics in Computer Science,
DOI 10.1007/978-1-4471-2503-7_7, © Springer-Verlag London Limited 2012

Fig. 7.1 (**a**) A binary image containing different shapes. (**b**) A binary image containing a human and some noise

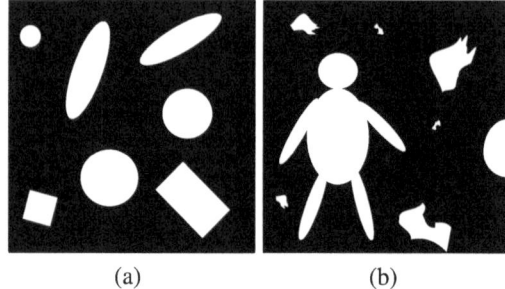

(a)   (b)

Fig. 7.2 4- and 8-connectivity. The effect of applying the two different types of connectivity

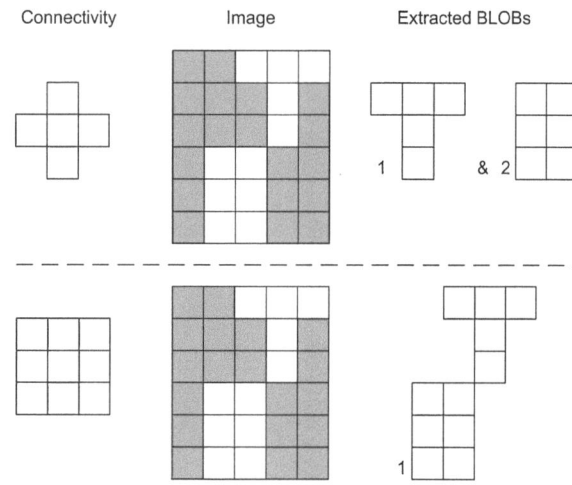

Connectivity   Image   Extracted BLOBs

7.1.1   The Recursive Grass-Fire Algorithm

The algorithm starts in the upper-left corner of the binary image. It then scans the entire image from left to right and from top to bottom, as seen in Fig. 4.28.

At some point during the scan an object pixel (white pixel) is encountered and the notion of grass-fire comes into play. In the binary image in Fig. 7.3 the first object pixel is found at the coordinate $(2, 0)$. At this point you should imagine yourself standing in a field covered with dry grass. Imagine you have four arms (!) and are holding a burning match in each hand. You then stretch out your arms in four different directions (corresponding to the neighbors in the 4-connectivity) and simultaneously drop the burning matches. When they hit the dry grass they will each start a fire which again will spread in four new directions (up, down, left, right) etc. The result is that every single straw *which is connected* to your initial position will burn. This is the grass-fire principle. Note that if the grass field contains a river the grass on the other side will not be burned.

Returning to our binary image, the object pixels are the "dry grass" and the non-object pixels are water. So, the algorithm looks in four different directions and if it finds a pixel which can be "burned", meaning an object pixel, it does two things.

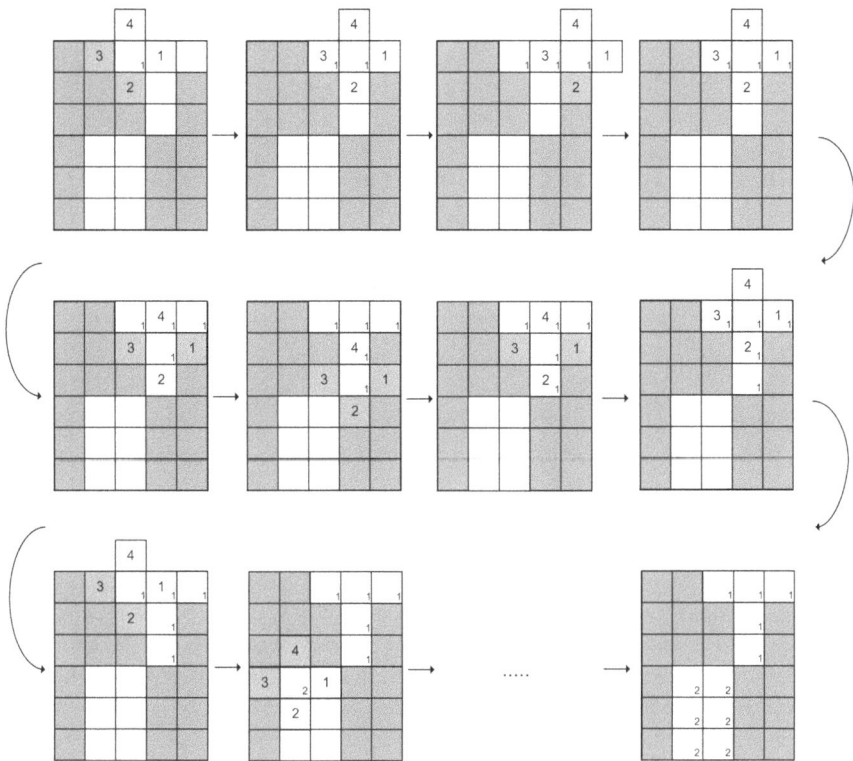

Fig. 7.3 The grass-fire algorithm. The "big" numbers indicate the order in which the neighbors are visited. The small numbers indicate the label of a pixel

Firstly, in the output image it gives this pixel an object label (basically a number) and secondly it "burns" the pixel in the input image by setting it to zero (black). Setting it to zero indicates that it has been burned and will therefore not be part of yet another fire. In the real grass field the fire will spread simultaneously in all directions. In the computer, however, we can only perform one action at the time and the grass-fire is therefore performed as follows.

Let us apply the principle on Fig. 7.3. The pixel at the coordinate $(2, 0)$ is labeled 1, since it is the first BLOB and then burned (marked by a 1 in the lower right corner). Next the algorithm tries to start a fire at the first neighbor $(3, 0)$, by checking if it is an object pixel or not. It is indeed an object pixel and is therefore labeled 1 (same object) and "burned". Since $(3, 0)$ is an object pixel, it now becomes the center of attention and its first neighbor is investigated $(4, 0)$. Again, this is an object pixel and is therefore labeled 1, "burned" and made center of attention. The first neighbor of $(4, 0)$ is outside the image and therefore per definition not an object pixel. The algorithm therefore investigates its second neighbor $(4, 1)$. This is not an object pixel and the third neighbor of $(4, 0)$ is therefore investigated $(3, 0)$. This has been burned and is therefore no longer an object pixel. Then the last neighbor of

Fig. 7.4 Two examples of
extracted BLOBs. Each
BLOB has a unique color

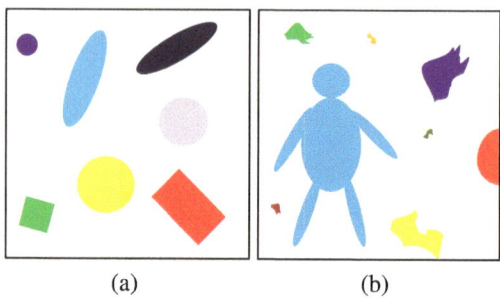

(a)   (b)

$(4, 0)$ is investigated $(4, -1)$. This is outside the image and therefore not an object
pixel. All the neighbors of $(4, 0)$ have now been investigated and the algorithm
therefore traces back and looks at the second neighbor of $(3, 0)$, namely $(3, 1)$. This
is an object pixel and is therefore labeled 1, burned and becomes the new focus of
attention. In this way the algorithm also finds $(3, 2)$ to be part of object 1 and finally
ends by investigating the fourth neighbor of $(2, 0)$.

All pixels which are part of the top object have now been labeled with the same
label 1 meaning that this BLOB has been segmented. The algorithm then moves on
following the scan path in Fig. 4.28 until it meets the next object pixel $(1, 3)$, which
is then labeled 2, and starts a new grass-fire. The result will be the image shown in
Fig. 7.2, where each BLOB has a unique label. In Fig. 7.4 the BLOBs from Fig. 7.1
have been extracted and color coded according to their BLOB label.

The algorithm can be implemented very efficiently by a function calling itself.
Such an algorithm is said to be recursive and care should be taking to ensure the
program is terminated properly as recursive algorithms have no built-in termination
strategy. Another danger is that a computer has a limited amount of memory allocated to function calls. And since the grass-fire algorithm can have many thousands
function calls queued up, the computer can run out of allocated memory.

7.1.2   The Sequential Grass-Fire Algorithm

The grass-fire algorithm can also be implemented in a sequential manner. This is
less efficient from a programming point of view, but it does not suffer from the
problems mentioned above for the recursive grass-fire algorithm.

The sequential grass-fire algorithm also scans the image from top left to bottom
right. When an object pixel is found it does two things. Firstly, in the output image
it gives this pixel an object label, 1, and secondly it "burns" the pixel in the input
image by setting it to zero (black). The next step is to check the neighbors (four or
eight pixels depending on the connectivity) and see if any of them is an object pixel.
So far this is exactly the same as the recursive grass-fire algorithm, but now comes
the difference. If any of the neighbors is an object pixel they are labeled 1 in the
output image and set to zero (burned) in the input image. Also, they are placed in
a list. Next step is to take the first pixel in the list and check its neighbors. If any
are object pixels they are labeled in the output, set to zero in the input and placed

in the list. This is continued until all pixels in the list have been investigated. The algorithm then continues following the scan path in Fig. 4.28 until it meets the next object pixel, which is then labeled 2, and starts a new grass-fire.

7.2   BLOB Features

Extracting the BLOBs is the first step when confronted with examples like those presented in Fig. 7.1. The next step is now to classify the different BLOBs. For the example with the circles, we want to classify each BLOB as either a circle or not a circle, and, for the other example, human vs. non-human BLOBs. The classification process consists of two steps. First, each BLOB is represented by a number of characteristics, denoted *features*, and second, some matching method is applied to compare the features of each BLOB with the features of the type of object we are looking for. For example, to find circles we could calculate the circularity of each BLOB and compare that to the circularity of a perfect circle. Below we will present how we can extract different features and in the next section then show how to compare features.

Feature extraction is a matter of converting each BLOB into a few representative numbers. That is, keep the relevant information and ignore the rest. But before calculating any features we first want to exclude every BLOB which is connected to the border of the image. The reason is that we in general have no information about the part of the object outside the image. For example, the semi-circle to the right of the human in Fig. 7.1 might look like a circle, but it might as well be the top of the head of a person lying down! Therefore, exclude all such BLOBs.

Having done so, a number of features can be calculated for each BLOB. Here follows a description of the most common features, but many others exist and new ones can be defined.[1]

Area of a BLOB is the number of pixels the BLOB consists of. This feature is often used to remove BLOBs that are too small or too big from the image. For example, in Fig. 7.1 (right) the human can be segmented by simply saying that all BLOBs with an area smaller than a certain value are ignored.

Bounding box of a BLOB is the minimum rectangle which contains the BLOB, see Fig. 7.5. It is defined by going through all pixels for a BLOB and finding the four pixels with the minimum x-value, maximum x-value, minimum y-value and maximum y-value, respectively. From these values the width of the bounding box is given as $x_{max} - x_{min}$ and the height as $y_{max} - y_{min}$. A bounding box can be used as a ROI.

Bounding circle of a BLOB is the minimum circle which contains the BLOB, see Fig. 7.5. It is found by first locating the center of the BLOB with one of the methods describe below. Next we search from the center and outwards in one direction until we find the point where the BLOB ends. The distance between this point and the

---

[1]In Sect. 9.3.1 features based on texture or color are described.

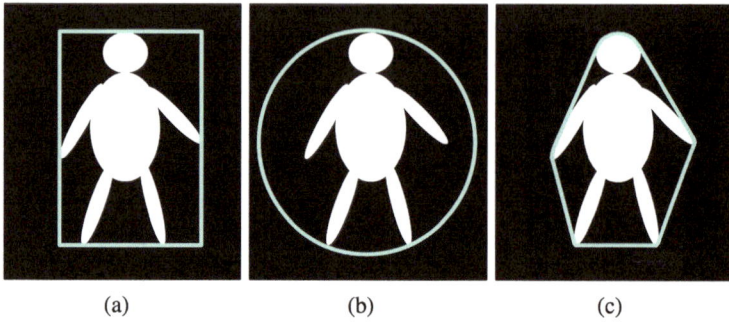

Fig. 7.5 (**a**) Bounding box. (**b**) Bounding circle. (**c**) Convex hull

center is the radius in this direction. We do this for all possible directions (for example with an angular resolution of $10°$) and the biggest radius defines the radius for the minimum circle.

Convex hull of a BLOB is the minimum convex polygon which contains the BLOB, see Fig. 7.5. It corresponds to placing a rubber band around the BLOB. It can be found in the following manner. From the topmost pixel on the BLOB search to the right along a horizontal line. If no BLOB pixel is found increase (clockwise) the angle of the search line and repeat the search. When a BLOB pixel is found the first line of the polygon is defined and a new search is started based on the angle of the previous search line. When the search reappears at the topmost pixel, the convex hull is completed. Note that morphology also can be applied to find the convex hull of a BLOB.

Bounding box ratio of a BLOB is defined as the height of the bounding box divided by the width. This feature indicates the elongation of the BLOB, i.e., is the BLOB long, high or neither.

Compactness of a BLOB is defined as the ratio of the BLOB's area to the area of the bounding box. This can be used to distinguish compact BLOBs from non-compact ones. For example, fist vs. a hand with outstretched fingers.

$$\text{Compactness} = \frac{\text{Area of BLOB}}{\text{width} \cdot \text{height}} \tag{7.1}$$

Center of mass (or center of gravity or centroid) of a physical object is the location on the object where you should place your finger in order to balance the object. The center of mass for a binary image is similar. It is the average x- and y-positions of the binary object. It is defined as a point, whose x-value is calculated by summing the x-coordinates of all pixels in the BLOB and then dividing by the total number of pixels. Similarly for the y-value. In mathematical terms the center of mass, (x_c, y_c) is calculated as

$$x_c = \frac{1}{N} \sum_{i=1}^{N} x_i, \qquad y_c = \frac{1}{N} \sum_{i=1}^{N} y_i \tag{7.2}$$

where N is the number of pixels in the BLOB and x_i and y_i are the x and y coordinates of the N pixels, respectively. In situations where the BLOB contains "appended parts" the median can replace Eq. 7.2. An example could be if you want to find the center of a person's torso. The configurations of the arms will effect the result of Eq. 7.2, but the median is less effected. The median is more computational demanding than the center of mass. An alternative to the median is to erode the BLOB with a large structuring element and then calculate the center of mass.

Center of the bounding box is a fast approximation of the center of mass. In mathematical terms the center of the bounding box, (x_{bb}, y_{bb}) is calculated as

$$x_{bb} = x_{min} + \frac{x_{max} - x_{min}}{2} = x_{min} + \frac{x_{max}}{2} - \frac{x_{min}}{2} = \frac{x_{min} + x_{max}}{2} \tag{7.3}$$

$$y_{bb} = y_{min} + \frac{y_{max} - y_{min}}{2} = y_{min} + \frac{y_{max}}{2} - \frac{y_{min}}{2} = \frac{y_{min} + y_{max}}{2} \tag{7.4}$$

Perimeter of a BLOB is the length of the contour of the BLOB. This can be found by scanning along the rim (contour) of an object and summing the number of pixels encountered. A simple approximation of the perimeter is to first find the outer boundary using the method from Sect. 6.3.4 (or another edge detection algorithm). Following this we simply count the number of white pixels in the image.

Circularity of a BLOB defines how circular a BLOB is. Different definitions exist based on the perimeter and area of the BLOB. Heywood's circularity factor is, for example, defined as the ratio of the BLOB's perimeter to the perimeter of the circle with the same area:

$$\text{Circularity} = \frac{\text{Perimeter of BLOB}}{2\sqrt{\pi \cdot \text{Area of BLOB}}} \tag{7.5}$$

A different way of calculating the circularity is to find the different radii as described for the bounding circle. The variance (see Appendix C) of the radii gives an estimate of the circularity. The smaller the variance the more circular the BLOB is.

In Fig. 7.6 two of the feature values are illustrated for the BLOBs in Fig. 7.4 (left). So after extraction of features a binary image has been converted into a number of feature values for each BLOB. The feature values can be collected in a so-called *feature vector*. For the BLOBs in Fig. 7.6, the feature vector for BLOB number one is

$$\vec{f_1} = \begin{bmatrix} 0.31 \\ 6561 \end{bmatrix} \tag{7.6}$$

Since we have seven BLOBs, we will also have seven feature vectors: $\vec{f_1}, \ldots, \vec{f_7}$.

Fig. 7.6 (**a**) The figure illustrates two features: Bounding Box and Center-of-Mass. (**b**) The table illustrates two other features: Circularity and Area. Note the order in which the BLOBs are labeled. This is a result of the scan-pattern in Fig. 4.28

BLOB number	Circu-larity	Area (pixels)
1	0.31	6561
2	0.40	6544
3	0.98	890
4	0.97	6607
5	0.99	6730
6	0.52	6611
7	0.75	2073

(a)   (b)

Fig. 7.7 2D feature space and position of the seven BLOBs from Fig. 7.6(a). The "x" represents the feature values of the prototype. The *dashed rectangle*: box classifier. *Red circle*: Euclidean distance classifier. *Blue ellipse*: weighted Euclidean distance classifier

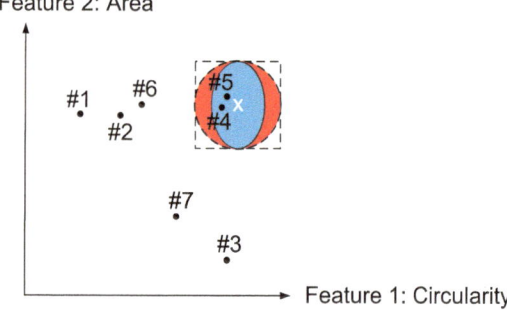

7.3   BLOB Classification

Each of the objects in Fig. 7.6 has now been identified as separate BLOBs using, for example, the Grass-Fire algorithm. The task is now to determine which BLOB is a circle and which is not. As suggested above we can use the circularity feature for this purpose. In Fig. 7.6 the values of the circularity of the different BLOBs are listed. The question is now how to define which BLOBs are circles and which are not based on their feature values. For this purpose we make a *prototype model* of the object we are looking for. That is, what are the feature values of a perfect circle and what kind of deviation will we accept? In a perfect world we will not accept any deviations from the prototype, but in practice the object or the segmentation of the object will not be perfect so we have to accept some deviations. For our example with the circles, we can define the prototype to have a circularity of 1 and a deviation of ± 0.15, meaning that BLOBs with circularity values in the range [0.85, 1.15] are accepted as circles.

What if we are looking for large circles? For this task one feature is not sufficient and we therefore use both the circularity and the area, see Fig. 7.6. These two features span a 2-dimensional *feature space* as seen in Fig. 7.7. The prototype model will now be two dimensional with each feature having an allowed range. Together these two ranges will form a rectangle and if a BLOB in an image has feature values inside the dashed rectangle, then it is a large circle otherwise it is not, see Fig. 7.7. This approach is known as a *box classifier* and the area of the rectangle is known as the *decision region*.

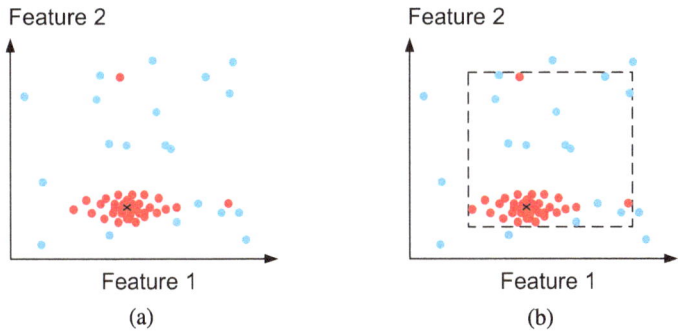

Fig. 7.8 A 2D feature space where each point is a feature vector, i.e., a BLOB. The *red points* are from the object we are trying to recognize while the *blue* are from non-object BLOBs. (**a**) Input. (**b**) The decision region in a box classifier where the maximum and minimum values are used to defined the decision region

Often it is not possible to define the prototype model beforehand and we therefore need to *learn* it, see Appendix C. The procedure is to run the developed system on typical input images (the more the better) and calculate the feature values for each BLOB (both large circles and any other BLOBs that might appear in the system). Each BLOB will result in a point in the feature space. In Fig. 7.8(a) an example is illustrated where the red points are from large circles and the blue points are from other BLOBs. The task we are faced with is to figure out the decision region of the prototype model so that as many correct BLOBs as possible are included in the decision region and at the same time exclude as many of the incorrect BLOBs as possible. We can see that the density of the red points is not uniform, but tends to be higher at the center of the "point cloud" of red points, indicated by a cross in the figure. This is a typical phenomenon independent of which features we are working with and the center is therefore a good representation of where the prototype is located in the feature space. The center can be calculated as the mean of all the red points, see Eqs. 7.2.

We can see in the figure that the red points are spread out differently in the x- and y-direction. This is also a typical phenomenon and by analyzing how the points are spread out we can learn the size of the decision region in Fig. 7.7. The simplest way is to find the minimum and maximum values of the features and let these values define the decision region. This can, however, lead to an incorrect classification if we have *outliers*. An outlier is a point that is far away from the other points in the feature space, see Fig. 7.8(b). A better approach is therefore is express the spreading of the points using the *variance*. Like the mean, the variance is a statistical measure that expresses something about the data. Concretely, the variance measures the average distance the points are from the mean. So a big variance means the points are spread out and a small variance means the points are gathered closely around the mean, see Appendix C.

When we have the means and variances of the different features the box classifier should be replaced by a *statistical classifier* since this is a more accurate approach. In the box classifier we have a binary decision; is a new feature vector (BLOB) inside or outside the rectangle? In a statistical classifier we instead measure a distance between a new feature vector (BLOB) and the prototype. The smaller the distance the more likely it is that the BLOB is the same type (here a large circle) as the prototype. To make this approach operational we need to threshold the distance and hence end up with a binary decision region like the dashed box in Fig. 7.7. The difference is that the region is now a more precise ellipse and not a rectangle, see Fig. 7.7. One statistical classifier is the *weighted Euclidean distance* in our case defined as

$$\text{WED}(\overrightarrow{f_i}, \text{prototype}) = \sqrt{\frac{(f_i(\text{cir}) - \text{mean}(\text{cir}))^2}{\text{variance}(\text{cir})} + \frac{(f_i(\text{area}) - \text{mean}(\text{area}))^2}{\text{variance}(\text{area})}}$$

$$(7.7)$$

where $\text{WED}(\overrightarrow{f_1}, \text{prototype})$ is the weighted Euclidean distance between feature vector $\overrightarrow{f_i}$, i.e., the ith BLOB, and the prototype. $f_i(\text{cir})$ and $f_i(\text{area})$ are the circularity and area of the ith BLOB, respectively. The rest of the parameters in the equation are the means and variances of the two features of the prototype. In the general case with p different features the weighted Euclidean distance measure is defined as

$$\text{WED}(\overrightarrow{f_i}, \text{prototype}) = \sum_{j=1}^{p} \sqrt{\frac{(f_i(m_j) - \text{mean}(m_j))^2}{\text{variance}(m_j)}} \qquad (7.8)$$

where m_j is the jth feature. If the variances of all features are the same, then we can ignore them and end up with the Euclidean distance measure (ED), where the decision region is a circle in 2D (see Fig. 7.7):

$$\text{ED}(\overrightarrow{f_i}, \text{prototype}) = \sum_{j=1}^{p} \sqrt{\left(f_i(m_j) - \text{mean}(m_j)\right)^2} \qquad (7.9)$$

It should be noticed that the three equations above assume that the scale of the features are the same. In our example the problem is that the area is measured in 1000 s and circularity is a value close to 1. This means that the area will dominate the distance measure completely. The solution is to normalize the features so they are scaled similarly and are in the same interval, e.g. [0, 1]. This can be obtained, for example, as

$$\text{Area feature} = \min\left\{\frac{\text{Area of BLOB}}{\text{Area of Model}}, \frac{\text{Area of Model}}{\text{Area of BLOB}}\right\} \qquad (7.10)$$

$$\text{Circularity feature} = \min\left\{\text{Circularity}, \frac{1}{\text{Circularity}}\right\} \qquad (7.11)$$

7.4   Further Information

The grass-fire algorithm can be modified to also operate on gray-scale and color images. The first modification is that the algorithm does not scan the entire image, but instead starts at a so-called *seed point* often defined interactively by a user. The second modification is that an object pixel is a pixel within a certain gray-scale or color range. The range can for example be defined as the value of the seed point ± a small value. A more robust approach is to define the range based on the statistics of the pixels located in the vicinity of the seed point, see Appendix C. The effect this algorithm will have is that a region centered around the seed point will be selected. One might think of the algorithm as a combination of thresholding and connected component analysis. The algorithm is known as *region growing* and can for example be applied to remove the red-eye effect in pictures.

The grass-fire algorithm is not the only connected component analysis algorithm that exits. But no matter which algorithm is used it is very often combined with the feature extraction process since both need to process each pixel in a BLOB. Combining them will speed up the system. Many other features than those described in this chapter exist, especially more advanced shape features such as Hu moments. Furthermore, many new features can be defined/optimized with respect to a concrete application.

A common question when doing BLOB classification is whether a simple box classifier is sufficient. The answer depends on the application. If the feature vectors of the non-object BLOBs and the object BLOBs are far apart in the feature space, then the exact position and shape of the decision region is not critical and hence a box classifier will suffice. This is the situation in Fig. 7.7. The accuracy of the box classifier goes down as the feature vectors becomes similar. This is illustrated in Fig. 7.9 where it can be seen that the weighted Euclidean distance classifier outperforms the box classifier.

Another line of argumentation is that the number of parameters needed to be defined in the box classifier (the shape of the rectangle) increases as the number of feature increase. In the weighted Euclidean distance classifier only one parameter (a threshold on the distance) has to be decided independent on how many features are used.

Sometimes we will have features that are dependent. *Dependency* means that if we know something about one feature we can say something about another feature. If for example we as features have area and perimeter, then it is very likely that the value of the perimeter increases as the area increases. Dependency in data can result in the point cloud having an orientation that is neither vertical nor horizontal, see Fig. 7.9(c). In these cases both the box classifier and the weighted Euclidean distance classifier will fail. Instead we must use the *Mahalanobis distance classifier*. It is a statistical classifier measuring the distance between an unknown feature vector and the prototype. So like the two other statistical classifiers presented above it only requires one parameter to be defined no matter how many features are used. In fact, the Euclidean distance classifier and the weighted Euclidean distance classifier are both special cases on the Mahalanobis distance classifier. In Fig. 7.9(c) the decision

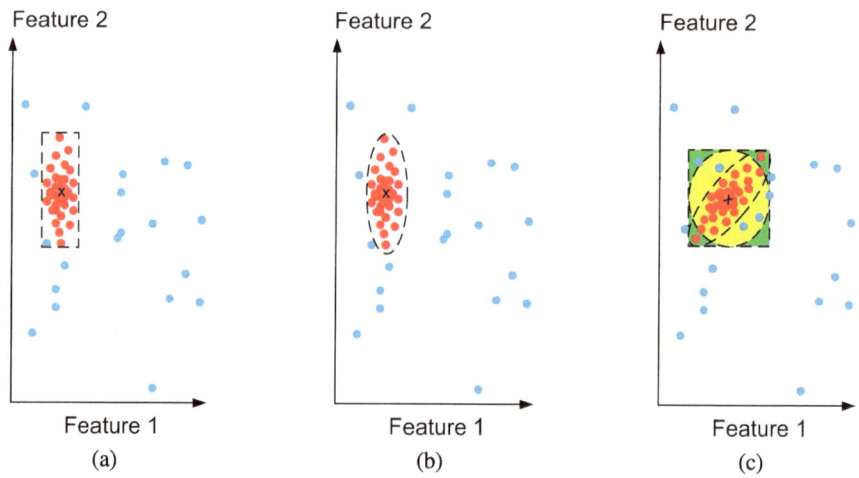

Fig. 7.9 A 2D feature space where each point is a feature vector, i.e., a BLOB. The *red points* are from the object we are trying to recognize while the *blue* are from non-object BLOBs. (**a**) Box classifier. (**b**) Weighted Euclidean distance classifier. (**c**) Mahalanobis distance classifier (*rotated ellipse*). Box classifier (*green rectangle*). Weighted Euclidean distance classifier (*yellow ellipse*)

regions for all three classifiers can be seen. Many other classifiers exist and are used in fields such as computer vision, machine learning and artificial intelligence. Many books can therefore be found on this matter, see for example [8].

No matter what, before choosing a particular classifier always capture a lot of training data and see how they spread out in the feature space. Just by looking at a figure like Fig. 7.9 you can often get a very good impression of how to proceed with the classification, but also, and equally important, an understanding of the quality of the chosen features.

7.5   Exercises

Exercise 1: Explain the following concepts: BLOB, connectivity, recursive grass-fire algorithm, sequential grass-fire algorithm, feature space, classification.

Exercise 2: How many BLOBs are present in Fig. 7.10 when 4-connectivity is applied?

Exercise 3: How many BLOBs are present in Fig. 7.10 when 8-connectivity is applied?

Exercise 4: In which order are the different pixels in Fig. 7.10 labeled when a recursive grass-fire algorithm with 4-connectivity is applied?

Exercise 5: Find the following features for each BLOB in Fig. 7.10: area, bounding box ration, compactness.

Exercise 6: Find the center of mass and center of the bounding box for each BLOB in Fig. 7.10 and discuss the differences.

Fig. 7.10 Object pixels are white (1). Background pixels are gray (0)

0	0	0	0	0	0	0	0	0	0	0	0
0	0	1	1	1	1	0	0	0	1	1	0
0	1	1	1	1	1	1	0	0	1	1	0
0	0	0	0	0	0	1	1	0	0	1	0
0	1	1	1	1	1	1	0	0	1	0	0
0	0	0	0	0	0	0	0	1	1	0	0
0	1	1	1	1	0	0	0	0	0	0	0
0	1	1	1	1	0	1	1	1	0	0	0
0	1	1	1	1	1	0	0	0	0	0	0
0	1	1	1	1	0	0	1	1	0	0	0
0	1	1	1	1	0	1	1	0	1	0	0
0	0	0	0	0	0	0	0	0	0	0	0

Additional exercise 1: What is region growing and how is it different from the recursive grass-fire algorithm?

Additional exercise 2: Suggest three features not defined in the chapter.

Additional exercise 3: Design an algorithm to calculate the convex hull of a BLOB.

Additional exercise 4: Design an algorithm to calculate the perimeter of a BLOB.

A video sequence is in principle a sequence of images. The methods presented in the previous chapters therefore apply equally well to a video sequence as an image. We simply process one image at a time. There are, however, two differences between a video sequence and an image. First, working with video allows us to consider temporal information and hence segment objects based on their motion. This is discussed below in Sect. 8.2. Moreover, temporal information is the cornerstone of *tracking*, which is described in the next chapter. Second, video acquisition and image acquisition may not be the same, and that can have some consequences. Below, this is discussed.

8.1   Video Acquisition

A video camera is said to have a certain *framerate*. The framerate is a measure for how many images the camera can capture per second and is measured in Hertz (Hz). The framerate depends on the number of pixels (and the number of bits per pixel) and the electronics of the camera. Usually the framerate is geared toward a certain transmission standard like USB, Firewire, Camera Link, etc. Each of these standards has a certain *bandwidth*, which is the amount of data that can be transmitted per second. With a fixed bandwidth we are left with a choice between high resolution of the image and a high framerate. When one goes up the other one goes down. In the end the desired framerate and resolution will always depend on the concrete application.

Say we have a system including a camera with a framerate of 20 Hz. This means that a new image is captured every 50 ms. But it also means that the image processing algorithms can spend a maximum of 50 ms per image. To underline this we often talk about two framerates; one for the camera and one for the image processing algorithms. The overall framerate of a system is the smallest of the two framerates.

Another important factor in video acquisition is compression. Very often the captured video sequence needs to be compressed in order to insure a reasonable framerate/resolution. The more the video is compressed, the higher the framerate/resolution, but the worse the quality of the decompressed video. The question

T.B. Moeslund, *Introduction to Video and Image Processing*,   117
Undergraduate Topics in Computer Science,
DOI 10.1007/978-1-4471-2503-7_8, © Springer-Verlag London Limited 2012

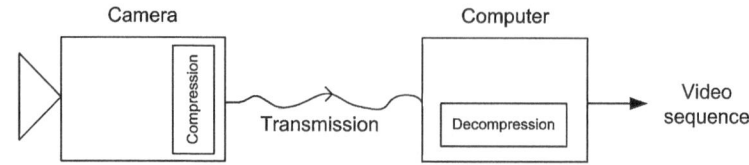

Fig. 8.1 Compression and decompression of video

is of course if the quality lose associated with video compression is a problem in a particular application or not? To be able to answer this we first need to understand what compression is, see Fig. 8.1.

Overall there exist two different types of compression; lossy and lossless. In the latter type the captured video in the camera and the decompressed video on the computer is exactly the same. This is virtually never used and hence not described further. In the former type of compression some information will be lost. Many different lossy video compression algorithms exist, but they all have a similar core. First of all they are developed with focus on the human mind in the sense that if a human looks at the captured video and the decompressed video, the difference should be as small as possible. That is, the information lost in video compression is optimized with respect to the human visual perception capabilities, i.e., a human will not notice the missing information. This may not be optimal from a computer's point of view, in the sense that the information lost in the compression can affect the image processing algorithms, but this is just how it is.

Humans are more sensitive to changes in the lighting than changes in the colors. The YC_bC_r color representation is therefore used, see Sect. 3.3.3, and the C_b and C_r components are compressed harder than the Y component. Another aspect of human perception involved in compression of video is the fact that humans are better at seeing gradual changes in an image as opposed to rapid changes. This fact is utilized by transforming the image into a new representation where the level of change is apparent. Rapid changes are then compressed harder than gradual changes.

Another main ingredient in video compression is to exploit that consecutive images usually do not change very much. To exploit this the image is first divided into a number of blocks. Each block is then used as a template to search for a matching block in the previous image. Template matching is used for this purpose, see Sect. 5.2.1. The two blocks are now subtracted and their difference is usually small and hence can be represented by fewer bits than the original block. This is done for all blocks in the input. The last component in video compression is similar to what is used for image, sound and text compression, namely *entropy coding*. This covers lossless methods that can compress based on the statistical nature of the data. For example, say we have the following pixel values: $2, 3, 3, 3, 3, 3, 3, 3, 67, 12, 12, 12, 12, 10$. Using entropy coding this can be written as $2, 3, 255, 6, 67, 12, 255, 3, 10$, where 255 indicates that the next value states the number of repetitions, that is: $3, 255, 6 = 3, 3, 3, 3, 3, 3, 3$. Originally we had 14 values and now we only have nine values, i.e., a compression factor of $14/9 = 1.56$.

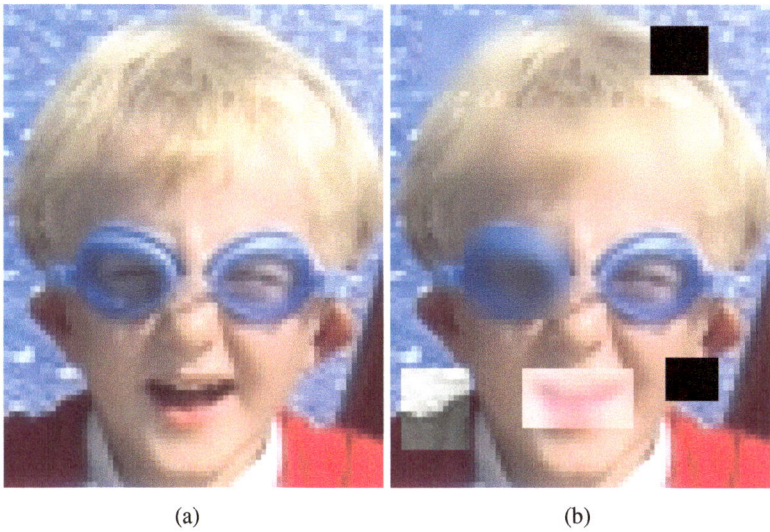

(a)   (b)

Fig. 8.2 Different blocking effects illustrated in a zoomed picture in order to increase visibility

How many bits needed to represent a compressed image in the video sequence depends on the content of the video. Sometimes we require more bits than are available in the bandwidth. This means that the compression method will have to delete some additional information, for example by a harder compression of the colors or by simply ignoring details of one or more blocks. The consequence of the latter can be that one or more blocks in the decompressed image contain less detail and hence appear blurry or do not contain any detail at all, i.e., will be black. Such phenomena are known as *blocking artifacts* and a few are illustrated in Fig. 8.2.

The point of all the above is that you as a designer need to look into these issues before doing video processing. It might be better to spend some extra money on a good camera (and transmission) producing good data compared to spending lots of time (in vain?) trying to compensate for poor data with clever algorithms. This is especially true if developing a system based on color processing. A compromise can be to use a cheap camera with poor quality video and then try to detect if blocking has occurred and if so delete such images from the video sequence.

No matter the type of camera and compression algorithm, the captured video sequence may contain motion blur due to motion in the scene, see Sect. 2.2. A similar problem is that the depth-of-field may not cover the entire FOV and hence moving objects may be blurred due to an incorrect focus. Processing video containing blur will possibly affect the results and should therefore be avoided is possible. One approach for doing so is to analyze each image and try to measure the level of blur. If too blurry the image should be deleted. The consequence of a blurred image is that the magnitudes of the edges in the image are small. So the blurriness can be measured by analyzing the edges in the image, see Sect. 9.3.1. Another approach is to compare the input image with a blurred version of the input image. If the input image contains a lot of edges, i.e., is sharp, then the two images will be significantly different. If they are similar it is likely that the input image was blurred in the first place.

8.2   Detecting Changes in the Video

In many systems we are interested in detecting what has changed in the scene, i.e., a new object enters the scene or an object is moving in the scene. For such purposes we can use image subtraction, see Chap. 4, to compare the current image with a previous image. If they differ, the difference defines the object or movement we are looking for. In the rest of this chapter we will elaborate on this idea and present an approach for detecting changes in video data.

8.2.1   The Algorithm

The algorithm for detecting changes in a video sequence consists of five steps:
1. Save reference image
2. Capture current image
3. Perform image subtraction
4. Thresholding
5. Filter noise

The algorithm can be performed in two different ways depending on the goal and assumptions. If the background in the scene can be assumed to be static then every new object entering the scene can in theory be segmented by subtracting an image of the background from the current image. This process is denoted *background subtraction* and illustrated in Fig. 8.3. The reference image of the background is captured as the first image when the system commences.

The other way the algorithm can be performed is when the assumption of a static background breaks down. For example if the light in the scene changes significantly, then an incoming image will be very different from the background even though no changes occurred in the scene. In such situations the reference image should be the previous image. The rationale is that the background in two consecutive images from a video sequence is probably very similar and the only difference is the new/moving object, see Fig. 8.4. Such methods are denoted *image differencing*.

The difference between the two ways the algorithm can be performed results in two different types of reference image: either the first in a sequence or the previous image. The remaining four steps in the algorithm are the same for the two algorithms and performed for each new image in the video.

Step Three

In *Step three* of the algorithm the reference image and current image are subtracted. Let us denote the reference image $r(x, y)$ and the current image $f(x, y)$. The resulting image, $g(x, y)$, is then given as

1. Save reference   2. Capture current   3. Perform image
   image   image   subtraction

4. Thresholding   5. Filter noise

Fig. 8.3 The five steps of segmenting video data through background subtraction

$$g(x, y) = f(x, y) - r(x, y) \qquad (8.1)$$

In Fig. 8.3 step three is shown. The car stands out in the resulting image since the pixel values of the car are different from the pixel values of the reference image. However, at some locations where a pixel in the reference image has a similar value to the pixel at the current image the resulting pixel value will be close to zero and hence will not stand out. This can for example be seen around the wheels of the car. As a designer you therefore need to introduce a background which is as different as possible from the object you intend to segment. For example, choosing a black background when segmenting white balls is a very good idea, whereas a white background is obviously not.

Another issue regarding image subtraction, is that negative values are very likely to appear in the resulting image $g(x, y)$. Say that your task is to segment objects when they pass by your camera. The objects are black and white, meaning that they have pixel values which are either black, $f(x, y) \cong 0$, or white $f(x, y) \cong 255$. You then design a gray background which has intensity values around 100, i.e., $r(x, y) \cong 100$, and perform image subtraction:

$$g(x, y) \cong \begin{cases} 0, & \text{where the object is not present;} \\ 155, & \text{where the object is white;} \\ -155, & \text{where the object is black} \end{cases} \qquad (8.2)$$

A common error is to set a negative pixel to zero. If this is done then only the white parts of the object is detected. Note that whether $g(x, y) = 155$ or $g(x, y) = -155$ is equally important. The correct solution is to apply the absolute value of $g(x, y)$, $Abs(g(x, y))$, see Appendix B.

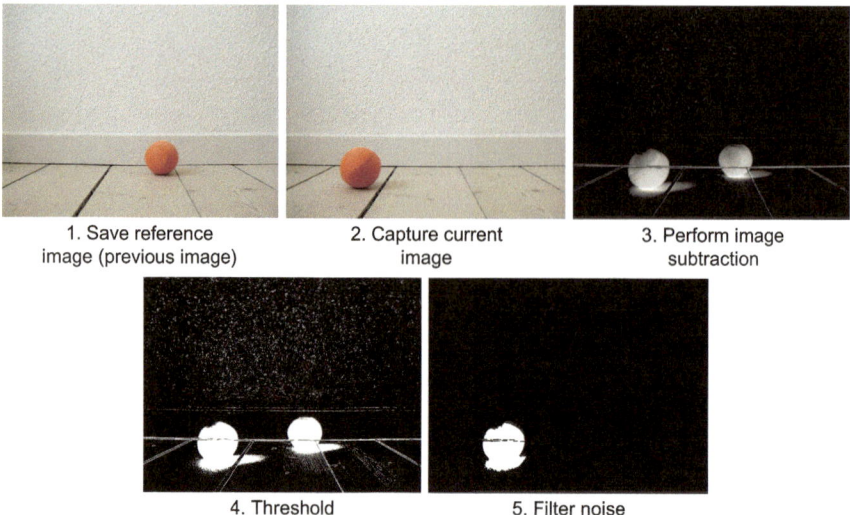

Fig. 8.4 The five steps of segmenting video data through image differencing

Step Four

Step four of the algorithm is simply a matter of binarizing the difference image $Abs(g(x, y))$ by comparing each pixel with a threshold value, T:

$$\text{Binary image} = \begin{cases} 0, & \text{if } Abs(g(x, y)) < T; \\ 255, & \text{otherwise} \end{cases} \qquad (8.3)$$

Step Five

The threshold in step four will, like any other threshold operation, produce noise due to an imperfect camera sensor, small fluctuations in the lighting, the object being similar to the background, etc. The noise will be in the form of missing pixels inside the silhouette of the object (false negatives, see Appendix C) and silhouette-pixels outside the actual silhouette (false positives). See Figs. 8.3 or 8.4 for examples.

The noise will in general have a negative influence on the quality of the results and *step five* therefore removes the noise (if possible) using some kind of filtering. Small isolated silhouette-pixels outside the actual silhouette can often be removed using either a median filter or a morphologic opening operation. The holes inside the silhouette can often be removed using a morphologic closing operation. Which method to apply obviously depends on the concrete application.

In the following, image differencing and background subtraction are explained in more detail.

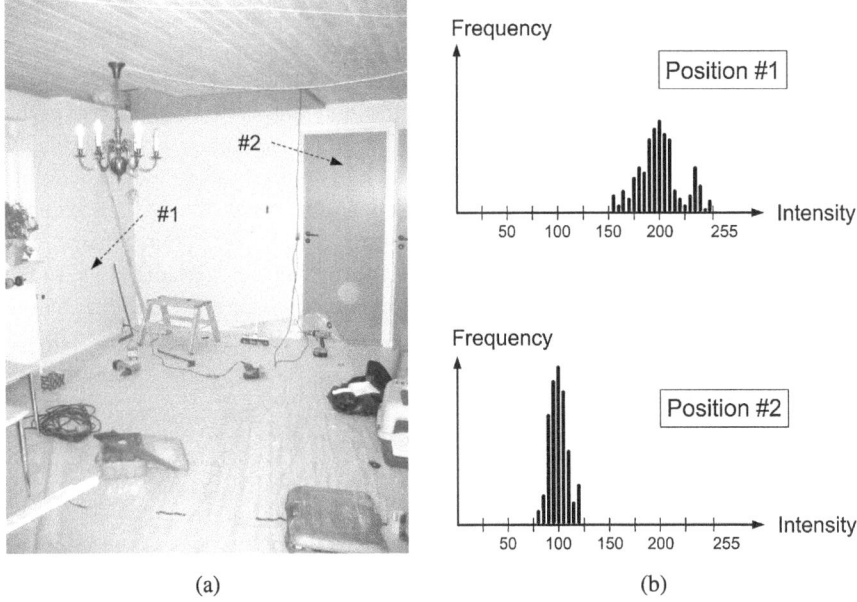

Fig. 8.5 (**a**) A static background image. The *two arrows* indicate the position of two pixels. (**b**) Histograms of the pixel values at the two positions. The data come from a sequence of images

8.3   Background Subtraction

Background subtraction is a simple and yet efficient method of extracting an object in a scene. This is especially true if the background can be designed to be uniform. In indoor and controlled setups this is indeed realistic, but for more complicated scenarios, other methods might be necessary. Even in the case of a controlled setup two issues must be considered:

1. Is the background really constant?
2. How to define the threshold value, which is used to binarize the difference image?

When you point a video camera at a static scene, for example a wall, the images seem the same. Very often, however, they are not. The primary reason being that artificial lighting seldom produces a constant illumination. Furthermore, if sunlight enters the scene, then this will also contribute to the non-constant illumination due to the randomness associated with the incoming light rays. The effect of this is illustrated in Fig. 8.5. To the left an image from a static scene is shown. To the right two histograms are shown. The first histogram is based on the pixel values at position #1 for a few seconds and similar for the second histogram. If the images are actually the same, the histograms would contain only one non-zero bin. As can be seen this is not the case and in general no such thing as a static background exists.

Say that the pixel at position #2 in the first image of the video sequence has a value of 80 (not very likely according to the histogram, but nevertheless possible). If the first image is used as the reference image, then typical background images (around 100 according to the histogram) will result in a difference around 20. Depending on the threshold value, this could actually be interpreted as an object in the scene, since it seems different from the reference image. This is obviously not desirable and each pixel in the reference image should therefore be calculated as the *mean* of the first N images, see Appendix C. The reference image at this particular position will then be around 100, which is much more appropriate according to the histogram. So to make the background subtraction more robust the first few seconds of processing should therefore be spent on calculating a good reference image.

Sometimes the background changes during processing. For example due to the changing position of the sun during the day or due to changes in the illumination sources, e.g., they are accidentally moved. In such situations a new reference image should be calculated. But how do we detect that this has happened? One way is, of course, if we can see that the performance of the system degrades. An automatic way is to gradually change the value of each pixel in the reference image in the following way:

$$r_{\text{new}}(x, y) = \alpha \cdot r_{\text{old}}(x, y) + (1 - \alpha) \cdot f(x, y) \tag{8.4}$$

where $r(x, y)$ is the reference image, $f(x, y)$ is the current image, and α is a weighting factor that defines how fast the reference image is updated. The value of α depends on the application, but a typical value is $\alpha = 0.95$.

8.3.1 Defining the Threshold Value

As for any other threshold operation, defining the actual threshold value is a trade-off between false positives and false negatives, see Appendix C, which is application-dependent.

It is important to notice that Eq. 8.3 is actually based on the assumption that the histograms for different pixel positions are similar and only differ in their mean values. That is, it is assumed that the variation in the histograms is similar. In order to understand the implications of this assumption let us have a closer look at the bottom histogram in Fig. 8.5 together with Eq. 8.3. Say we define the threshold value to 25. This means that an object in an image needs to have a value below 75 or above 125 in order to be segmented as an object pixel and not a background pixel. This seems fine. But then have a look at the top histogram in Fig. 8.5. Clearly this histogram has a larger variation and applying a threshold of 25 will result in incorrect segmentation of pixel values in the intervals: [150, 175] and [225, 255].

In many situations different histograms will occur simply because the different parts of the scene are exposed to different illumination conditions, which yields histograms with different variations. For example, you could have some parts of the background which move slightly (due to a draft for instance) and this will create a larger variation. So to sum up the above, the problem is that each position in the image is a associated with the same *global threshold* value.

The solution to this potential problem is to have a unique threshold value for each pixel position! Finding these manually, is not realistic simply due to the number of pixels and the threshold values are therefore found automatically by the use of the standard deviation for each pixel position, see Appendix C. So when the mean of each pixel is calculated, so is the standard deviation. Equation 8.3 is therefore reformulated as

$$\text{Binary image} = \begin{cases} 0, & \text{if } Abs(g(x, y)) < \beta \cdot \sigma(x, y); \\ 255, & \text{otherwise} \end{cases} \tag{8.5}$$

where β is a scaling factor and $\sigma(x, y)$ is the standard deviation at the position (x, y). Since β is the same for every position, we have no more parameters to define than above, but now the thresholding is done with respect to the actual data, hence a *local threshold*.

8.4   Image Differencing

If the assumption of a static background is violated significantly then background subtraction will produce incorrect results. In such situations we can apply image differencing to detect changes in a scene. As stated above, image differencing operates as background subtraction, except for the fact that the reference image is now a previous image.

Image differencing is simple and can efficiently measure changes in the image. Unfortunately the method has two problems. The first is a lack of detecting new objects which are not in motion. Say a new object enters a scene. As long as the object moves, image differencing detects this in the image subtracting process, but if the object stops moving, the reference image will be equal to the current image and hence nothing is detected. This is a clear weakness compared to background subtraction, which is indifferent to whether the new object is moving or not, as long as the appearance of the object is different from the background.

The other problem associated with image differencing is the notion of *ghost objects* illustrated in Fig. 8.6. The figure contains artificial images from a sequence where an object is moving horizontally through a scene. To make it simple, the object is a square with uniform gray-scale value. What can be seen is that the image differencing produces two segments (smaller objects). One originates from the current object and the other one from the object in the reference image—where the object was. This latter segment type is denoted a ghost object, since no object is present. A ghost object can also be seen in Fig. 8.4.

If the goal is only to obtain the coarse motion in the image, then this does not matter. If, however, we are only interested in the position of the object in the current image, then we need to remove ghost objects. One approach for doing so is if we know the moving direction of the object. We can then infer which is the object and which is the ghost. Another approach is if we know that the object is always brighter than the background. Then the pixels belonging to the ghost will have negative values after the image subtraction.

Fig. 8.6 Image differencing.
The effect of changing the
reference image

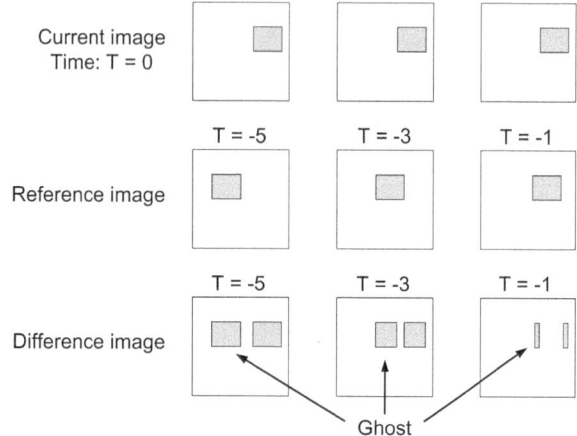

It should also be noticed that when the object is overlapping in the reference and current image, then we only detect a part of the object, as seen in Fig. 8.6. If we know the size and speed of the object we can calculate how long time there should be between the reference image and the current image to avoid overlap. Or in other words, the reference image need not be the previous image $T = -1$, it can also be for example $T = -5$, see Fig. 8.6.

8.5   Further Information

Video compression has for a long time been a cornerstone in video acquisition and allowed for transmission and storage of video data. Video compression is a research field in its own right and contains many more aspects than those basics presented in this chapter. The interested reader is referred to a textbook dedicated to exactly this field, see for example [17]. As the hardware and software has matured it has become possible to capture, transmit and store larger and larger amounts of video data. But even with today's fast computers, clever transmission systems, and huge storage facilities, the handling of video data can still be too difficult and a reduced framerate/resolution/quality is necessary. To appreciate this fact just imagine the amount of video data captured, transmitted and stored in a surveillance setup with for example 100 cameras.

Background subtraction can be a powerful allied when it comes to segmenting objects in a scene. The method, however, has some build-in limitations that are exposed especially when processing video of outdoor scenes. First of all, the method requires the background to be empty when learning the background model for each pixel. This can be a challenge in a natural scene where moving objects may always be present. One solution is to median filter all training samples for each pixel. This will eliminated pixels where an object is moving through the scene and the resulting model of the pixel will be a true background pixel. An extension is to first order all training pixels (as done in the median filter) and then calculate the average of the pixels closest to the median. This will provide both a mean and variance per pixel. Such approaches assume that each pixel is covered by objects less than half the time in the training period.

Another problem that is especially apparent when processing outdoor video is the fact that a pixel may cover more than one background. Say we have a background pixel from a gray road. Imagine now that the wind sometime blows so a leaf covers the same pixel. This will result in two very different backgrounds for this pixel; a greenish color and a grayish color. If we find the mean for this pixel we will end up with something in between green and gray with a huge variance. This will render a poor segmentation of this pixel during background subtraction. A better approach is therefore to define two different background models for this pixel; one for the leaf and one for the road, see [12, 18] for specific examples and [9] for a general discussion.

Yet another problem in outdoor video is shadows due to strong sunlight. Such shadow pixels can easily appear different from the learnt background model and hence be incorrectly classified as object pixels. Different approaches can be followed in order to avoid such misclassifications. First of all, a background pixel in shadow tends to have the same color as when not in shadow—just darker. A more detailed version of this idea is based on the notion that when a pixel is in shadow it often means that it is not exposed to direct sunlight, but rather illuminated by the sky. And since the sky tends to me more bluish, the color of a background pixel in shadow can be expected to be more blueish too. Secondly, one can group neighboring object pixels together and analyze the layout of the edges within that region. If that layout is similar to the layout of the edges in the background model, then the region is likely to be a shadow and not an object. For more information please refer to [6, 15].

8.6 Exercises

Exercise 1: Explain the following concepts: framerate, compression, background subtraction, local vs. global thresholding, image differencing, ghost object.

Exercise 2: What is the compression factor of the following sequence of pixels if we apply entropy coding? 14, 14, 14, 7, 14, 14, 14, 7, 7, 7, 7, 7, 7, 7, 7, 7, 7, 7, 7, 4, 4, 4, 4.

Exercise 3: A camera has a framerate of 125 Hz. How many images does the camera capture per minute?

Exercise 4: A camera captures a new image every 125 ms. What is the framerate of the camera?

Exercise 5: A function is defined as $y = abs(x - 1)$. Draw this function for $x \in [-10, 10]$.

Exercise 6: The reference image $r(x, y)$ in background subtraction is updated gradually with a weight (α) of 0.9. At one point in time a pixel at position (50,50) in the reference image has the value 100, that is, $r(50, 50) = 100$. In the next five images we have: $f(50, 50) = 10$, $f(50, 50) = 12$, $f(50, 50) = 12$, $f(50, 50) = 14$, $f(50, 50) = 15$. What is $r(50, 50)$ after these five frames?

A reference image is being learned for background subtraction. After the learning period two pixel positions have the histograms seen in the figure below.

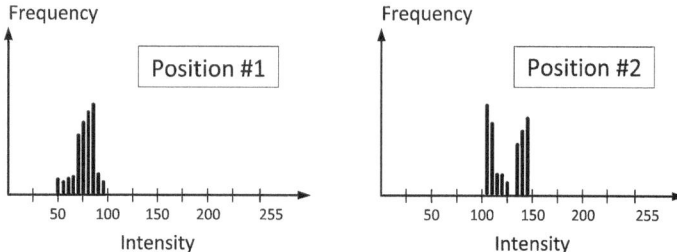

Exercise 7: Which histogram has the highest mean?
Exercise 8: Which histogram has the smallest standard deviation?
Exercise 9: Which pixel position comes from the most static background?
Additional exercise: What is MPEG and how does it work?

One of the central questions in video processing is how to follow an object over time. Imagine you are designing a game where the position of the hand is used as a controller. What you need from your video processing software is then the position of the hand in each image and hence a temporal sequence of coordinates, see Table 9.1.

We can also illustrate this as a number of points in a coordinate system. If we connect these points we will have a curve through time, see Fig. 9.1. This curve is denoted the *trajectory* of the object.

The notion of a trajectory is not limited to the position of the object. We can generalize the concept and say that the object is represented by a so-called *state vector*, where each entry in the vector contains the value of a certain parameter at a particular time step. Besides position, such entries could be velocity, acceleration, size, shape, color etc. Formally we define tracking to be a matter of finding the trajectory of an object's state. This chapter will define a framework for tracking, namely the so-called *predict-match-update* framework, see Fig. 9.6. Without loss of generality we will below assume the state is only the position of the object, meaning that the state vector we seek to find is $\vec{s}(t) = [x(t), y(t)]$. Below the framework is built up one block at a time.

9.1   Tracking-by-Detection

We can use some of the methods described previously in the book to detect an object. If we do this in each image and simply concatenate the positions we could argue that we are doing tracking. This approach is, however, *not* considered tracking since each detection is done independently of all other detections, i.e., no temporal information is included.

The most simple form of tracking is when the estimated position is updated using previous states. The current and previous states are combined in order to smooth the current state. The need for this is motivated by the fact that noise will always appear in the estimated position.

T.B. Moeslund, *Introduction to Video and Image Processing*,
Undergraduate Topics in Computer Science,
DOI 10.1007/978-1-4471-2503-7_9, © Springer-Verlag London Limited 2012

Table 9.1 The position of an object over time

Time	1	2	3	4	5	6	7	8	9	10	11	12	13	
X	1	2	4	5	4	6	8	9	9	7	3	2	2	⋯
Y	10	8	8	7	6	4	4	3	2	2	2	2	4	⋯

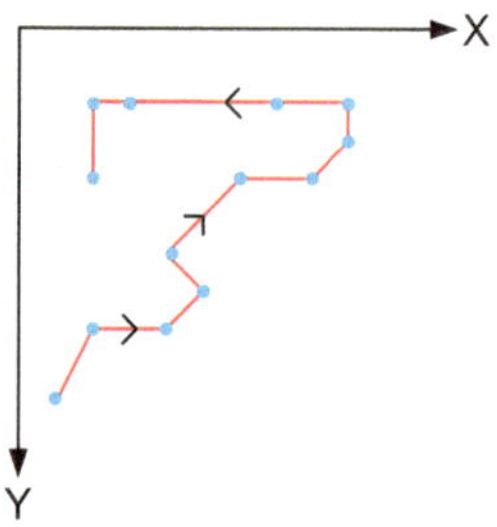

Fig. 9.1 The trajectory of an object over time

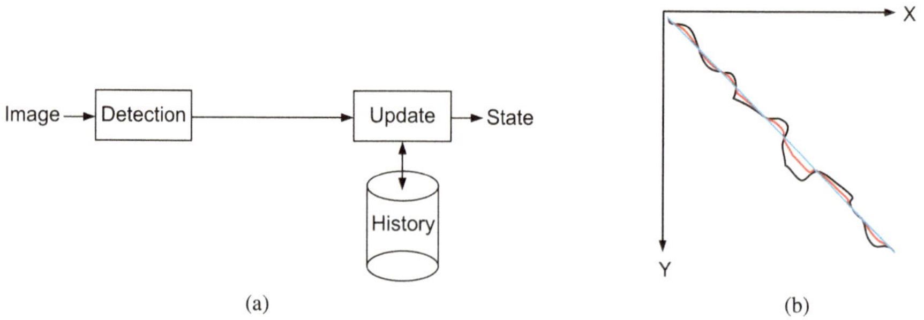

(a)   (b)

Fig. 9.2 (**a**) Framework for updating the state. (**b**) The effect of updating the states. The *blue curve* is the true trajectory of the object. The *black curve* is the detected trajectory and the *red curve* is the smoothed trajectory

Smoothing can be implemented by calculating the average of the last N states. The larger N is, the more smooth the trajectory will be. As N increases so does the latency in the system, meaning that the updated state will react slow to rapid position changes. For example if you are tracking a car that is accelerating hard or is doing an emergency break. This slow reaction can be counteracted by also including future states in the update of the current state, but such an approach will delay the output from the system. Whether this is acceptable or not depends on the application. Another way of counteracting the latency is to use a weighted smoothing filter. Instead of adding N positions together and dividing by N, we weight each position according to its age. So the current state has the highest weight, the second newest state has the second highest weight etc. No matter which smoothing method is used to update the state, it is a compromise between smoothness and latency. In Fig. 9.2 the updating of the state is illustrated. The history-block contains previous states.

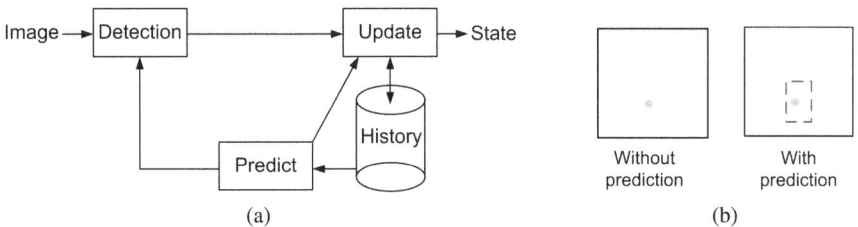

Fig. 9.3 (**a**) Framework for updating and predicting the state. (**b**) The effect of predicting the position of the object in the next image

9.2 Prediction

Very often the object we want to follow is moving much slower than the framerate of the camera. As a consequence the object is not moving very much from one image to the next. So, having located an object in one image will allow us to *predict* where the object will approximately be in the next image. We want to exploit this fact when detecting the object. This is done by introducing a ROI centered at the position where we predict the object to be and only analyze the pixels within the ROI, see Fig. 9.3. This will save a significant amount of processing time.

The question is now *where* we predict the object to be. For this purpose a *motion model* is introduced, that is, a model explaining how the object is moving. The most simple model is a *zeroth order linear motion model*. It predicts the object to be exactly at the same position in the next image as it is in the current image. The next of the linear motion models is the *first order linear motion model*, which includes the velocity of the object. Given the current position $\vec{p}(t) = [x(t), y(t)]$ and velocity $\vec{v}(t) = [v_x(t), v_y(t)]$ of the object, the predicted position will be

$$\vec{p}(t+1) = \vec{v}(t) \cdot \Delta t + \vec{p}(t) \tag{9.1}$$

where $\vec{p}(t+1)$ is the predicted position and Δt is the time between $\vec{p}(t)$ and $\vec{p}(t+1)$. Often the framerate is constant and Δt is simply the number of images predicted into the future. Usually we are just interested in predicting one image ahead and hence Δt can be removed from the equation.

The *second order linear motion model* also includes the current acceleration of the object $\vec{a}(t) = [a_x(t), a_y(t)]$ and the predicted position is given as

$$\vec{p}(t+1) = \frac{1}{2} \cdot \vec{a}(t) \cdot \Delta t^2 + \vec{v}(t) \cdot \Delta t + \vec{p}(t) \tag{9.2}$$

Again, with a fixed framerate and only predicting the next image, the two Δ terms become 1 and can therefore be ignored.

Motion models are not necessarily linear. If we for example are following an object being thrown, we need a model that includes gravity. Another example could be when tracking an object moving in a circle, the motion model would of course be that of a circle, or if we are tracking a drunken human, the motion model might be more like a sinus curve than a straight line.

Sometimes the movement of an object cannot be explained by just one motion model. If we for example are tracking a fish in an aquarium, we will need two motion models. One model for when the fish is just swimming slowly around and another model for when the fish needs to get away from something fast. The first type of movement could be modeled by a first order linear model, while the other type of movement could be modeled by a random direction with maximum acceleration. Having two (or more) motion models will result in two (or more) ROIs.

No matter how good our motion model is, it is still just a model of the movement, i.e. an approximation. The object is therefore not likely to be located exactly at the predicted location. For this reason we look for the object within a ROI. The question is now how to define the size of the ROI. The simplest approach is to try different sizes and see which works best. A more scientific approach, which will render a smaller ROI and hence save processing time, is to define the size based on the *uncertainty* of the prediction. Say we in the last image predicted the x-position of the object to be at position 370, but found the object at position 350. Whether this difference is due to a bad prediction or a bad detection we do not know. What we *do* know is that there is some uncertainty in the x-direction. The bigger the uncertainty is, the bigger the ROI should be in the x-direction. Normally it is not recommended to let the difference control the ROI directly since it is sensitive to noise. A more conservative way of changing the ROI based on the difference is here shown for the width of the ROI:

$$\text{width}(t+1) = \alpha \cdot \left| \underline{x}(t) - x(t) \right| + (1-\alpha) \cdot \text{WIDTH} \tag{9.3}$$

where α is a small value, $\underline{x}(t)$ is the predicted x-value of the object at time t, $x(t)$ is the detected x-value of the object at time t, and WIDTH is a predefined minimum width of the ROI. The same can of course be done in the vertical direction.

Similar to the uncertainty of the prediction, we also have an uncertainty associated with the detection. Imagine that we in one image have a bad segmentation of the object we are tracking. The effect of this could be that we only detect a small part of the object. We can still calculate the position of the object, but the number of object pixels used in this calculation is much smaller than in previous images, see Fig. 9.4. This would suggest that the detection has become more uncertain and ultimately we could have a situation where the object is not found and hence no detection is available. In both cases it might be better using the prediction than the detection when updating the state. Following along this line of thinking, the update of the state could be

$$\vec{s}(t) = \frac{w_1}{w_1 + w_2} \cdot \underline{\vec{p}}(t) + \frac{w_2}{w_1 + w_2} \cdot \vec{p}(t) \tag{9.4}$$

where w_1 should be controlled by the uncertainty associated with the prediction and w_2 by the uncertainty associated with the detection.

Fig. 9.4 The number of
object pixels as a function of
time. Note how the number
suddenly drops

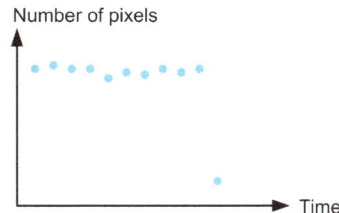

Number of pixels

Time

Predicting is a delicate matter as we are talking about foreseeing the future. Care should therefore be taken before using any of the methods and equations presented above. But prediction in its simple form with a zeroth order or first order motion model, and a large ROI, is nearly always a good idea. So is the notion of including predicted values in the update when no detection is available.

9.3 Tracking Multiple Objects

Sometimes we need to track multiple objects at the same time. If the objects are different we can duplicate the methods mentioned above and track each object individually. When the objects are similar, however, we need a coherent framework that can simultaneous track multiple objects.

In the top row of Fig. 9.5 we see two similar objects that we want to track. Remember that tracking is about finding the trajectory of the object over time, meaning that we need to figure out which object is which in each image. This is known as a *data association* problem in the sense that we need to assign some data (here two detected objects) to their respective trajectories. In the figure it is obvious that we have an object to the left moving downwards while the object to the right moves upwards, but how does the computer infer this? The solution is to predict the ROI for each object, as discussed above, and investigate which of the two objects best *match* the respective ROIs. This is illustrated in the bottom row in Fig. 9.5. By including the matching block into the tracking framework, we have now arrived at its final structure, see Fig. 9.6. This tracking framework is denoted the *predict-match-update* framework.

Unfortunately, tracking of multiple objects is not always as simple as illustrated in Fig. 9.5. When objects move they are likely to occlude each other, which will result in objects disappearing or new objects appearing. Moreover, sometimes the

Fig. 9.5 Top row shows four
consecutive images
containing two moving
objects. In the bottom row the
dashed red boxes indicate the
predicted ROIs. The numbers
(#1 *and* #2) indicate which
trajectory an object is found
to belong to

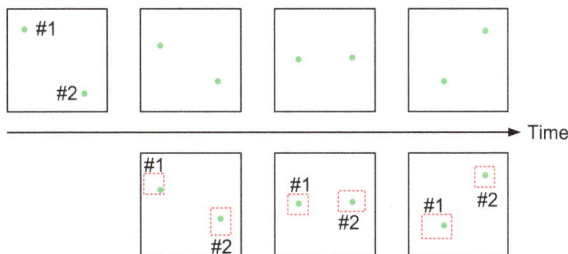

Time

Fig. 9.6 The
predict-match-update
tracking framework

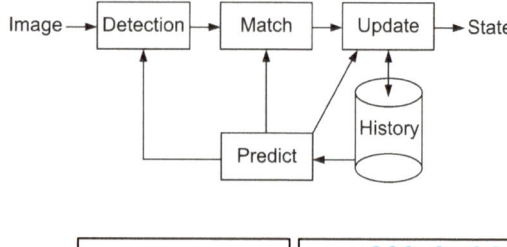

Fig. 9.7 (**a**) Illustration of
merged and split objects.
(**b**) Illustration of noise, new
object and lost objects

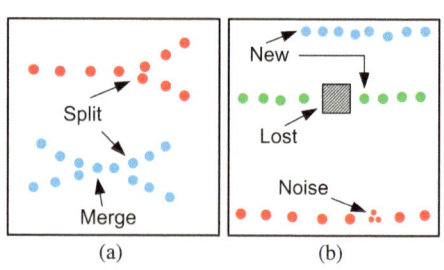

segmentation algorithm might fail resulting in an object being lost and/or new objects appearing. All these issues might occur simultaneously clouding the matter
further. In Fig. 9.7 some of these phenomena are illustrated. In Fig. 9.7(a) we have
a situation where one object is occluded by another object when entering the image's field of view. This continues until they split into two objects. We also see a
situation where two objects merge into one and later split into two objects again. In
Fig. 9.7(b) we first see a situation where a new object is detected in the middle of
the scene and below a situation where an object disappears behind a static object in
the scene before reappearing again. Last we see a situation where the detection of an
object is incorrect resulting in the predicted object being lost and three new objects
appearing.

One approach for resolving these issues is to measure how many of the detected
objects are within each predicted ROI. In Fig. 9.8(a) we show an example where we
have predicted five objects and detected five objects.

The zeros and ones in the table in Fig. 9.8(b) indicate if a detected object is within
a predicted object's ROI. The numbers in the row (green) and column (red) outside
the table indicate the sum of a particular row or column. Entries in the table those
row and column sums are both one, have a unique match and can be assigned to each
other. This will give that object 1 is assigned to trajectory B and object 2 to trajectory A. The row sum of the detected object 5 is equal to 0 meaning that this is a new
object. The column sum of the predicted object E is 0 meaning that object E is lost.
Next we look at non-assigned predicted objects with a column sum equal to 1 and
assign these objects. In our example this will mean that detected object 4 is assigned
to trajectory D. We therefore set entry $(C, 4) = 0$ in the table and can now assign
object 3 to trajectory C since both its row and column sums are one. The final result
for this image is shown to the right in Fig. 9.8(b). Looking at Fig. 9.8(a) it might be
reasonable to assume that object 5 should be assigned to trajectory E. We can handle
such situations by increasing the size of the ROI, but this is a dangerous path to fol-

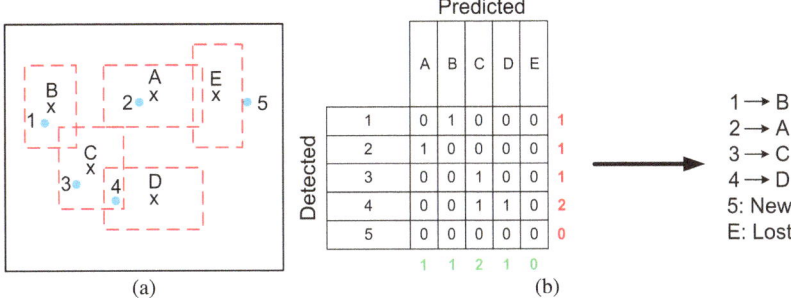

Fig. 9.8 (**a**) The *blue dots* are the detected objects and X illustrates the predicted objects. The *dashed red boxes* indicate the predicted ROIs. (**b**) A table indicating which detected objects that match which predicted objects

low since this will in general increase the number of ambiguities. A better approach is to delay the decision about whether an object is new or lost for some time.

If a lost object is present in an image, the trajectory is updated with the predicted value instead of the missing detection. The more times this is done, the more uncertain this trajectory becomes and hence the size of the ROI should be increased accordingly. Moreover, if no detections have been associated to a trajectory for some time, it should be concluded that the object is lost and its trajectory terminated.

For a new object to be accepted as a truly new object the following can be done. The first time a new object is detected a temporary trajectory is defined and the object is being tracked. When it has been successfully tracked for a certain amount of time it can be concluded that this is indeed a new object and the trajectory is no longer temporary. If no detected object is associated to the temporary trajectory for some time, the temporary trajectory is terminated.

9.3.1 Good Features to Track

Instead of only focusing on the position when tracking objects we can also include the features we are using to classify the different objects. This basically means we are combining the matching problem describe above with the feature classification problem discussed in Chap. 7. In practice we base the matching on the approach from Sect. 7.3 and simply add the x- and y-positions of the object as two additional features. The binary table in Fig. 9.8(b) is then replaced by a table where each entry indicates the distance from a predicted object and to a detected object. The uncertainties related to the predicted and detected objects could/should be incorporated as weights as discussed in Sect. 7.4. To binarize this new table each entry is thresholded and we can therefore apply the same matching mechanisms as described above.

When tracking objects we can of course use any of the features described in Chap. 7. But when it comes to tracking multiple objects we usually require more details features. Below we describe two approaches namely color-based and texture-based.

Fig. 9.9 A color histogram with ten bins and how an object will be represented using the color histogram bins as features

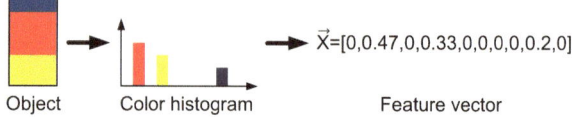

Object   Color histogram   Feature vector

The average color of an object can be a strong feature as it is relatively independent on how the shape and size of an object changes. Also, if a color space, where the intensity and chromaticity are separated, is used, the color feature is relatively robust to changes in the lighting. Sometimes an object contains multiple colors and the average may not be the best way to represent such an object. Instead a color histogram can be used. No matter which color space is used the different color components are concatenated and hence results in one histogram. Each histogram bin is normalized so the sum of all bins is equal to one. This makes the color histogram invariant to the scale of the object. To reduce the number of features, the resolution of the histogram bins is usually coarse. An example of a color histogram with ten bin, i.e., ten features, can be seen in Fig. 9.9.

While a color histogram is a better representation than the average color, it does not contain any information about spatial distribution of the different colors. Another approach is therefore to divide the object into a number of regions (usually horizontal dividers) and then represent each region by its average color (or color histogram). This approach is obvious sensitive to object rotation and care should therefore be taking before applying it.

As mentioned above the framerate will often be high compared to the movement of the object and it can therefore be assumed that the object does not change significantly from image to image. Inspired by this notion we can simply represent the object by its pixels and try to refind the object in the next image using template matching, see Sect. 5.2.1. For this to work the object (or a part of it) needs to be represented by a rectangle, but more importantly it is assumed that this rectangle is unique compared to the surroundings. Uniqueness here means the rectangle contains texture—the more the better—which is not repeated in the background. The level of textureness can be investigated by looking at the amount of edges in the rectangle. If many strong edges are present with different orientation, then there is a high likelihood that the rectangle is unique and can be refound in the next image. One concrete way of measuring this is to correlate the rectangle with the Sobel kernels from Sect. 5.2.2. This will produce two edge images. For each edge image the absolute value of each edge pixel is found and all these values are summed, and checked if the sum is above a threshold value. We do the same for the other edge image and if both sums are above the threshold value the rectangle is concluded to contain a high level of textureness, hence be a good template to track.

No matter which of these features are applied in tracking, care should be taking when combining them with the position and/or other features in order to ensure the different features are scaled properly, see Sect. 7.3. Another important issue is that the model for a particular object is very likely to change over time and should therefore be updated from image to image. The simple solution is to replace the model with the detection, but this is dangerous since the detection could be incorrect. A gradual update scheme, like in Eq. 9.3, is therefore suggested.

9.4 Further Information

An excellent way of implementing the predict-match-update framework is through the *Kalman filter* [19]. It does not cover the detection and matching blocks, but it has built-in mechanisms for updating the state based on the detections, the predictions and the related uncertainties. When is comes to tracking noisy detections, a branch of methods exist, which do not only predict where the objects are most likely to be, but also predict a number of likely hypotheses and maintain those over time. Such methods are known as Particle Filters, the Condensation algorithm, Sequential Monte Carlo filtering, or Multiple Hypothesis filters. One place to start a journey into such methods is [11].

Color features can be improved by also including information about position. One such method is the color correlogram [20]. But when it comes to more advanced tracking, texture is often preferred over color. A good tracking framework based on texture is the KLT-tracker [16]. It finds candidate rectangles containing a high level of texture and tracks these rectangles over time. The rectangles are small and a number of these should therefore be used to track a large object. The tracker detects when the texture of a particular rectangle has changed too much compared to when it was initiated and the tracker then reinitializes a new rectangle to be tracked.

If the texture changes too much between two images, template matching-based methods will not suffice and more advanced methods are required. A good example is the SIFT algorithm [13]. It represents the pixels in a rectangle by their gradient information. This is done in a clever way making the representation invariant to rotation and scale. In Fig. 9.10 an example is shown where the object is standing still, but the camera is moving. This is equivalent to when the camera is fixed and the object is moving. The SIFT algorithm is here used to find and track 100 points between two images. Note that such approaches often refer to the process of relocating features as *finding the correspondence* rather than tracking.

9.5 Exercises

Exercise 1: Explain the following concepts: state vector, trajectory, prediction, motion model, tracking, tracking-by-detection, data association, predict-match-update framework.

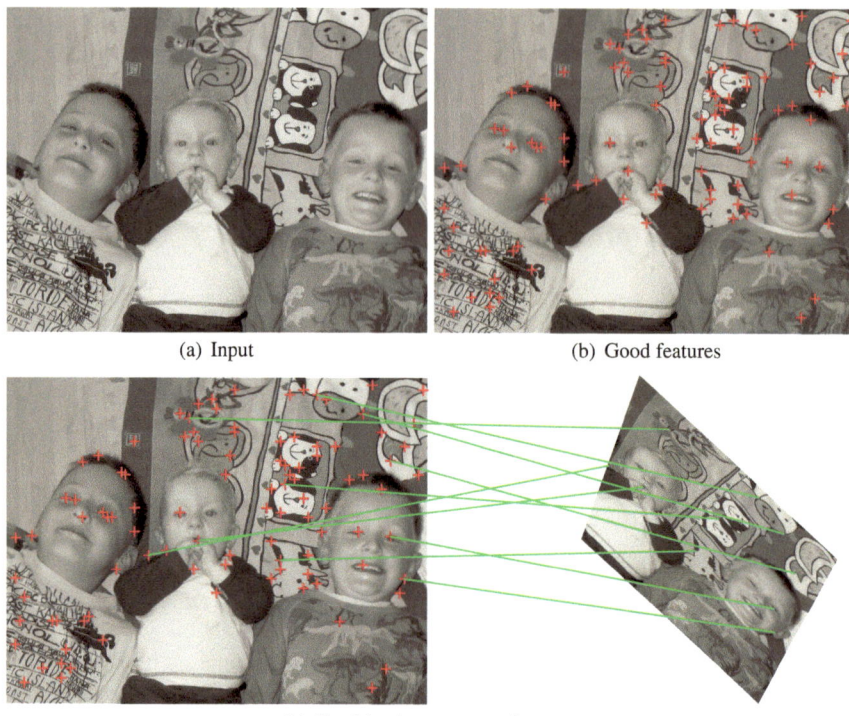

(a) Input   (b) Good features

(c) Tracking between two images

Fig. 9.10 Tracking using SIFT. (**a**) Input. (**b**) Each *red cross* corresponds to the center of a small rectangle containing pixels with high gradient information, i.e., a good region to track. 100 good features are shown. (**c**) The *green lines* illustrate where the features have been refound in the new image. Note that only ten features are shown to increase visibility

The following positions of an object have been detected:

Time	1	2	3	4	5	6	7	8	9	10	11	12	13
X	1	2	4	5	4	6	8	9	9	7	3	2	2
Y	10	8	8	7	6	4	4	3	2	2	2	2	4

Exercise 2: What is the velocity of the object at time = 12?

Exercise 3: What is the acceleration of the object at time = 12?

Exercise 4: Where will the object be predicted to be at time = 12, if a first order motion model is applied?

Exercise 5: Where will the object be predicted to be at time = 12, if a second order motion model is applied?

Exercise 6: It is desired to find the state of the object using information from both the detection and the prediction. The uncertainty associated with the prediction should be twice as high as the uncertainty associated with the detection. A first order motion model is applied. What is the state at time = 12?

Exercise 7: A system is tracking multiple objects. In one frame the relationship between predicted and detected objects is as shown below. Find the matching between detected and predicted objects together with any new/lost objects.

Detected \ Predicted	A	B	C	D	E	F	G	H
1	0	0	0	0	1	0	0	0
2	1	0	1	0	0	0	0	0
3	0	0	0	1	1	0	0	0
4	1	0	0	0	0	0	0	0
5	0	0	0	0	0	1	0	0
6	1	1	1	0	0	0	0	0
7	0	0	0	0	0	0	0	0

Additional exercise: What is the Kalman Filter and how does it operate?

Geometric Transformations 10

Most people have tried to do a geometric transformation of an image when preparing a presentation or when manipulating an image. The two most well-known are perhaps rotation and scaling, but others exist. In this chapter we will describe how such transformations operate and discuss the issues that need to be considered when doing such transformations.

The term "geometric" transformation refers to the class of image transformation where the geometry of the image is changed but the actual pixel values remain unchanged.[1]

Let us recall from the previous chapters that an image is defined as $f(x, y)$, where $f(\cdot)$ denotes the intensity or gray-level value and (x, y) defines the position of the pixel. After a geometric transformation the image is transformed into a new image denoted $g(x', y')$, where the tic (') means position in $g(x, y)$. This might seem confusing, but we need some way of stating the position before the transformation (x, y) and after the transformation (x', y').

As mentioned above the actual intensity values are not changed by the geometric transformation, but the positions of the pixels are (from (x, y) to (x', y')). So if $f(2, 3) = 120$ then in general $g(2, 3) \neq 120$. A geometric transformation basically calculates where the pixel at position (x, y) in $f(x, y)$ will be located in $g(x', y')$. That is, a mapping from (x, y) to (x', y'). We denote this mapping as

$$x' = A_x(x, y) \tag{10.1}$$

$$y' = A_y(x, y) \tag{10.2}$$

where $A_x(x, y)$ and $A_y(x, y)$ are both functions, which map from the position (x, y) to x' and y', respectively.

---

[1]For readers interested in a quick refreshment or introduction to linear algebra—in particular vectors and matrices—please refer to Appendix B.

T.B. Moeslund, *Introduction to Video and Image Processing*,
Undergraduate Topics in Computer Science,
DOI 10.1007/978-1-4471-2503-7_10, © Springer-Verlag London Limited 2012

10.1   Affine Transformations

The class of *affine transformations* covers four different transformations, which are illustrated in Fig. 10.1. These are: translation, rotation, scaling and shearing.

10.1.1 Translation

Let us now look at the transformations in Fig. 10.1 and define their concrete mapping equations. Translation is simply a matter of shifting the image horizontally and vertically with a given off-set (measured in pixels) denoted Δx and Δy. For translation the mapping is thus defined as

$$
\begin{aligned}
x' &= x + \Delta x \\
y' &= y + \Delta y
\end{aligned}
\quad \Rightarrow \quad
\begin{bmatrix} x' \\ y' \end{bmatrix} =
\begin{bmatrix} x \\ y \end{bmatrix} +
\begin{bmatrix} \Delta x \\ \Delta y \end{bmatrix}
\tag{10.3}
$$

So if $\Delta x = 100$ and $\Delta y = 100$ then each pixel is shifted 100 pixels in both the x- and y-direction.

10.1.2 Scaling

When scaling an image, it is made smaller or bigger in the x- and/or y-direction. Say we have an image of size 300×200 and we wish to transform it into a 600×100 image. The x-direction is then scaled by: $600/300 = 2$. We denote this the x-scale factor and write it as $S_x = 2$. Similarly $S_y = 100/200 = 1/2$. Together this means that the pixel in the image $f(x, y)$ at position $(x, y) = (100, 100)$ is mapped to a new position in the image $g(x', y')$, namely $(x', y') = (100 \cdot 2, 100 \cdot 1/2) = (200, 50)$. In general, scaling is expressed as

$$
\begin{aligned}
x' &= x \cdot S_x \\
y' &= y \cdot S_y
\end{aligned}
\quad \Rightarrow \quad
\begin{bmatrix} x' \\ y' \end{bmatrix} =
\begin{bmatrix} S_x & 0 \\ 0 & S_y \end{bmatrix} \cdot
\begin{bmatrix} x \\ y \end{bmatrix}
\tag{10.4}
$$

10.1.3 Rotation

When rotating an image, as illustrated in Fig. 10.1(d), we need to define the amount of rotation in terms of an angle. We denote this angle θ meaning that each pixel in $f(x, y)$ is rotated θ degrees. The transformation is defined as

$$
\begin{aligned}
x' &= x \cdot \cos\theta - y \cdot \sin\theta \\
y' &= x \cdot \sin\theta + y \cdot \cos\theta
\end{aligned}
\quad \Rightarrow \quad
\begin{bmatrix} x' \\ y' \end{bmatrix} =
\begin{bmatrix} \cos\theta & -\sin\theta \\ \sin\theta & \cos\theta \end{bmatrix} \cdot
\begin{bmatrix} x \\ y \end{bmatrix}
\tag{10.5}
$$

(a) Input   (b) Translate

(c) Scale   (d) Rotate

(e) Shear   (f) Affine

Fig. 10.1 Different transformations

Note that the rotation is done counterclockwise since the y-axis is pointing down-wards. If we wish to do a clockwise rotation we can either use $-\theta$ or change the transformation to

$$
\begin{aligned}
x' &= x \cdot \cos\theta + y \cdot \sin\theta \\
y' &= -x \cdot \sin\theta + y \cdot \cos\theta
\end{aligned}
\quad \Rightarrow \quad
\begin{bmatrix} x' \\ y' \end{bmatrix} =
\begin{bmatrix} \cos\theta & \sin\theta \\ -\sin\theta & \cos\theta \end{bmatrix} \cdot
\begin{bmatrix} x \\ y \end{bmatrix}
\tag{10.6}
$$

10.1.4 Shearing

To shear an image means to shift pixels either horizontally, B_x, or vertically, B_y. The difference from translation is that the shifting is not done by the same amount, but depends on where in the image a pixel is. In Fig. 10.1(e) $B_x = -0.5$ and $B_y = 0$. The transformation is defined as

$$
\begin{aligned}
x' &= x + y \cdot B_x \\
y' &= x \cdot B_y + y
\end{aligned}
\quad \Rightarrow \quad
\begin{bmatrix} x' \\ y' \end{bmatrix} =
\begin{bmatrix} 1 & B_x \\ B_y & 1 \end{bmatrix} \cdot
\begin{bmatrix} x \\ y \end{bmatrix}
\tag{10.7}
$$

10.1.5 Combining the Transformations

The four transformations can be combined in all kinds of different ways by multiply-ing the matrices in different orders, yielding a number of different transformations. One is shown in Fig. 10.1(f). Instead of defining the scale factors, the shearing fac-tors and the rotation angle, it is common to merge these three transformation into one matrix. The combination of the four transformations is therefore defined as

$$
\begin{aligned}
x' &= a_1 \cdot x + a_2 \cdot y + a_3 \\
y' &= b_1 \cdot x + b_2 \cdot y + b_3
\end{aligned}
\quad \Rightarrow \quad
\begin{bmatrix} x' \\ y' \end{bmatrix} =
\begin{bmatrix} a_1 & a_2 \\ b_1 & b_2 \end{bmatrix} \cdot
\begin{bmatrix} x \\ y \end{bmatrix} +
\begin{bmatrix} a_3 \\ b_3 \end{bmatrix}
\tag{10.8}
$$

and this is the affine transformation. Below the relationships between Eq. 10.8 and the four above mentioned transformations are listed.

	a_1	a_2	a_3	b_1	b_2	b_3
Translation	1	0	Δ_x	0	1	Δ_y
Scaling	S_x	0	0	0	S_y	0
Rotation	$\cos\theta$	$-\sin\theta$	0	$\sin\theta$	$\cos\theta$	0
Shearing	1	B_x	0	B_y	1	0

Often *homogeneous coordinates* are used when implementing the transformation since they make further calculations faster. In homogeneous coordinates, the affine transformation becomes

$$
\begin{bmatrix} x' \\ y' \\ 1 \end{bmatrix} =
\begin{bmatrix} a_1 & a_2 & a_3 \\ b_1 & b_2 & b_3 \\ 0 & 0 & 1 \end{bmatrix} \cdot
\begin{bmatrix} x \\ y \\ 1 \end{bmatrix}
\tag{10.9}
$$

where $a_3 = \Delta x$ and $b_3 = \Delta y$.

Fig. 10.2 (**a**) Forward
mapping. (**b**) Backward
mapping

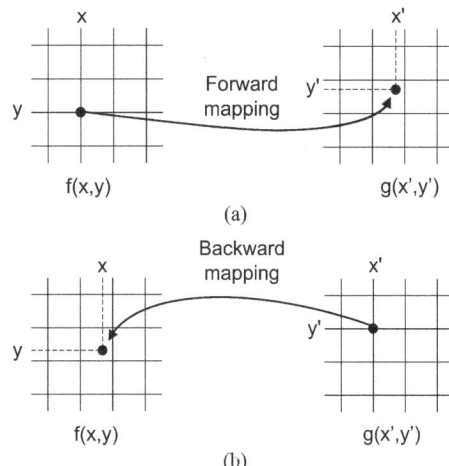

(a)

(b)

10.2   Making It Work in Practice

In terms of programming, the affine transformation consists of two steps. First the
coefficients of the affine transformation matrix are defined. Second we go though all
pixels in the image $f(x, y)$ one at a time (using two for-loops as seen in Sect. 4.7)
and for each pixel we find its new position in $g(x', y')$ using Eq. 10.9. This process
is known as *forward mapping*, i.e., mapping each pixel from $f(x, y)$ to $g(x', y')$,
see Fig. 10.2(a).

At first glance this simple process seems to be fine, but unfortunately it is not! Let
us have a closer look at the scaling transformation in order to understand the nature
of the problem. Say we have an image of size 300×200 and want to scale this to
510×200. From above we can calculate the scaling factors as $S_x = 510/300 = 1.7$
and $S_y = 200/200 = 1$. Using Eq. 10.4 the pixel positions in a row of $f(x, y)$ are
mapped in the following manner:

x	0	1	2	3	4	5	6	7	8	$\cdots$	300
x'	0	1.7	3.4	5.1	6.8	8.5	10.2	11.9	13.6	$\cdots$	510

We can observe that "holes" are present in $g(x', y')$. If for example 10.2 is
rounded off to 10 and 11.9 to 12, then $x' = 11$ will have no value, hence a hole
in the image output. In Fig. 10.3 we have used forward mapping to scale image
10.1(a). The holes can be seen as the black pattern.

If the scaling factor is smaller than 1 then a related problem would occur, namely
that multiple pixels from $f(x, y)$ are mapped to the same pixel in $g(x', y')$. This is
not critical in terms of how the output would look like, but mapping multiple pixels
to the same pixel in $g(x', y')$ is computationally inefficient. Both these issues are
present in all geometric transformations.

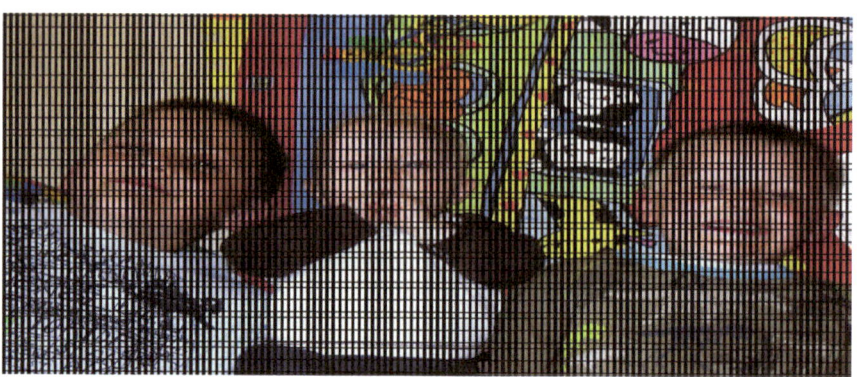

Fig. 10.3 Image scaling using forward mapping. Notice the black pattern, which is a result of the inherent problem related to forward mapping

10.2.1 Backward Mapping

The solution is to avoid forward mapping and instead use *backward mapping*. Backward mapping maps from $g(x', y')$ to $f(x, y)$. That is, it goes through the *output image*, $g(x', y')$, one pixel at a time (using two for-loops) and for each position (x', y') it uses the *inverse transformation* to calculate (x, y). That is, it finds out where in the input image a pixel must come from in order to be mapped to (x', y'). The principle is illustrated in Fig. 10.2(b). The inverse transformation is found by matrix inversion of the transformation matrix as

$$\begin{bmatrix} x \\ y \\ 1 \end{bmatrix} = \begin{bmatrix} a_1 & a_2 & a_3 \\ b_1 & b_2 & b_3 \\ 0 & 0 & 1 \end{bmatrix}^{-1} \cdot \begin{bmatrix} x' \\ y' \\ 1 \end{bmatrix} \qquad (10.10)$$

For scaling, rotation and shearing the inverse matrices look like the following:

$$\text{Scaling:} \quad \begin{bmatrix} 1/S_x & 0 & 0 \\ 0 & 1/S_y & 0 \\ 0 & 0 & 1 \end{bmatrix}, \qquad \text{Rotation:} \quad \begin{bmatrix} \cos\theta & \sin\theta & 0 \\ -\sin\theta & \cos\theta & 0 \\ 0 & 0 & 1 \end{bmatrix}$$

$$\text{Shearing:} \quad \frac{1}{1 - B_x B_y} \begin{bmatrix} 1 & -B_x & 0 \\ -B_y & 1 & 0 \\ 0 & 0 & 1 - B_x B_y \end{bmatrix}$$

So, if we want to implement a program that as input takes an image f(x,y) and as output gives a scaled image g(x',y'), then it could look something like this in C-code:

```
Image_Width_Output  = Image_Width_Input  * Sx;
Image_Height_Output = Image_Height_Input * Sy;
```

```
for (y_output = 0; y_output < Image_Height_Output;
     y_output++)
{
  for (x_output = 0; x_output < Image_Width_Output;
       x_output++)
  {
    x_input = 1/Sx * x_output;
    y_input = 1/Sy * y_output;
    g(x_output,y_output) = f(x_input,y_input);
  }
}
```

where Sx and Sy are the scale factors and (x', y') is written as (x_output,y_output) and (x,y) is written as (x_input,y_input).

10.2.2 Interpolation

As can be seen in Fig. 10.2 backward mapping is very likely to result in a value of (x, y) which is not possible. For example, what is the intensity value of $f(3.4, 7.9)$? It is undefined and we therefore *interpolate* in order to find an appropriate intensity value. The most simple form of interpolation is called *zeroth-order interpolation*. It rounds off to the value of the nearest possible pixel, i.e., $f(3.4, 7.9) \rightarrow f(3, 8)$. A better, but also more computational demanding, approach is to apply first-order interpolation (a.k.a. bilinear interpolation), which weights the intensity values of the four nearest pixels according to how close they are. The principle is illustrated in Fig. 10.4. The area of the square wherein (x, y) is located is 1. Now imagine that we use the position (x, y) to divide this square into four sub-regions. The area of each of these sub-regions define the weight of one of the four nearest pixels. That is, the area $dx \cdot dy$ becomes the weight for the pixel $f(x_1, y_1)$ and so forth. The final intensity value is then found as

$$
\begin{aligned}
g(x', y') = {} & f(x_0, y_0) \cdot (1 - dx)(1 - dy) \\
& + f(x_1, y_0) \cdot (dx)(1 - dy) \\
& + f(x_0, y_1) \cdot (1 - dx)(dy) \\
& + f(x_1, y_1) \cdot (dx \cdot dy)
\end{aligned}
\tag{10.11}
$$

Note that this equation can be rewritten more compactly for an efficient software implementation. Note also that more advanced methods for interpolation exist, but this is beyond the scope of this text.

Fig. 10.4 Bilinear interpolation. The final pixel value becomes a weighted sum of the four nearest pixel values

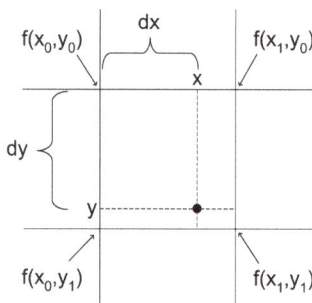

10.3   Homography

Geometric transformation can also be used to correct errors in images. Imagine a telescope capturing an image of a star constellation. The image is likely to be distorted by the fact that light is bent in space due to the gravitational forces of the stars and also by the changing conditions in the Earth's atmosphere. Since the nature of these phenomena is known, the transformation they enforced on the image can be compensated for by applying the inverse transformation.

Another, and perhaps more relevant, error that can be corrected by a geometric transformation is *keystoning*. A keystone is the top-most block in an arch, i.e., an arch-shaped doorway. Since the keystone is wedge-shaped it is used to describe wedge-shaped images. Such an image is obtained when capturing a square using a tilted camera or when projecting an image onto a tilted plane, see Fig. 10.5. Since this is a common phenomenon, most video projectors have a built-in geometric mapping function, which can correct for keystoning.

Let us investigate the correction of keystoning in more depth by looking at a concrete example. Imagine you are designing a simple game where a projector projects circles onto a table and a camera captures your finger when touching the table. The

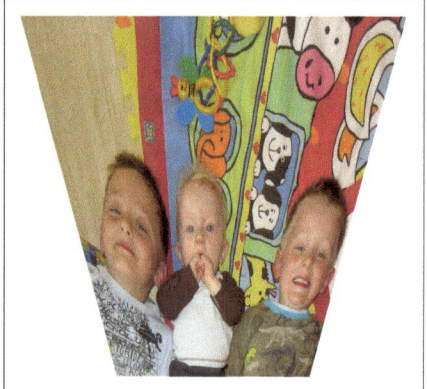

        (a) Input   (b) Keystoned image

Fig. 10.5 Keystoning

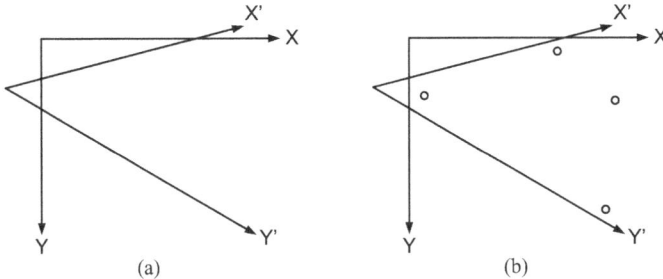

Fig. 10.6 The coordinate system of the image (x, y) and the coordinate system of the projector (x', y') seen from the image's point of view. (**b**) The circles are projected from the projector in order to find corresponding points in the two coordinate systems

purpose of the game could then be to see how many circles you can touch in a predefined time period. For such a system to work you need, among other things, to know what a detected pixel coordinate (the position of the finger) corresponds to in the image projected onto the table. If both camera and projector are tilted with respect to the table, then two keystone errors are actually present. In general, the geometric transformation which maps from one plane (camera image) to another (projected image) is known as a *projective transformation* or *homography*. It can be calculated in the following way using the *Direct Linear Transform* [10].

First have a look at Fig. 10.6(a) to see what we are dealing with. To the left you see an illustration of two coordinate systems. The (x, y) coordinate system is the coordinate system of the image and the (x', y') coordinate system is the coordinate system of the projector seen from the image's point of view. Or in other words, if you make the projector project two perpendicular arrows onto a plane (for example a table) and capture a picture of the table, then the perpendicular arrows will look like the x' and y' arrows. So the transformation we are after should map from (x, y) to (x', y').

The use of a homography is not limited to finding the correspondence between an image and a projector. Imagine we have a robot arm that should pick something up from a table. A camera captures an image of the table, finds the object of interest and send its position to the robot. The table is the robot's coordinate system meaning that the origin is one of the corners and the x' and y' axes are two perpendicular edges of the table. The image's coordinate system is now x and y, and we need to find a transformation from (x, y) to (x', y'). So the exact same situation as with the projector and hence the exact same solution.

From the theory of homography we know that the mapping between the two coordinate systems is

$$
\begin{bmatrix} h \cdot x' \\ h \cdot y' \\ h \end{bmatrix} = \begin{bmatrix} a_1 & a_2 & a_3 \\ b_1 & b_2 & b_3 \\ c_1 & c_2 & 1 \end{bmatrix} \cdot \begin{bmatrix} x \\ y \\ 1 \end{bmatrix}
\tag{10.12}
$$

From this it follows that

$$\frac{h \cdot x'}{h} = x' = \frac{a_1 \cdot x + a_2 \cdot y + a_3}{c_1 \cdot x + c_2 \cdot y + 1} \tag{10.13}$$

$$\frac{h \cdot y'}{h} = y' = \frac{b_1 \cdot x + b_2 \cdot y + b_3}{c_1 \cdot x + c_2 \cdot y + 1} \tag{10.14}$$

Rewriting into matrix form we have

$$\begin{bmatrix} x' \\ y' \end{bmatrix} = \begin{bmatrix} x & y & 1 & 0 & 0 & 0 & -x \cdot x' & -y \cdot x' \\ 0 & 0 & 0 & x & y & 1 & -x \cdot y' & -y \cdot y' \end{bmatrix} \cdot \vec{d} \tag{10.15}$$

where $\vec{d} = [a_1, a_2, a_3, b_1, b_2, b_3, c_1, c_2]^T$.

In order to find the values of the coefficients we need to know the positions of four points in both coordinate systems, i.e., eight equations with eight unknowns. We could for example send out four points from the projector and then find their positions (automatic or manual) in the image, see Fig. 10.6(b). Then we would have the positions of four corresponding points in both coordinate systems:

$$(x_1, y_1) \leftrightarrow (x_1', y_1') \quad (x_2, y_2) \leftrightarrow (x_2', y_2') \quad (x_3, y_3) \leftrightarrow (x_3', y_3')$$

$$(x_4, y_4) \leftrightarrow (x_4', y_4') \tag{10.16}$$

If we enter these points into the equations we end up with the following linear system $\vec{e} = \mathbf{K}\vec{d}$:

$$\begin{bmatrix} x_1' \\ y_1' \\ x_2' \\ y_2' \\ x_3' \\ y_3' \\ x_4' \\ y_4' \end{bmatrix} = \begin{bmatrix} x_1 & y_1 & 1 & 0 & 0 & 0 & -x_1 \cdot x_1' & -y_1 \cdot x_1' \\ 0 & 0 & 0 & x_1 & y_1 & 1 & -x_1 \cdot y_1' & -y_1 \cdot y_1' \\ x_2 & y_2 & 1 & 0 & 0 & 0 & -x_2 \cdot x_2' & -y_2 \cdot x_2' \\ 0 & 0 & 0 & x_2 & y_2 & 1 & -x_2 \cdot y_2' & -y_2 \cdot y_2' \\ x_3 & y_3 & 1 & 0 & 0 & 0 & -x_3 \cdot x_3' & -y_3 \cdot x_3' \\ 0 & 0 & 0 & x_3 & y_3 & 1 & -x_3 \cdot y_3' & -y_3 \cdot y_3' \\ x_4 & y_4 & 1 & 0 & 0 & 0 & -x_4 \cdot x_4' & -y_4 \cdot x_4' \\ 0 & 0 & 0 & x_4 & y_4 & 1 & -x_4 \cdot y_4' & -y_4 \cdot y_4' \end{bmatrix} \cdot \begin{bmatrix} a_1 \\ a_2 \\ a_3 \\ b_1 \\ b_2 \\ b_3 \\ c_1 \\ c_2 \end{bmatrix} \tag{10.17}$$

The coefficients of the transformation are now found as $\vec{d} = \mathbf{K}^{-1}\vec{e}$, which is solved using linear algebra, see Appendix B. So, what we end up with are values for the coefficients a_1, a_2 etc. If we insert these into Eqs. 10.13 and 10.14 we can insert a point (x, y) and calculate where that point will end up in the other coordinate system, i.e., (x', y'). If we want to reverse the mapping, so we can go from (x', y') to (x, y), we simply reverse the four points so that x_1' become x_1, x_2' become x_2 etc. These new points are inserted into Eq. 10.17 and we can find the coefficients of the reverse mapping.[2]

---

[2]In Chaps. 12 and 13 homography is used in two concrete examples.

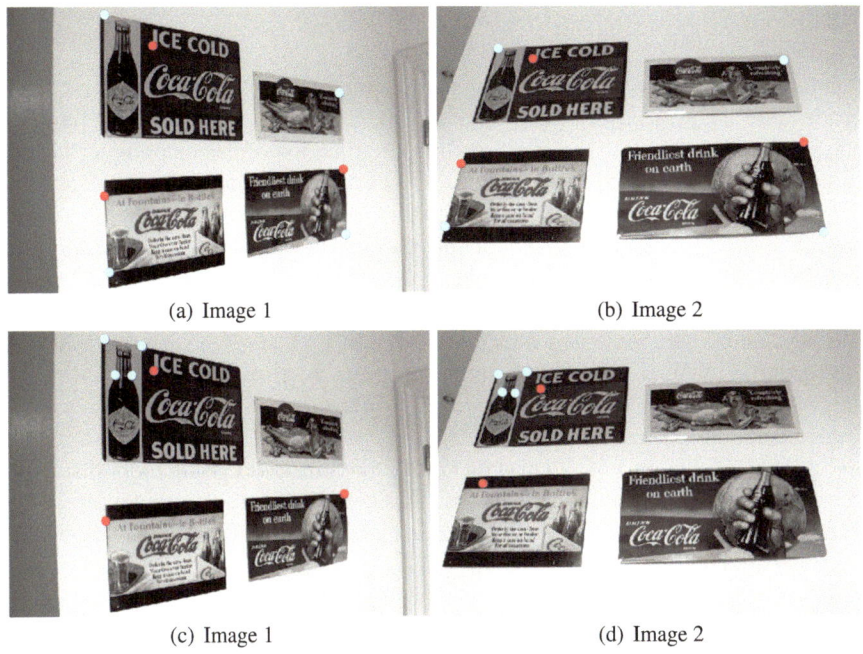

(a) Image 1   (b) Image 2

(c) Image 1   (d) Image 2

Fig. 10.7 The importance of choosing the four points far apart. The *blue points* are used for calculating the mapping between the two coordinate systems, whereas the *red points* are mapped from image 1 to image 2 using this mapping

It is important that the four points we use are spread out across the entire image. This will ensure a good transformation. If your points are too close together, then the transformation might not be applicable for the entire image, but only for the region wherein the points are located. This is illustrated in Fig. 10.7. The top row shows two images of the same scene but captured from two different viewpoints. In order to learn the mapping between the two, the coordinates of the blue points are measured in the two images. From these points we can solve Eq. 10.17 and hence obtain the two Eqs. 10.13 and 10.14. We now use these equations to map the red points in image 1 to image 2. We can see that the mapped points in image 2 are in agreement with the red points in image 1. The same is now done for the images in the second row only now the blue points are located close to each other. The effect of this is that when mapping the red points from image 1 to image 2, they end up in incorrect locations. The further away from the blue points a red point is in image 1, the worse the mapping. In fact, the red point furthest away in image 1 is mapped to a position outside image 2 and therefore not present in image 2. This example should underline the very important point about choosing the four points as far away from each other as possible.

10.4   Further Information

Equation 10.12 might seem a bit strange an unmotivated. An explanation requires insides into the projective aspects of a camera, meaning how a 3D world point is mapped into the sensor in the camera. An approximation of this mapping is the so-called *pin-hole model* and from that Eq. 10.12 can be derived. The pin-hole model is an approximation meaning that the equation is not a perfect mapping. If a more precise mapping is required, then look into the field of (geometric) *camera calibration*. While the resulting math is a bit hard, the solution is simple. You print a paper containing a chessboard and glue it onto a rigid object. Capture a number of images where you hold the chessboard at different angles with respect to the camera and let a program do the rest. The output from the program is a function that maps between the two coordinate systems (x, y) and (x', y'). Both OpenCV and Matlab have good implementations of this method.

Equation 10.12 can actually also be made more precise by using more than four corresponding points, the more the better. This corresponds to expanding Eq. 10.17 by adding more equations. We will then have more equations than unknowns, which is known as an overdetermined system.

Yet another method for finding the mapping between two coordinate systems is the use of a look-up-table (LUT). We find a number of corresponding points (usually many more than four), but instead of using them to calculate the mapping we simply store them in a file. Later when the system needs to map a known point $P(x, y)$ from $f(x, y)$ to a point $P'(x', y')$ in the other coordinate system $g(x', y')$, we first find the four points in the file that are closest to $P(x, y)$ and then combine their respective mappings into $P'(x', y')$. Say the four closest points are $P_1(x, y)$, $P_{10}(x, y)$, $P_4(x, y)$, and $P_7(x, y)$. One approach is then to calculate the Euclidean distance between each point and $P(x, y)$, yielding d_1, d_{10}, d_4, and d_7. The mapping of $P(x, y)$ can now be calculated as

$$P'(x', y') = \frac{1/d_1}{w} \cdot P_1'(x', y') + \frac{1/d_{10}}{w} \cdot P_{10}'(x', y')$$

$$+ \frac{1/d_4}{w} \cdot P_4'(x', y') + \frac{1/d_7}{w} \cdot P_7'(x', y') \qquad (10.18)$$

$$w = \frac{1}{d_1} + \frac{1}{d_{10}} + \frac{1}{d_4} + \frac{1}{d_7}$$

where $P_1'(x', y')$ is the mapping value for $P_1(x, y)$ found in the LUT.

10.5   Exercises

Exercise 1: Explain the following concepts: homogeneous coordinates, interpolation, homography.

Exercise 2: Explain the following concepts and the underlying math: Translation, scaling, rotation, shearing, affine transformation.

Exercise 3: An image is first rotated $10°$ and then scaled with a factor 2 in both horizontal and vertical direction. Next, the image is scaled with a factor 0.5 in both horizontal and vertical direction and rotated $-10°$. Do we now have the same image as we started out with?

Exercise 4: An image is first rotated $10°$ and then scaled with a factor 2 in both horizontal and vertical direction. Would the same image appear if the order of the rotation and scaling is reversed (i.e., first scaling and then rotation)?

Exercise 5: An input image $f(x, y)$ consists of a black background with a white rectangle on top. The corners of the rectangle are located at: $(50, 50)$, $(50, 60)$, $(60, 50)$ and $(60, 60)$. We want to scale the image with a factor 2 in the horizontal direction and a factor 1.5 in the vertical direction. What will the area of the white rectangle be after the scaling?

Exercise 6: $f(x, y)$ is rotated $15°$ around the point $(55, 55)$. Where will the corner $(50, 50)$ be located after the rotation?

Exercise 7: $f(x, y)$ is sheared with $B_x = 2$ and $B_y = -1.5$. Where will the corner $(50, 50)$ be located after the shearing?

Exercise 8: In an image the following pixel values are present: $f(10, 10) = 10$, $f(10, 11) = 12$, $f(11, 10) = 11$ and $f(11, 11) = 9$. During a backward mapping it is found that $g(100, 100) = f(10.3, 10.8)$. What value will $g(100, 100)$ have if we use i) zero-order interpolation? ii) first-order interpolation?

Exercise 9: The mapping between two coordinate systems (x, y) and (x', y') is defined via the LUT below. Which position does the point $(x, y) = (8, 6)$ correspond to in (x', y')?

(x, y)	$(1, 4)$	$(3, 4)$	$(6, 4)$	$(10, 4)$	$(2, 7)$	$(5, 7)$	$(10, 7)$	$(3, 10)$	$(5, 10)$	$(9, 9)$
(x', y')	$(0, 1)$	$(3, 1)$	$(5, 1)$	$(10, 2)$	$(1, 4)$	$(4, 4)$	$(9, 5)$	$(1, 7)$	$(3, 8)$	$(7, 7)$

Additional exercises: What is camera calibration? What can it be used for and how does it work?

In some situations the end goal of video and image processing is not to extract information, but rather to create some kind of visual effect. Or in other words, just for the fun of it. This can be done in many different ways, where some are more interesting than others. In this chapter we present ten different methods for creating visual effects. The first five are based on manipulation of the actual pixel values and the last five on geometric transformations. The different effects are illustrated on one of the two images in Fig. 11.1.

11.1 Visual Effects Based on Pixel Manipulation

The number of different methods based on manipulating the actual pixel values is endless, but obviously some have a better effect that others. Below we first focus on utilizing some of the methods presented in earlier chapters and see how they can be used to create visual effects. Hereafter, we present two methods based on specific algorithms developed just for the purpose of creating a visual effect.

(a)　　　　　　　　　　　　(b)

Fig. 11.1 Input images for the visual effects

T.B. Moeslund, *Introduction to Video and Image Processing*,
Undergraduate Topics in Computer Science,
DOI 10.1007/978-1-4471-2503-7_11, © Springer-Verlag London Limited 2012

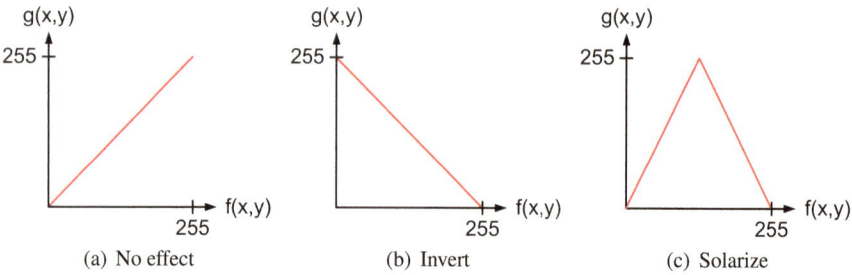

(a) No effect   (b) Invert   (c) Solarize

Fig. 11.2 Three different gray-level mappings

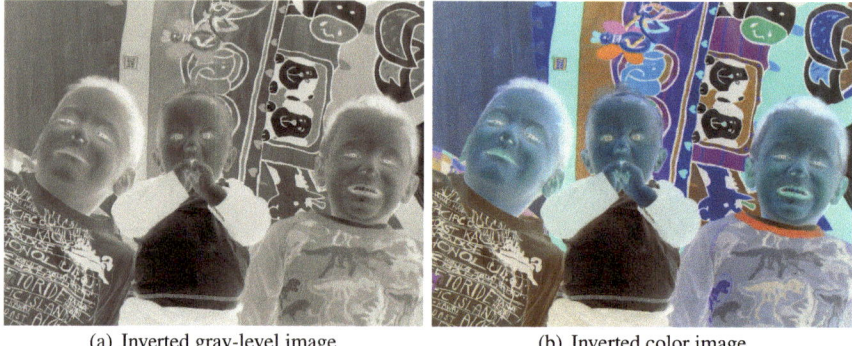

(a) Inverted gray-level image   (b) Inverted color image

Fig. 11.3 Inverting an image

(a) Solarize effect on a gray-level image   (b) Solarize effect on a color image

Fig. 11.4 Solarize filter

11.1.1 Point Processing

The simplest way to create visual effects is to play around with the gray-level mapping. Two classic gray-level mappings are illustrated in Fig. 11.2 and the visual effects of these mappings are illustrated in Figs. 11.3 and 11.4.

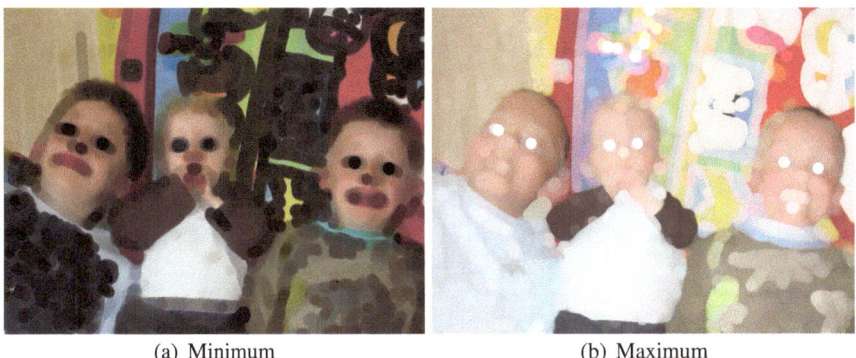

      (a) Minimum   (b) Maximum

Fig. 11.5 Rank filters

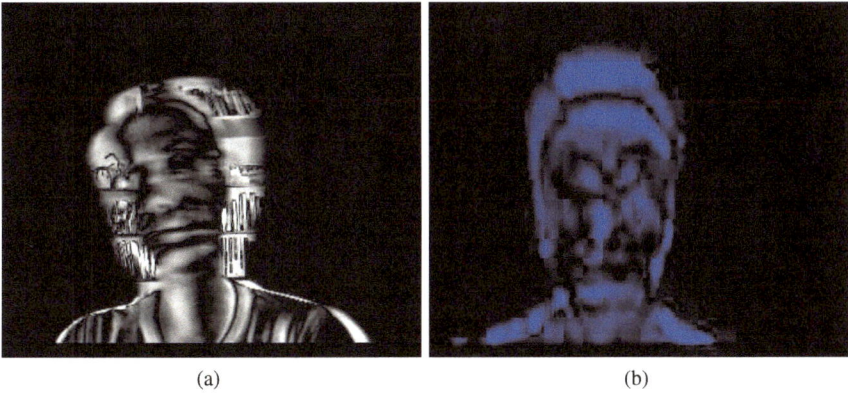

           (a)   (b)

Fig. 11.6 Using object motion to create visual effects

11.1.2 Neighborhood Processing

The different neighborhood processing methods can sometimes also result in nice visual effects. In Fig. 11.5 the effects of the two first rank filters listed in Sect. 5.1.1 are shown.

11.1.3 Motion

The image differencing method described in Sect. 8.4 is a simple yet efficient way of creating visual effects in video. The ghost objects illustrated in Fig. 8.6 are in general unwanted in video processing, but when it comes to creating an interesting visual effect they can be quite interesting. Furthermore, if the difference image is *not* thresholded, the "ghosty" appearance is even more profound.

(a) Eight colors   (b) Two colors

(c) Eight colors with enhanced edges   (d) Two colors with enhanced edges

Fig. 11.7 Reducing the number of colors in the output

In Fig. 11.6 two examples are shown. The left image is a result of subtracting the current image from a previous image (and taking the absolute value) in a sequence where a person moves his head from one side to the other. In the right image the difference image is used as the blue channel in an RGB image where the red and green channels are set to zero. The sequence used to generate the difference image contains the head of a person moving upwards.

11.1.4 Reduced Colors

Changing the colors in an image is an easy way to create a visual effect. Examples were shown above in Sect. 11.1.1. Another way is simply to reduce the number of colors applied in the image. This is illustrated in Figs. 11.7(a) and 11.7(b) where only eight and two different colors are used, respectively. To spice it up a bit the effects can be even more profound by enhancing the main edges. This can be done by first making a gray-scale copy of the input and then do an edge detection. Small edges (BLOBs) are removed and the remaining edges dilated and superimposed on the output. The effect is that the output appears a bit as a cartoon drawing. Examples are illustrated in Figs. 11.7(c) and 11.7(d).

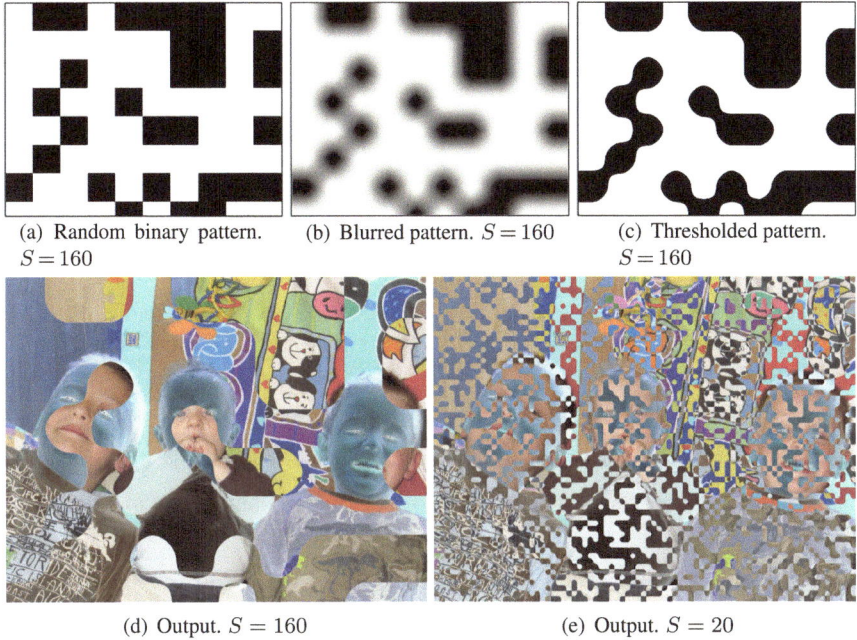

(a) Random binary pattern. $S = 160$ (b) Blurred pattern. $S = 160$ (c) Thresholded pattern. $S = 160$

(d) Output. $S = 160$ (e) Output. $S = 20$

Fig. 11.8 Random inversions

11.1.5 Randomness

It can often be interesting to add some randomness in order to create a visual effect. This can be done in many different ways and only the imagination of the designer sets the limit. The output will be different from time to time even though the input in the same. This adds a nice uniqueness to visual effects involving randomness. Below we describe one concrete example, namely an algorithm denoted *random inversions*.

The algorithm is based on the idea of generating a random binary pattern and then using this to apply image inversion locally. First the output image is divided into squares of equal size $S \times S$. For each square we draw a random number between zero and one. If this number is above 0.5 then the square is set to white; otherwise to black. This will result in an intermediate output like the one in Fig. 11.8(a). In the next step the intermediate output in blurred by a mean filter in order to obtain softer shapes, see Fig. 11.8(b). The kernel size is equal to $S/2$. The blurred squares are now thresholded, using a threshold value of 128, to ensure the edges of the shapes are sharp, see Fig. 11.8(c). For each white pixel we now invert the corresponding RGB pixel in the input and place that in the output. For each black pixel we simply

Fig. 11.9 Representation of
a point (P_x, P_y) using polar
coordinates (θ, r)

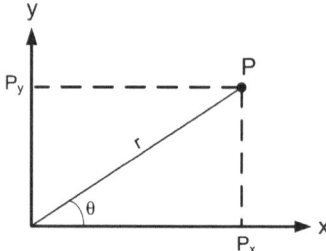

copy the corresponding input pixel to the output. In Figs. 11.8(d) and 11.8(e) the
effect of the algorithm is illustrated.

11.2 Visual Effects Based on Geometric Transformations

One could argue that the geometric transformations presented in Chap. 10 all create visual effects. They are, however, not characterized as such, but rather as image
manipulation. Other geometric transformations exist that are aimed at creating visual effects. These transformations can be compared to the magic mirrors found in
entertainment parks, where for example the head of the person facing the mirror is
enlarged in a strange way while the legs are made smaller. Such transformations
are said to be *non-linear* as opposed to the transformations in Chap. 10, which are
linear. What is meant is that transformations which can be written as a product
between a vector and a matrix (for example as in Eq. 10.9) are said to be *linear*.
Transformations involving, for example, trigonometric operations, square roots, etc.
are said to be *non-linear*. Below four such transformations are presented followed
by a so-called local transformation.

11.2.1 Polar Transformation

A point P in 2D can be represented as (P_x, P_y) see Fig. 11.9. But we can also
represent it by an angle θ and length r, see Fig. 11.9. From the law of right-angled
triangles, see Sect. B.8, we can write

$$P_x = r \cdot \cos(\theta) \tag{11.1}$$

$$P_y = r \cdot \sin(\theta) \tag{11.2}$$

This is denoted a polar transformation. When using this to create a visual effect,
we use the image coordinates (x, y) as θ and r, respectively. That is, the forward
mapping is given as

$$x' = y \cdot \cos(x) \tag{11.3}$$

$$y' = y \cdot \sin(x) \tag{11.4}$$

As discussed in Sect. 10.2 the forward mapping needs to be replaced by the backward mapping. For the polar transformation, this can be found in the following way:

$$\frac{y'}{x'} = \frac{y \cdot \sin(x)}{y \cdot \cos(x)} = \frac{\sin(x)}{\cos(x)} = \tan(x) \quad \Rightarrow$$

$$x = \arctan\left(\frac{y'}{x'}\right) \tag{11.5}$$

$$x'^2 + y'^2 = y^2 \cdot \cos(x)^2 + y^2 \cdot \sin(x)^2 = y^2 \cdot \left(\cos(x)^2 + \sin(x)^2\right) = y^2 \quad \Rightarrow$$

$$y = \sqrt{x'^2 + y'^2} \tag{11.6}$$

To implement this a few things need to be done. First of all the angle, θ, needs to be scaled so that its maximum value is 360. This is done by replacing x by

$$\frac{x \cdot 360}{width} \tag{11.7}$$

where *width* is the width of the input image. The height and width of the output image will be two times the radius, i.e. two times the height of the input image. Normally the size of the output image is therefore scaled by replacing y by $y/2$. This will result in an output image where the height and width are equal to the height of the input image.

The function arctan() behaves differently depending on the quadrant wherein it is applied. This needs to be handled when implementing the function, but many software libraries luckily have a built-in function that handles that, for example *ATAN2()* in the C language.

The origin of the polar transform, $(0, 0)$, is located in the center of the output image which is $(height/2, height/2)$. When going through the output image (using two for loops) we therefore need to subtract $height/2$ from both x' and y'. Lastly, we need to ensure that only valid values are processed. The invalid values can be seen as the four white regions in the corners in Fig. 11.10. We do this by only processing pixels (x', y') those distance to the center of the image is equal to or below the maximum radius $height/2$.

Combining all of the above we can rewrite Eqs. 11.5 and 11.6 as

$$x = \frac{width}{360} \cdot \arctan\left(\frac{\Delta y}{\Delta x}\right) \tag{11.8}$$

$$y = 2 \cdot r \tag{11.9}$$

where $\Delta x = x' - x_c$, $\Delta y = y' - y_c$, $x_c = height/2$ and $y_c = height/2$ are the center of the input image, and $r = \sqrt{\Delta x^2 + \Delta y^2}$ is the radius. These equations only hold when

$$r \leq r_{max} \tag{11.10}$$

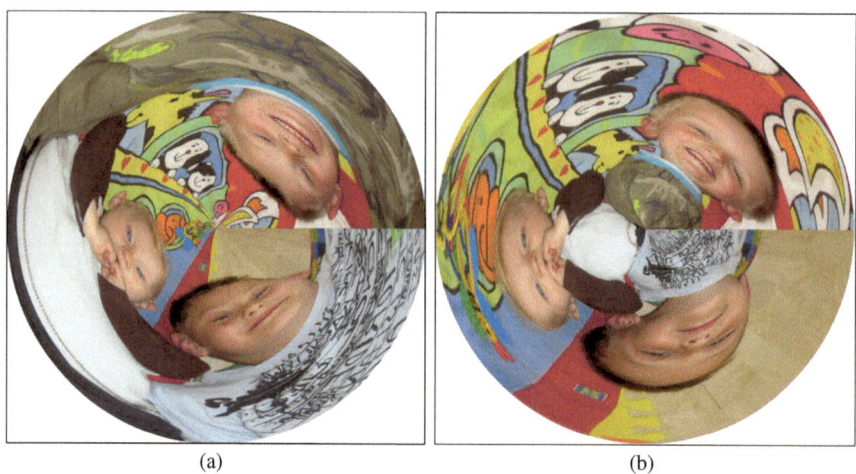

(a)   (b)

Fig. 11.10 (**a**) A polar transformed image. (**b**) A polar transformed image with the y-axis pointing upwards

where r_{max} is half the height of the output image. When $r > r_{max}$ we simply say $g(x', y') = 255$. In Fig. 11.10 two polar images are illustrated. The first is calculated as described above. For the other one the y-axis (the radius) is pointing up as opposed to down.

11.2.2 Twirl Transformation

Geometric transformations can easily become so complicated that the backward mapping is very hard or even impossible to derive. Such transformations are therefore often defined directly in the output domain, meaning that the forward mapping is *not* defined but only the backward mapping. The next three transformations are of this type. The first is the *twirl transformation*, which is inspired by the polar transformation, see Eqs. 11.1 and 11.2. The rotation angle θ is now defined as

$$\theta = \arctan\left(\frac{\Delta y}{\Delta x}\right) + \phi \cdot \left(\frac{r_{max} - r}{r_{max}}\right) \qquad (11.11)$$

where ϕ is the rotation baseline and the other parameters are defined as for the polar transformation. The effect of the transformation is that the center remains at the same position and the rest of the pixels are rotated around the center with a rotation angle that is maximum (ϕ degrees) near the center and becomes smaller the closer to the image corners a pixel is. The final backward mapping is defined as

$$x = x_c + r \cdot \cos(\theta) \qquad (11.12)$$
$$y = y_c + r \cdot \sin(\theta) \qquad (11.13)$$

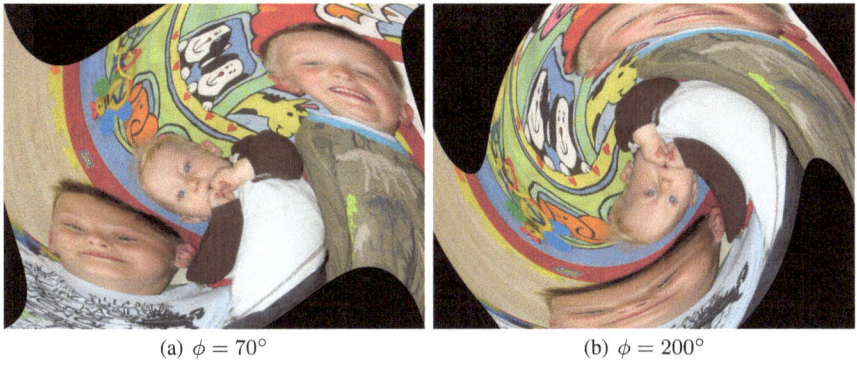

(a) $\phi = 70°$ (b) $\phi = 200°$

Fig. 11.11 The twirl transformation

So, for each pixel (x', y') in the output image, we calculate a pixel position in the input image (x, y) using Eqs. 11.12 and 11.13. If the calculated pixel position is not within the input image, we set (x', y') to black. In Fig. 11.11 the twirl transformation is illustrated.

11.2.3 Spherical Transformation

This transform zooms in on the center of the image. The size of the zoomed area is defined by S. The actual zoom effect is similar to how a lens would bend the light. This is normally referred to as the refractive index, n. The backward mapping is defined as

$$x = x' - t \cdot \tan(\alpha_x) \tag{11.14}$$

$$y = y' - t \cdot \tan(\alpha_y) \tag{11.15}$$

where $t = \sqrt{S^2 - r^2}$ and

$$\alpha_x = \left(1 - \frac{1}{n}\right) \cdot \sin^{-1}\left(\frac{\Delta x}{\sqrt{\Delta x^2 + t^2}}\right),$$

$$\alpha_y = \left(1 - \frac{1}{n}\right) \cdot \sin^{-1}\left(\frac{\Delta x}{\sqrt{\Delta y^2 + t^2}}\right) \tag{11.16}$$

where S and n are defined by the user, and Δx and Δy are defined as above. Equations 11.14 and 11.15 are only defined for $r < S$. When this is not the case the transformation is reduced to $x = x'$ and $y = y'$. As for the transformation above, we will insert a black pixel if the transformation results in a pixel outside the input image. In Fig. 11.12 the spherical transformation is illustrated.

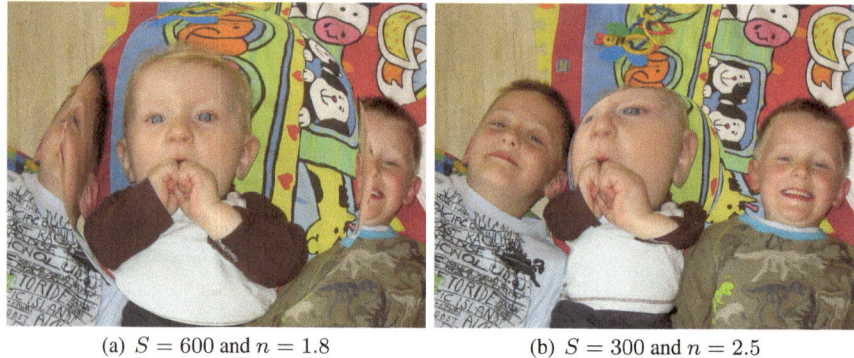

(a) $S = 600$ and $n = 1.8$ (b) $S = 300$ and $n = 2.5$

Fig. 11.12 The spherical transformation

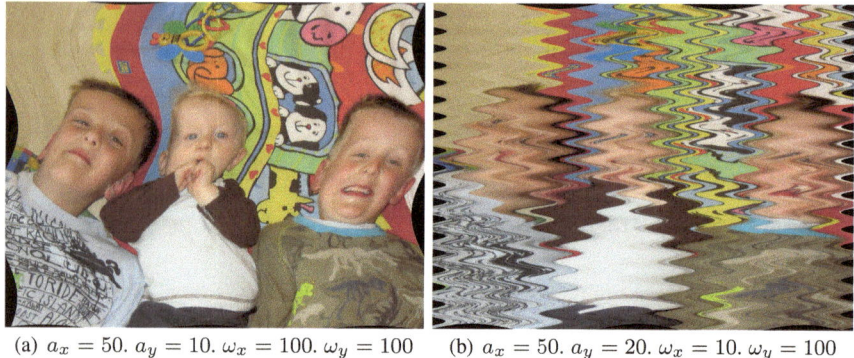

(a) $a_x = 50.\ a_y = 10.\ \omega_x = 100.\ \omega_y = 100$ (b) $a_x = 50.\ a_y = 20.\ \omega_x = 10.\ \omega_y = 100$

Fig. 11.13 The ripple transformation

11.2.4 Ripple Transformation

Another interesting non-linear geometric mapping is the ripple transformation. It distorts the image locally using a sinus function. The effect is that an overall wave pattern is introduced to the image. The backward mapping for the ripple transformation is defined as

$$x = x' + a_x \cdot \sin\left(\frac{y' \cdot 2\pi}{\omega_x}\right) \tag{11.17}$$

$$y = y' + a_y \cdot \sin\left(\frac{x' \cdot 2\pi}{\omega_y}\right) \tag{11.18}$$

where a_x and a_y are the amplitudes of the wave pattern in the x- and y-directions, respectively and ω_x and ω_y control the frequencies of the waves in the x- and y-directions, respectively. In Fig. 11.13 the ripple transformation is illustrated.

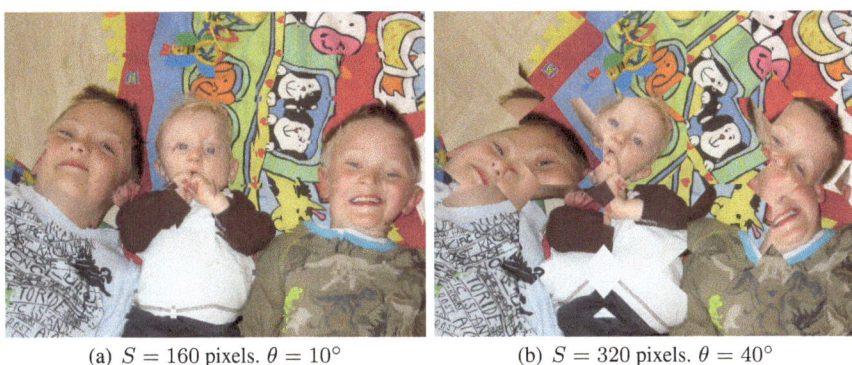

(a) $S = 160$ pixels. $\theta = 10°$ (b) $S = 320$ pixels. $\theta = 40°$

Fig. 11.14 A local geometric transformation based on rotation

11.2.5 Local Transformation

In the four geometric transformations above, all pixels go through the same mapping process and we can therefore refer to such transformations as global. This need not be the case and we can apply different transformations locally, hence a *local transformation*. Obviously this can result in many different outputs by combining the four transformations above plus those presented in Chap. 10. Here we provide an example based on rotation.

First we copy the input image to the output image in order to avoid empty pixels in the output. Next we divide the input image into a number of squares each having the size $S \times S$. Each square in the input is now rotated and mapped to the output image. The rotation angle is either θ degrees or $-\theta$ degrees, depending on its position in the input. That is, the first square is rotated θ degrees. The second $-\theta$ degrees. The third θ degrees and so on. The actual rotation is done using backward mapping. The effect is shown in Fig. 11.14 for two different parameter settings.

11.3 Further Information

An alternative approach to perform a local geometric transformation is to use *warping*. If we recall the analogy to magic mirrors, warping corresponds to the glass of the mirror being shaped differently depending on its position on the mirror. Compared to the local approach described above, warping ensures that we do not have abrupt changes in the output as seen in Fig. 11.14(b). In warping, the input image is divided into a number of triangles, which are then each mapped by an affine transformation, see Sect. 10.1, to the output image, see Fig. 11.15.

Another use of warping is found in *morphing*. Morphing is the process of mapping one image into another image. This is seen in for example TV commercials where a wild animal is mapped into a beautiful woman. Morphing is based on knowing where a number of keypoints in one image should end up in the other image, for example the position of eyes, ears and mouth. These points are used to calculate

Fig. 11.15 An example of
warping, where an image is
divided into 32 triangles each
having its own affine
transformation

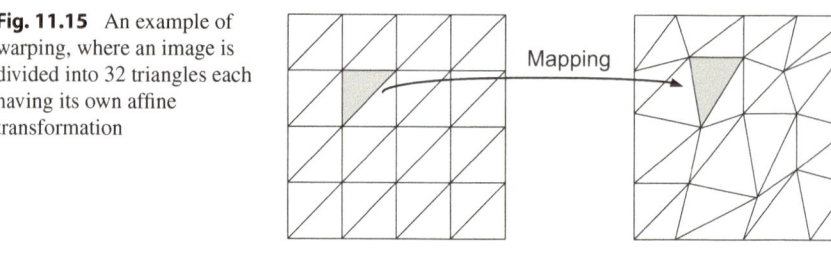

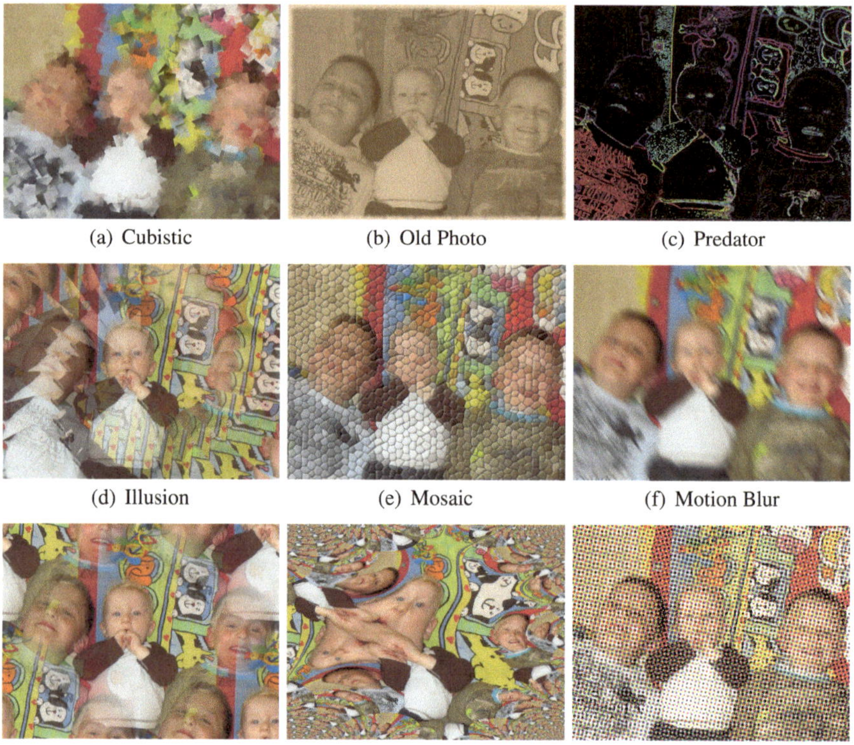

Mapping

(a) Cubistic	(b) Old Photo	(c) Predator
(d) Illusion	(e) Mosaic	(f) Motion Blur
(g) Seamless	(h) Fractal Trace	(i) Newsprint

Fig. 11.16 Different visual effects

appropriate coefficients for the warping. Besides changing the shape of the image
using warping, morphing also interpolates the intensities of the two images using
alpha blending, see Sect. 4.6.

As mentioned above an endless number of different effects can be created based
on pixel manipulation and/or geometric transformations. In Fig. 11.16 the effects of
nine additional methods are illustrated.

11.4 Exercises

Exercise 1: Explain the following concepts: pixel manipulation vs. geometric transformation, warping, morphing.

Additional exercise 1: Design your own method/algorithm that creates a visual effect.

Additional exercise 2: How is arctan() defined?

It was late Friday night in a local bar downtown in IP-valley. Mick and SB were hanging out and debating who had the most miserable life. At one point the bartender interrupted them and basically told them to shut the fuck up or leave the bar. "Too depressing," he said.

Mick looked at him with a puzzled expression and wondered why the normally gentle and polite bartender suddenly lost his temper. Later that evening when only a few customers remained, the bartender again approached Mick and SB. Fearing they might actually be kicked out of their favorite place, they quickly sobered up and smiled innocently at the man.

"Sorry guys," he started, while looking a bit pale. He opened three beers and began to talk.

When Mick and SB were walking home that night they agreed to try and help the frustrated bartender. He had explained how his only kid under-performed in school and had a very hard time concentrating. The bartender had blamed all the hours his kid spent playing computer games and he explained that he had tried everything, but after his wife died the kid detached himself more and more from the rest of the world, and the bartender couldn't take his son's one remaining pleasure from him.

"What can we do?" Mick asked SB.

"Oh come on man, that's obvious," SB replied, "we develop some kind of edutainment game where the kid can learn something while playing."

SB went on to explain his theory about the butterfly-effect of teaching, namely that students need small islands of knowledge, which they are good at, in order to learn new stuff.

"If you have solid steppingstones, you can do anything," SB concluded.

Mick was about to argue and ask what that had to do with butterflies, but since he had no better idea (and he actually also had to admit that there was some logic in the argument) he agreed to the overall idea and promised to come up with an idea over the weekend.

T.B. Moeslund, *Introduction to Video and Image Processing*,
Undergraduate Topics in Computer Science,
DOI 10.1007/978-1-4471-2503-7_12, © Springer-Verlag London Limited 2012

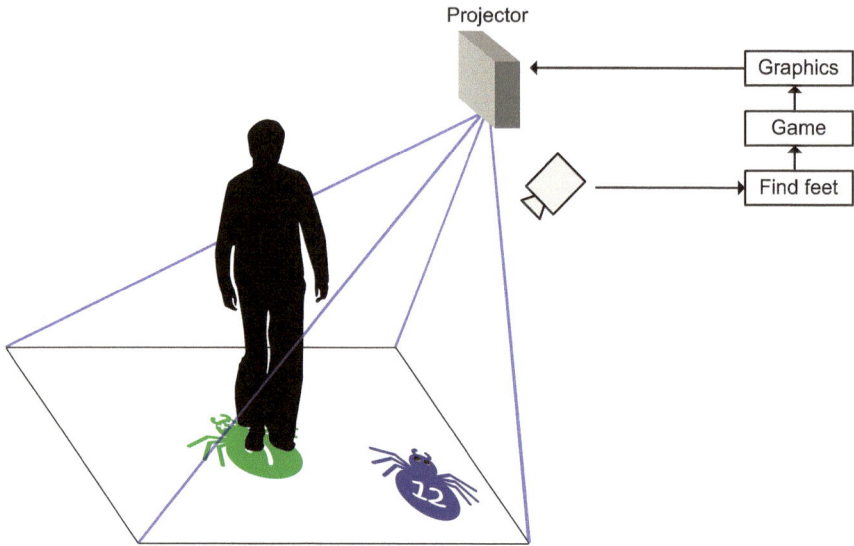

Fig. 12.1 The overall concept of the edutainment game

12.1   The Concept

SB immediate liked the concept Mick had developed.[1] It was simple and involved a small game where you had to 1) move physically and 2) solve math exercises. The idea was to use a projector to project math exercises on the floor. The correct answer to the question together with some incorrect ones were also displayed on the floor. To spice it up a bit, the possible answers were presented on the back of small creatures and the kid now has to step on the correct creature before it crawls out of the scene and a new question is asked.

Mick showed a block-diagram, see Fig. 12.1, to SB and explained the different components of the system:

Game In this block, the math exercises are generated together with the possible answers. The movements of the creatures are also controlled from this block. Lastly it is decided whether the kid answers correctly by figuring out if one of his feet touches the correct answer, an incorrect answer, or nothing.

Graphics This block generates the graphics.

Projector The physical projector, which projects the graphics.

Find feet This block takes input images from the camera and uses image processing to find the position of the feet of the player.

Camera A camera filming the player.

"Damnation, you've been busy!" SB said, smiling at Mick.

"Well, that was the easy part, now comes the hard part," SB replied seriously.

---

[1]Please note that the concept, ideas and images in this chapter are heavily inspired by [3]. The interested reader can find additional information at the book's web site.

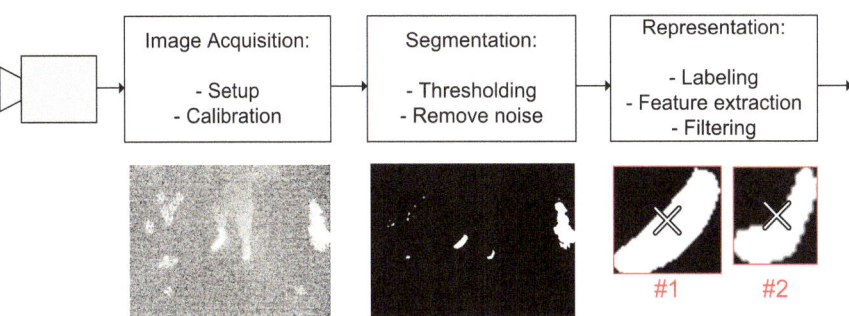

Fig. 12.2 The block-diagram of the image processing. The input is an image from the camera—very noisy one might add. In the *center* of the image the lower part of a person is present). The output is the position of each foot (indicated by the two ×)

They quickly agreed that the first three blocks where no problem and therefore focused their energy on the image processing block: Find Feet.

"Hmmm, any ideas on how to..." SB began, before he was interrupted by a big smile on Mick's face.

"What!" SB started before he realized the answer himself and continued: "of course, let's look in *the* book".

They ventured into Chap. 1 and soon found an overall structure for the image processing. After studying the different book chapters they also managed to figure out which algorithms to apply in the different sub-blocks, see Fig. 12.2. Below we shall have a closer look at how SB and Mick pulled it off.

12.2   Setup

12.2.1 Infrared Lighting

SB and Mick quickly realized that such a simple thing—for humans—as to find the feet of a person can be quite complicated for a computer. The simplest solution they came up with was to ask the user to wear distinctly colored socks/shoes and then do thresholding in some color space. However, for some reason Mick didn't like touching other people's shoes (!) and therefore came up with an alternative solution.

He had earlier in his life been puzzled about the fact that his TV remote control sends out light in order to control the TV and that he could not see the light. He learned that, this was because the remote was sending out infrared light, which the human eye cannot see, i.e., humans can only see light of certain wavelengths, see Fig. 2.2. He then tried to see if different cameras could actually see this light and learned that some can and some can't—strange. He asked an expert who explained that a camera is produced in order to capture the same as the human sees and hence a filter is usually inserted into the camera that prevents the infrared light from entering the sensing chip. In general, the better the filter the more expensive the camera. Mick tried to take some cameras apart and actually found out that the filter is sometimes

Traditional camera   Camera without any filters   Camera with visual-light filter

Fig. 12.3 *Left*: Standard camera. Center: Standard camera with the infrared filter removed. *Right*: Standard camera where a visual-light filter has been inserted instead of the infrared filter

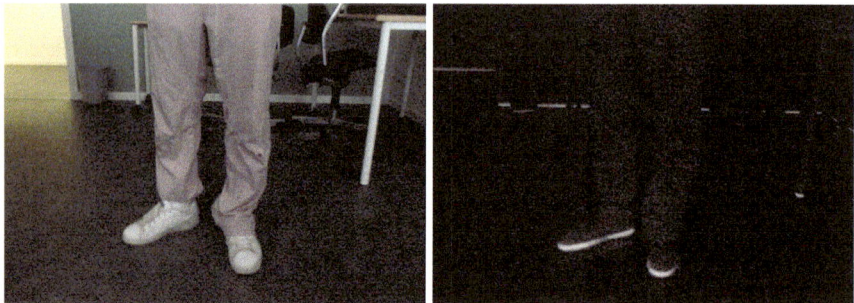

Fig. 12.4 *Left*: Image of a person's lower body. *Right*: Same image captured by a camera with a visual-light filter inserted *and* with infrared light sent out in a plane elevated a few centimeters above the floor

a physical piece of material that can be removed *and* more interesting a new filter can be inserted. He showed SB Fig. 12.3 to illustrate his point.

The three images are of a scene containing a battery casing to the right, a circuit-board with an infrared light to the left, and some wires in the middle. The left figure is captured with a standard camera, where the infrared light is slightly visible. In the center image the infrared filter has been removed, meaning that there is nothing to block the infrared light. Finally the image to the right shows the situation when a visual-light filter is inserted into the camera, meaning that only infrared light is being captured by the camera.

"Impressive!" SB exclaimed, "so you want to place these infrared light sources on the feet of the person?"

"No, that would be similar to asking the users to wears colored socks/shoes."

"Oh, but what then?" SB asked, a bit puzzled.

"The infrared light source can be forced to send light out only in a plane. We do this and then place a couple of them on the floor. In this way infrared lighting is only present in a plane a few centimeters above the floor and this is where the feet are, when they are touching the floor. In the Fig. 12.4 you can see an image with ordinary lighting and one with my suggestion. Of course this means that no other objects can be placed on the floor inside the area where the game is played. But I think that's a reasonable assumption."

Fig. 12.5 The camera image containing the graphics projected on to the floor. The two coordinate systems have been added to underline the misalignment of the coordinate system of the camera and the coordinate system of the graphics. Note the four light sources placed on the floor at the corners of the graphics

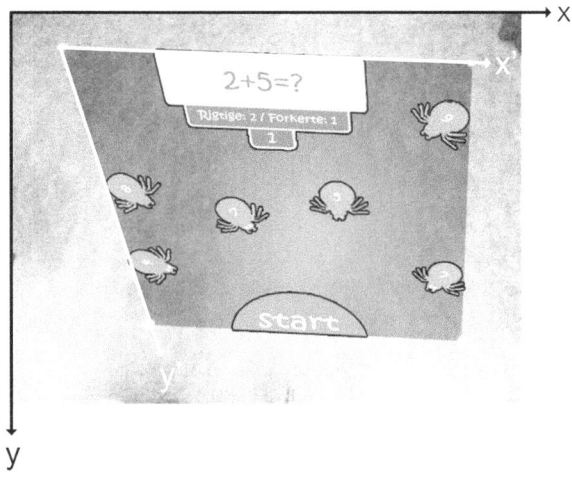

SB stared at Mick while his jaw started to drop and said: "I'm not worthy. That is fucking brilliant, man."

"I know," Mick said, smiling.

12.2.2 Calibration

"How will the Game-block know if the player steps on the right answer?" Mick asked.

After a moment of silence they looked at each other and realized that a calibration was needed. They both knew the basics about calibration, but calibration involves math, which neither of them was particular fond of.

What they had realized was that the coordinate system of the projector and the coordinate system of the camera were different. To better understand the problem they created Fig. 12.5. This figure shows what the camera sees, i.e., the coordinate system of the image from the camera is a standard orthogonal one: (x, y). The graphics projected by the projector is of course also represented in a standard coordinate system denoted (x', y'). But since the projector is tilted and rolled a bit with respect to the floor, graphics projected on the floor is a bit "off" in the sense that the opposite sides are not of equal length. Moreover, the camera is also tilted and rolled with respect to the floor adding to the "off-ness" of the graphics when captured by the camera. To sum up, the two different coordinate systems are not aligned. But why is this a problem?

Imagine the player is standing on the correct answer. The Game-block might have told the graphics to place that answer at $(x', y') = (100, 200)$. The Find Feet-block now takes an image and (correctly) locates the position of the foot as $(x, y) = (307, 298)$. How can the Game-block now compare (x', y') and (x, y) and figure out if the player is standing on the correct answer? It cannot. It simply does not know how to map from one coordinate system to the other. So what a calibration

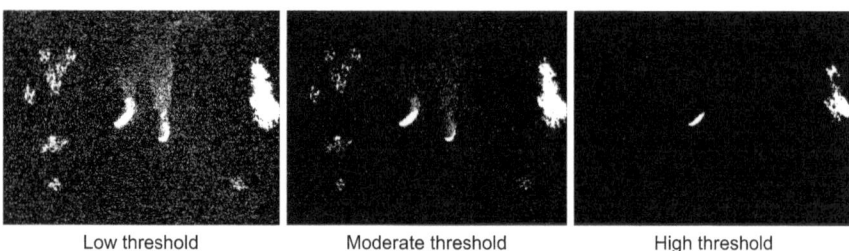

Low threshold   Moderate threshold   High threshold

Fig. 12.6 The effect of applying different threshold values

does is to find a mapping between two different coordinate systems—here between (x, y) and (x', y'). This mapping is known as a homography, see Sect. 10.3. Once the calibration is done and the mapping function found, this function is then applied to each found foot before the Game-block assesses whether the player steps on the right answer or not. Assuming neither the camera nor the projector are moved, the calibration only has to be done ones. Good practice is, however, to do a calibration each time the system is started.

The solution to the calibration problem is given in Sect. 10.3. It requires knowledge of the position of the same four points in the two camera systems. SB and Mick found these four points by placing an infrared light source at each of the four positions where the four corners of the graphics are projected onto the floor, see Fig. 12.5. The positions of these four corners in the (x', y') coordinate system are equal to the (known) size of the projected graphics: $(0, 0)$, $(0, Y_{MAX})$, $(X_{MAX}, 0)$, and (X_{MAX}, Y_{MAX}). The corresponding (x, y) positions of these four corners are found manually.

12.3   Segmentation

Mick and SB decided to apply a thresholding approach as the first step in segmenting the feet from the rest of the image. Unfortunately, when they set up the system at the bartender's house it turned out that the infrared images where not always as nice as those produced in Mick's living room, see Fig. 12.4. In fact, the images were heavily contaminated by noise, see Fig. 12.2, and choosing a suitable threshold value turned out to be a delicate matter. On one hand, a low threshold value would segment the feet but also produce a lot of noise. On the other hand, a high threshold value would eliminate noise, but also parts of the feet. In the end, a moderate threshold value was chosen, see Fig. 12.6. They tried to eliminate the remaining noise by morphology and/or a median filter, while at the same time thinking about the framerate. None could do a perfect job and the conclusion was a 7×7 median filter and then remove the final groups of noise pixels in the Representation sub-block, see Fig. 12.2. In Fig. 12.7 the effect of different median filters is illustrated.

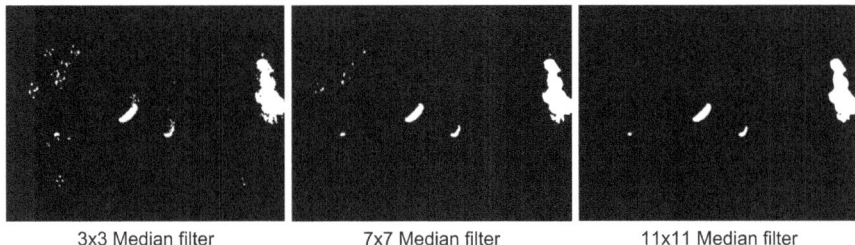

| 3x3 Median filter | 7x7 Median filter | 11x11 Median filter |

Fig. 12.7 The effect of applying different sized median filters

12.4 Representation

When SB and Mick finally arrived at this sub-block they were pretty content with themselves. They knew that once the input image could be converted into a binary image where the objects of interest were isolated from all other objects, then the goal was close. First, of course, they had to combine the object pixels (the white pixels) into the groups of connected object pixels—the labeling process.

"Mick, I can't find anything about labeling in the book."

"It's called BLOB extraction in there," Mick replied while gesturing at the book.

"Of course it is", SB said in an ironic tone. He found the section and started to read. "Should we use 4-connectivity or 8-connectivity?"

"After we have median filtered the binary image, the objects are quite smooth."

"Meaning?"

"Meaning that the connectivity will not make a big difference, hence use 4-connected."

"Ehh, why?"

"It's faster, and as I just said, it won't make a big difference."

"I see." SB quickly implemented the BLOB extraction algorithm and now had a number of labeled BLOBs. Two things now remained, finding the BLOBs representing the feet and finding the center point of each foot. To this end some features needed to be extracted from each BLOB.

While filtering the noise they had realized that the size of a BLOB is an excellent feature when classifying BLOBs as feet or noise. So they ignored BLOBs that were too small and too big, and now only the feet remained. In the book, Eq. 7.2 showed how to calculate the center of the BLOB (foot). When SB saw the equations, however, he became pale. He hated when an equation contained a Greek letter. "Why can't they just use ordinary letters?", he was asking himself, when he suddenly got an idea (anything to avoid using Greek letters).

"Mick, the position of the feet, is that critical?"

"What do you mean?"

"Does it matter if it's a few pixels off?"

"No, not really."

"Then why don't we use the center of the bounding box instead of the center of mass?"

Mick thought about it for a moment before replying: "Good idea and it is actually also less computationally demanding."

30 minutes later. "Done, the code is done," SB said proudly.

"Excellent, I have just arranged for a meeting with the bartender tomorrow night."

12.5   Postscript

The bartender loved the game developed by SB and Mick, and actually had great fun playing it himself. His son, however, tried it twice and then announced that it was stupid and left.

Some months later the bartender, now in a much better mood, had his son with him in the bar (on a Friday night!). He gently pushed the kid toward SB and Mick, who was a bit surprised to see him.

"So you like the game?" Mick tried.

"No", he said and a awkward silence occurred. The bartender then stepped forward and explained that his son one day had asked him how the game had known where his feet were. The bartender had then repeated some of the stuff Mick and SB explained to him when he asked them a similar question, namely that it was software that analyzed the images from the camera. He had continued explaining that the software was based on math. His son had looked at him with big eyes and said: "So you are saying that math can actually be used for something in the real world?"

The following day the kid had approached his (very surprised) math teacher and asked if he knew some of the math that was used in software. The teacher (after recovering) had asked why, heard the story and smiling told the kid that all aspects of math are applied in software nowadays. To follow it up, the teacher created a mini-project for his class where aspects of how math are used in software was the topic. The students (including the bartender's son) loved it and several "lost" students (including the bartender's son) picked up a new interest in math. "And this in turn," the bartender continued, "has had a positive effect on my son's attitude in school." Smiling he looked at his son and said: "well?"

The kid looked a bit shy when addressing Mick and SB: "Thanks."

SB looked at Mick with his killer smile and said while blinking: "I rest my case."

"What?"

"The butterfly effect!"

Application Example: Coin Sorting Using a Robot

Mick and SB were talking quietly in their local bar when the bartender's nephew, Fred, approached them.

"I just inherited a robot," he said out of the blue.

"Well, of course you have, terminator or R2D2?" Mick said while laughing.

"You inherited a what?" SB tried a bit more polite.

"A robot."

"What do you mean a robot?"

"Well actually just a robot arm."

"Ohh, just the arm," Mick said ironically while laughing so hard the guests at the nearby tables turned. He got up an went loudly to the restroom while saying *I'll be back* in his best Arnold impression.

"Well more like a controllable mechanical arm," Fred continued undaunted. Still not quite taking it in SB couldn't help himself and asked who was wearing it before Fred got it.

"Very funny," Fred said flatly. "My farther bought it at a foreclosure auction some years back. He had this idea of using it to sort all the coins he inherited from his brother. But he dies before finishing the job." SB didn't know what to say, but after a few moments the silence was broken when Mick returned from the restroom.

"I bet you'll be good at arm wrestling if you put it on."

"Seriously, I want to complete what my farther set out to do."

"Ok, how far did he get."

"Well, he moved it into his garage five years ago and that's about it."

"Oh. But why didn't he just sort the coins by hand?"

"Too many."

"How about those machines at the bank?" "Only works on newer coins and besides, that would be cheating. I spent last month moving it to my basement and getting it up and running. Now I can control it from a remote program and it can pick up objects on the table—if I know exactly where they are located."

"Really! Why don't you bring it here so it can grab another beer for me?" Mick said. SB gave him a look and he continued. "Ok, sorry, so when will you be done, I'll like to see a robot sorting coins."

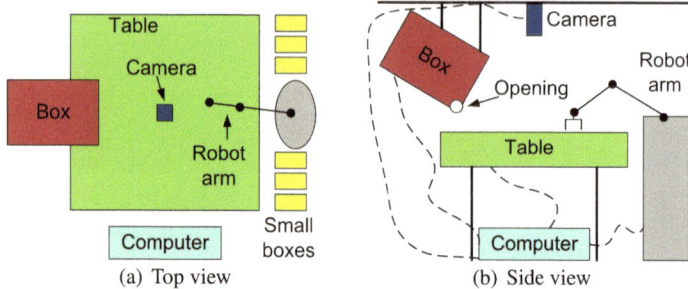

(a) Top view   (b) Side view

Fig. 13.1 An illustration of the concept. The *dashed lines* indicate that the computer can control the table, the box, the robot, and receive data from the camera. Note that the small boxes are not shown in the side view to simplify the visualization

"Well that's the thing, I need a way of informing the robot exactly where the coins are located and their type."

"Ahh, you need to do image processing, good, very good my young apprentice," Mick said smiling.

"True, but I don't know anything about it, so I though you might help me. My uncle suggested asking you since you did such a good job some years back with that math game. And he even said he would give you a discount on your bills if you helped."

The week after they all met at Fred's house to see the robot and know a bit more about the coins and concept.

13.1 The Concept

Mick and SB were very impressed by the setup in Fred's basement. They had obviously seen robots before on TV, but never met one in person, so to speak. While Fred showed them around he explained the concept of his automatic coin sorting system. Mick made two drawings so he would be able to remember when they got back home, see Fig. 13.1.

The concept was the following. The robot, or rather the robot arm, was equipped with a "hand" allowing it to pick up objects located on the table in front of it. It was no ordinary table, but a so-called vibrating table that was controlled from the computer. At first Mick and SB were puzzled by the purpose of a vibrating table, but later they realized that it played a central role in the setup.

"Look at that box up there", said Fred. "That is where I place the coins. The computer can then control the small opening in the bottom of the box and thereby release coins onto the table. The box can hold around 2000 coins at a time and with my 50,000 coins I just need to fill it up 25 times. When the coins are dropped onto the table they often end on top of each other. This is problematic when the robot tries to pick them up because it assumes the coins are located exactly on the table and not some mm above. The computer therefore commands the table to vibrate, which ensured the coins don't overlap."

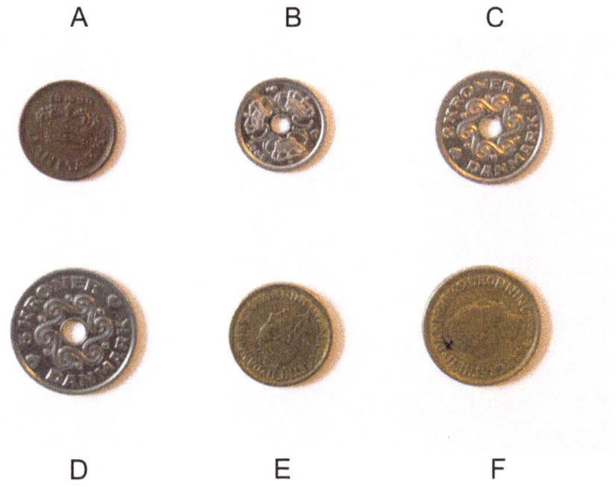

Fig. 13.2 The six different types of coins

"How does the robot know where a coin is?" Mick asked. Both Fred and SB looked at him with surprise until he realized why. "Ahh, through image processing, got it," he said smiling.

"What are those small boxes for?" SB asked.

"That is where the robot places the sorted coins. Type one goes into the first box, type two into the second and so on. I have six different types of coins (see Fig. 13.2) and hence 6 small boxes."

"So the concept is the following," SB recapitulated, "you have a program running that can tell the box to release a portion of coins onto the table. The table then vibrates in order to avoid coins laying on top of each other. The camera then captures an image of the table and finds the coins and determines their type. The type and position of each coin is then send to the computer that controls the robot to pick up the coins one at a time and place them in the small boxes. When the image processing cannot find any more coins a new portion of coins is released onto the table. This is repeated until no more coins remain in the box. The robot, the vibrating table and the box are already operational and you want us to make some image processing finding the type and position of the coins, correct?"

"Yes, can you do it?"

"Of course" Mick and SB said at the same time. SB continued cocky, "after the success we had with the system we built for your uncle this should be a-walk-in-the-park."

"Careful now," Mick warned, "this is a different problem."

"But we still have *the* book," SB replied smiling. They revisited the old system they built for the bartender to find inspiration. After a few initial tests they decided on the block diagram in Fig. 13.3.

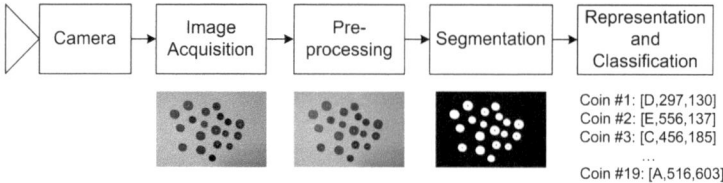

Fig. 13.3 The block diagram of the image processing part of the system. The output for each coin is its type and center

Fig. 13.4 The field-of-view of the camera and how it relates to the setup

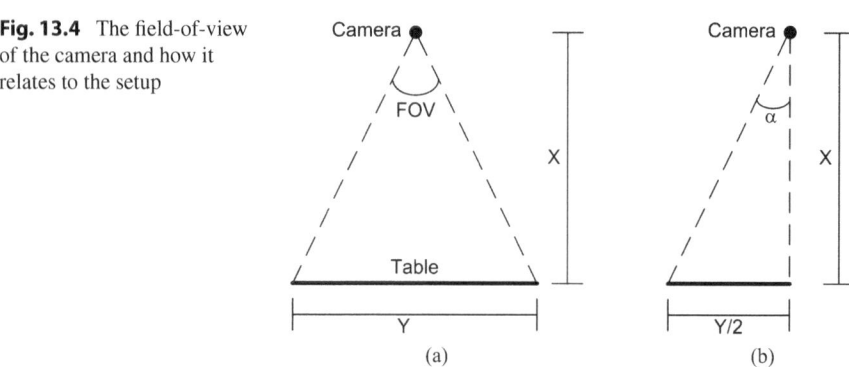

13.2   Image Acquisition

Fred had a cousin selling electronics online and Fred had convinced the cousin to give him a good deal on a camera. He sent the link to the different cameras to Mick and SB, and asked them to pick one. Fred had already decided that the camera should be located 0.5 meter above the center of the vibrating table, which had the dimensions 0.5 m × 0.5 m. The only requirement for the camera was that it should be able to see the entire table. SB therefore made a drawing to figure out what the field-of-view (FOV) of the camera should be, see Fig. 13.4(a). When SB had been staring at it for 15 min he asked Mick if he had any ideas.

"You did not pay much attention in math classes did you?"

"Will you help me or not?" SB said irritated."

"No, but I'll give you a hint," Mick said and drew a vertical line. "Look at that triangle (see Fig. 13.4(b)) and then multiply the solution by two." SB slapped his own face while wondering where his mind had been in all those math classes back in high school. He soon wrote the following equation and found out that they should get a camera with a FOV of at least 53.1°.

$$\text{FOV} = 2 \cdot \alpha = 2 \cdot \tan^{-1}\left(\frac{Y/2}{X}\right) = 2 \cdot \tan^{-1}\left(\frac{0.5 \text{ m}/2}{0.5 \text{ m}}\right) = 53.1° \qquad (13.1)$$

where Y is the width of the table and X is the distance between the camera and table.

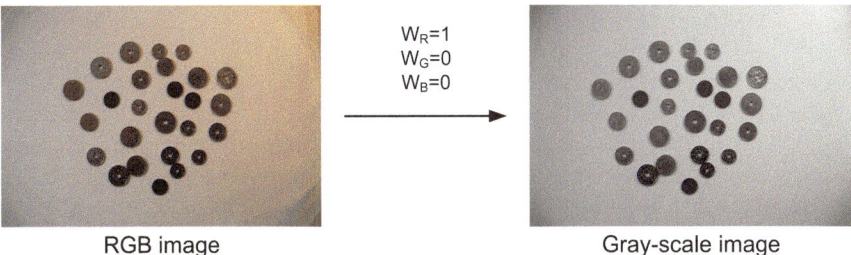

$$W_R=1$$
$$W_G=0$$
$$W_B=0$$

RGB image   Gray-scale image

Fig. 13.5 Converting the RGB image to a gray-scale image

Fred had calibrated the robot to the table, so that the robot could pick up coins if their position on the table were provided. The position of the coins found by the image processing software therefore needed to be mapped into the coordinate system of the table, i.e. the robot. From the system they developed for the bartender they knew the solution was to find four corresponding points in the two coordinate systems and then find the mapping using the theory of homography. To increase the precision of the mapping they decided to use 16 points instead of four. They placed 16 coins on the table in a regular grid spanning the entire table. They first measured the position of each coin with respect to the origin of the table (defined to be the lower left corner) and then measured their positions in the image. They now had 16 corresponding points, which they loaded into a program they found on the web and hocus-pocus, out came the coefficients of Eq. 10.12. They put the coefficients into Eqs. 10.13 and 10.14 and they could now map from the image coordinates to the coordinates of the robot. Now they just needed to find the coins and their type.

13.3 Preprocessing

The first idea that came to mind when they discussed how to distinguish the different types of coins from each other was to use the color of the coins. Fred, however, quickly undermined that idea by showing them how the color of a coin can change after being exposed to different circumstances such as extensive sunlight or acid. Having accepted that they decided to convert the input RGB image to a gray-scale image in order to reduce the amount of data. They played around with different weighting schemes, see Eq. 3.3, but in the end it turned out that simply using the red part of the image, that is $W_R = 1$ and $W_G = W_B = 0$, gave the best result. They argued among themselves that the reason was that the coins contains more red material.[1] In Fig. 13.5 the conversion is illustrated.

---

[1] The explanation could of course also be that the lighting in the scene is more reddish, but they never investigated that.

13.4   Segmentation

Mick and SB realized after some struggle that a standard thresholding approach with
a fixed threshold value would not suffice. Primarily because the system should run
for a long period of time where the lighting in the basement changed significantly
due to the many windows and Fred's unwillingness to cover these windows. After
reading about thresholding in the book they looked at each other.

"It seems we need automated thresholding, right?" asked Mick.

"Agreed, but which one of the two methods mentioned, the global or the local?"
After a short break SB continued, "well, we known that the lighting on the table
can differ from position to position, which suggests applying the local thresholding method. But we also know that the overall lightning in the room may change,
which suggests using automatic thresholding." They played around with the two
methods and finally arrived at the conclusion that they needed both. First they used
the subtracting approach from the local method to remove the effect of the uneven
illumination within the image and then they applied the global method to the resulting image. It worked very robustly independent on how the lightning changed, but
was not perfect. Some small holes appeared inside the coins due to strong refections
of the light from the metal surfaces. They applied a morphologic closing operation
to remove these holes. The different steps Mick and SB went through can be seen in
Fig. 13.6.

13.5   Representation and Classification

With good binarized images, SB and Mick now turned to the problem of defining
features that would allow for a classification of the different types of coins. First,
of course, they had to locate the different BLOBs in the image. For this purpose
they reused their BLOB extracting algorithm from their previous system. Next they
removed all small BLOBs, like those in the corners of Fig. 13.6(f), by introducing a
minimum threshold value on the BLOB size.

"Mick?" SB called, "have you noticed that the coins sometimes touch each and
hence two BLOBs are merged into one?"

"Yes. We need to calculate the circularity and ignore all BLOBs with a circularity
far from one. Could you look into that?" SB agreed and found the equation for
circularity (Eq. 7.5). It contained both the area and perimeter. SB didn't know how to
calculate those features for a BLOB with holes inside and therefore first performed
a closing with a big kernel to remove the hole. That did the trick. Armed with the
circularity he could easily detect merged BLOBs and ignore them based on their
circularity values. He proudly showed the result to Mick who liked his solution.
Mick had in the meanwhile been investigating which features that could separate
the different types of coins. He knew that different lighting situations and different
placements of a coin would result in slightly different feature values. So in order
to understand the effect of these factors he placed ten different coins of each type
different places in the scene (under different lighting conditions) and measured their
feature values, see Fig. 13.7.

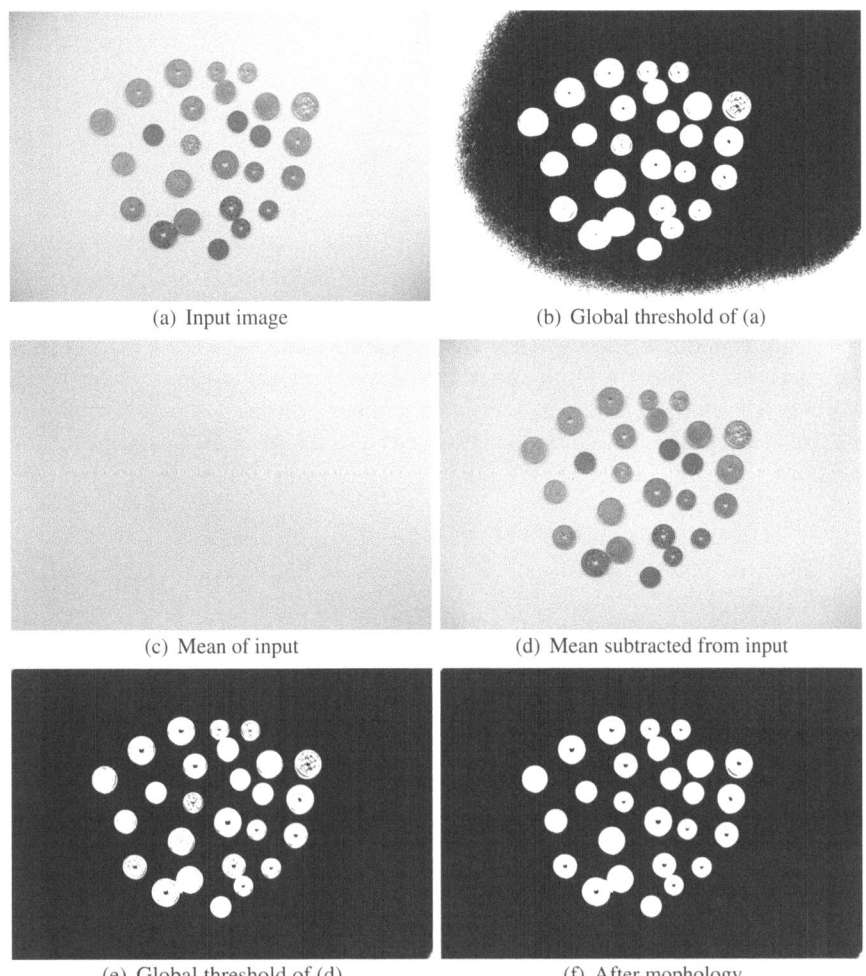

(a) Input image   (b) Global threshold of (a)

(c) Mean of input   (d) Mean subtracted from input

(e) Global threshold of (d)   (f) After mophology

Fig. 13.6 The different segmentation steps. (**a**) The input image. (**b**) The input thresholded using the global method. (**c**) The mean of the input image calculated with a 200×200 kernel. (**d**) The result of subtracting the mean from the input. (**e**) Image (**d**) thresholded using the global method. (**f**) The effect of applying morphologic closing with a kernel of 7×7 to the binary image in (**e**)

"I started out using just the size, but that was not enough and I therefore ended up also using the number of holes in the BLOB."

"But how will you figure out if a BLOB contains a hole or not?"

"I'll find the center of the BLOB and see if that pixel is black or white," Mick said glooming.

"But what if the center pixel is black due to noise that is not removed in the segmentation process?" Mick felt quiet. "Argh, didn't think about that". Silence.

Fig. 13.7 The feature space and the distribution of the 60 coins used for training

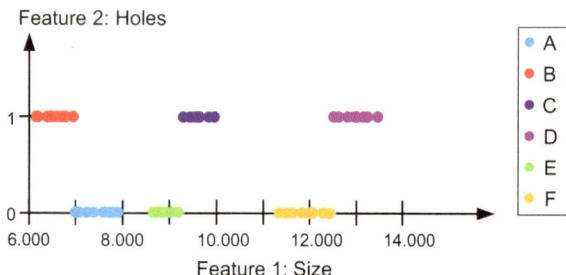

"I have an idea," SB said, "if the center pixel is white we don't have a hole. If the center pixel is black we start a connected component analysis in this pixel where object pixels are black. If the BLOB found in this way has a size corresponding to the size of a hole and...". SB stopped when he noticed Mick wasn't paying attention anymore.

"What?"

"How can a hole have a size?" Mick said with a wolfish smile.

"Idiot," SB said and continued, "if the size of the BLOB is acceptable we have found a hole."

"But a hole is something that is not there, so how can you then find it?" laughed Mick, while SB left the room to get some air. When he returned they finished implementing the hole detection algorithm. Next they looked at the feature space, see Fig. 13.7.

"Why can a certain type of coin have different sizes from image to image? I mean, a certain type of coin has a fixed size" SB wondered aloud.

"First of all, the further away from the camera a coin is the smaller it will look."

"Really?" SB asked doubtfully.

"Yes. Imagine a coin 10 m away, then it would be very small in the image."

"Ahh, I get it, that is due to the perspective geometry of the camera." Mick looked really impressed at SB while wondering where he picked up such a fancy term.

"Second, and more importantly," Mick continued, "due to changes in the lighting and the different surfaces of different coins, the segmentation will not perform equally well on different coins and hence the area of even the same type of coins will change. But if you look at the feature space and focus on the coins with a hole, you can see that there is a relatively large difference between the sizes of the different types. From this follows that we can simply classify the coins without a hole by a few if-then-else statements. You can see the same is true for the coins with a hole. This classification strategy gives us the type of a particular BLOB. The center of a coin we can find using Eq. 7.2. And no, we can't use one of the approximations of the center like last time, since we need as precise a center as possible."

They implemented this and the resulting information sent to the robot was as in Table 13.1.

The last step was to test their algorithm and they therefore captured a number of images in different lighting conditions and with different coins located at different locations. They found that sometimes the lighting resulted in poor segmentation

Table 13.1 An example of the information sent to the robot after an image has been processed. X_c and Y_c are the x and y positions of the center of the BLOB

Type	D	B	D	D	F	C	$\cdots$
X_c	780	1099	599	1363	1186	843	$\cdots$
Y_c	277	277	364	427	423	434	$\cdots$

of particular coins in particular locations. The consequence was that such coins could not be accepted as coins since their circularity would be too far from one. It happened rarely, so they didn't care too much about this problem. Besides, the next time the table was vibrated the problematic coins would change position and hence the problem disappeared. Happy with their image processing algorithm they handed over the code to Fred who then merged it with his own system for controlling the robot. The day after he started the system.

13.6 Postscript

Some months later Mick and SB ran into Fred in the local bookstore.

"Hey guys, been meaning to talk to you for some time, but been so busy."

"No problem, how did it go with the robot?" SB asked.

"She works like a charm. I filled up the box each morning and when I returned from work all the coins from the box were placed in the respective small boxes according to their type. So after a month or so all the coins were sorted."

"So you packed the robot away then?" Mick asked.

"Well, when I turned her off I kind of got the feeling I have killed her," Fred said with a weird voice, "so I turned her on again...". SB and Mick looked at each other.

"Do you also talk to it?" Mick asked smiling.

"Well, no, of course not," Fred said in a nervous voice, "I just go sit in the basement at nights so she is not getting lonely, but never mind, now I have found a new job for her. I have bought ten big boxes of old stamps and I want her to sort them. Do you have plans for the weekend?"

Bits, Bytes and Binary Numbers

When working with images it is useful to know something about how data are stored in the memory of the computer. Most values associated with images are closely related to the internal representation of the numbers. The value of one pixel is often stored as one byte for example.

The memory of the computer can basically be seen as an enormous amount of switches that can either be turned on or off. Each switch is called a bit (binary digit) and can therefore be assigned either the value 0 or the value 1. So if you just wanted to store values of either 0 or 1 it would be perfectly fine. However, this is rarely the case and bits are combined to represent other types of number.

The binary number system is also called a base-2 system, since the basic unit only has two values. Our *normal* system is a base-10 system and is called the decimal system. To understand the base-2 system better, let us first have a look at the base-10 system. When you see the following two numbers, 137 and 209814, you should actually think like this in terms of the base-10 system:

$$1 \cdot 10^2 + 3 \cdot 10^1 + 7 \cdot 10^0 = 100 + 30 + 7 = 137 \tag{A.1}$$

$$2 \cdot 10^5 + 0 \cdot 10^4 + 9 \cdot 10^3 + 8 \cdot 10^2 + 1 \cdot 10^1 + 4 \cdot 10^0$$
$$= 200000 + 0 + 9000 + 800 + 10 + 4 = 209814 \tag{A.2}$$

To generalize the formula we have

$$\cdots x_n \cdot 10^n + x_{n-1} \cdot 10^{n-1} + \cdots + x_2 \cdot 10^2 + x_1 \cdot 10^1 + x_0 \cdot 10^0 \tag{A.3}$$

The x values are the *coefficients* of the base-10 system and they define the final decimal number. This formula is similar no matter what base you use. Below the general formulas for calculating a decimal number for base-16 (hexadecimal numbers) and base-2 (binary numbers) can be seen:

Base-16: $\cdots x_n \cdot 16^n + x_{n-1} \cdot 16^{n-1} + \cdots + x_2 \cdot 16^2 + x_1 \cdot 16^1 + x_0 \cdot 16^0$
$$\tag{A.4}$$

Base-2: $\cdots x_n \cdot 2^n + x_{n-1} \cdot 2^{n-1} + \cdots + x_2 \cdot 2^2 + x_1 \cdot 2^1 + x_0 \cdot 2^0 \tag{A.5}$

T.B. Moeslund, *Introduction to Video and Image Processing*,   187
Undergraduate Topics in Computer Science,
DOI 10.1007/978-1-4471-2503-7, © Springer-Verlag London Limited 2012

The number of different values the coefficient can take is equal to the base, hence for base-10, ten different values are possible $(0, 1, 2, 3, 4, 5, 6, 7, 8, 9)$ and for base-2, two values are possible $(0, 1)$.

Eight bits together is called a byte. A byte is shown as a row of eight bits (having values 0 or 1). The bit to the left is called the most-significant bit (MSB) and the bit to the right the least-significant bit (LSB). Converting a byte into a decimal number is done by inserting the coefficients into the following equation (the eight right-most terms of Eq. A.5):

Decimal number

$$= x_7 \cdot 2^7 + x_6 \cdot 2^6 + x_5 \cdot 2^5 + x_4 \cdot 2^4 + x_3 \cdot 2^3 + x_2 \cdot 2^2 + x_1 \cdot 2^1 + x_0 \cdot 2^0 \quad \Rightarrow$$

Decimal number

$$= x_7 \cdot 128 + x_6 \cdot 64 + x_5 \cdot 32 + x_4 \cdot 16 + x_3 \cdot 8 + x_2 \cdot 4 + x_1 \cdot 2 + x_0$$

Some example byte values:

Binary	Decimal
00000000	0
00000001	1
00000010	2
00000100	4
00000101	5
00001111	15
00010101	21
01010101	85
10000000	128
11111111	255

As can be seen a byte is defined to have values from 0 to 255 (256 values in total). Sometimes bytes are also appended to create numbers larger than 255. A common example is two bytes together that spans the values $0 - 65535$ ($2^{16} = 65536$ in total).

A.1   Conversion from Decimal to Binary

A simple routine exists for getting the binary representation of a decimal number. Initially, the largest power of two that is less than the decimal number is found. If the decimal number is 137, the largest power of two is 128 (2^7). This is then subtracted from the original number and the corresponding bit is set. This is repeated until the decimal number is reduced to zero. In our example, 137 is found to be a sum of 128, 8, and 1 and therefore the binary representation of 137 is 10001001. Another example:

Decimal	Max power of two	Binary	Resulting binary number
85	64 (2^6)	01000000	01000000
21 (85–64)	16 (2^4)	00010000	01010000
5 (21–16)	4 (2^2)	00000100	01010100
1 (5–4)	1 (2^0)	00000001	01010101

Mathematical Definitions

This appendix provides some basic mathematical definitions. The appendix is intended for readers who do not have a mathematical background or readers who need a "brush-up".

B.1 Absolute Value

The *absolute value* of a number, z, is written as $Abs(z)$ or $|z|$. It is calculated by deleting the "minus" in front of the number. This means that $|-150| = 150$. Mathematically the absolute value of a number, z, is calculated as

$$|z| = \sqrt{z^2} \tag{B.1}$$

In terms of programming it can be written as

```
if (z < 0)
    z = -1 * z;
```

B.2 min and max

The *min* value of a set of numbers is written as $\min\{x_1, x_2, \ldots, x_n\}$ and simply means the smallest number in the set. For example, $\min\{7, 3, 11, 2, 42\} = 2$. The *max* value of a set of numbers is written as $\max\{x_1, x_2, \ldots, x_n\}$ and simply means the biggest number in the set. For example, $\max\{7, 3, 11, 2, 42\} = 42$. In terms of programming the max operation can be written as follows, where we assume that N numbers are present in the list and that they are stored in *list*[]:

```
MaxValue=list[0];
for (i = 1; i < N; i = i+1)
{
   if (list[i] > MaxValue)
      MaxValue = list[i];
}
```

T.B. Moeslund, *Introduction to Video and Image Processing*,
Undergraduate Topics in Computer Science,
DOI 10.1007/978-1-4471-2503-7, © Springer-Verlag London Limited 2012

Table B.1 Different rational numbers and three different ways of converting to integers

x	Floor of x	Ceiling of x	Round of x
3.14	3	4	3
0.7	0	1	1
4.5	4	5	5
−3.14	−4	−3	−3
−0.7	−1	0	−1
−4.5	−5	−4	−4

B.3   Converting a Rational Number to an Integer

Sometimes we want to convert a rational number into an integer. This can be done in different ways, where the three most common are:

Floor simply rounds a rational number to the nearest smaller integer. For example: Floor of $4.2 = 4$. Mathematically it is denoted $\lfloor 4.2 \rfloor = 4$. In C-programming a build-in function exists: *floor()*.

Ceiling is the opposite of floor and rounds off to the nearest bigger integer. For example: Ceiling of $4.2 = 5$. Mathematically it is denoted $\lceil 4.2 \rceil = 5$. In C-programming a build-in function exists: *ceil()*.

Round finds the nearest integer, i.e., Round of $4.2 = 4$ and Round of $4.7 = 5$. In terms of C-code the following expression is often used: $int(x + 0.5)$. That is, we add 0.5 to the number and then typecast it to an integer.

In Table B.1 some examples are provided.

B.4   Summation

Say you want to add the first 12 positive integers:

$$1 + 2 + 3 + 4 + 5 + 6 + 7 + 8 + 9 + 10 + 11 + 12 = 78 \qquad \text{(B.2)}$$

This is no problem writing down, but what if you want to add the first 1024 positive integers? This will be dreadful to write down. Luckily there exists a more compact way of writing this using *summation*, which is denoted as $\sum$. Adding the first 1024 positive integers can now be written as

$$\sum_{i=1}^{1024} i \qquad \text{(B.3)}$$

where i is the summation index. Below the summation sign we have $i = 1$, which means that the first value of i is 1. Above the summation sign we have 1024. This actually means $i = 1042$, but we virtually always skip $i =$. Either way, it means that the last value of i is 1042. You can think of i as a counter going from 1 to 1042 in steps of one: $1, 2, 3, 4, 5, \ldots, 1040, 1041, 1042$. What comes after the summation is a function, which is controlled by i and it is the values of this function (for each i) that are added together. Below, some examples of different summations are given:

$$\sum_{i=1}^{12} i = 1+2+3+4+5+6+7+8+9+10+11+12 = 78 \quad (B.4)$$

$$\sum_{i=0}^{4} 2 \cdot i = 0+2+4+6+8 = 20 \quad (B.5)$$

$$\sum_{i=-2}^{1} i^2 = 4+1+0+1 = 6 \quad (B.6)$$

Say that you want to sum the pixel values of the first row in an image with width $=$ 200. This is then written as

$$\sum_{i=0}^{199} f(i, 0) \quad (B.7)$$

In general the summation is written as

$$\sum_{i=n}^{m} h(i) \quad (B.8)$$

In terms of C-programming the summation is implemented as a *for-loop*:

```
Result=0;
for (i = n; i < (m+1); i = i+1)
{
    Result = Result + h(i);
}
```

We can also do a summation using more indices than i. For example, if we want to add all pixel values in an image, then we need two indices representing rows and columns. Concretely we would write

$$\sum_{j=0}^{M-1} \sum_{i=0}^{N-1} f(i, j) \quad (B.9)$$

where N is the number of columns and M is the number of rows. In terms of C-programming the double summation is implemented as two *for-loops*:

Fig. B.1 (**a**) Point
representation. (**b**) Vector
representation

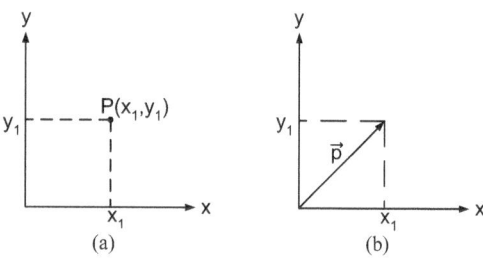

(a)   (b)

```
Result=0;
for ( j = 0; j < M; j = j+1)
{
    for (i = 0; i < N; i=i+1)
    {
        Result = Result + GetPixel(input, i, j);
    }
}
```

B.5   Vector

In the 2D coordinate system in Fig. B.1 a point is defined as $P(x_1, y_1)$. The same point can be represented as a *vector*:

$$\vec{p} = \begin{bmatrix} x_1 \\ y_1 \end{bmatrix} \tag{B.10}$$

A vector is often written as a lowercase letter with an arrow above. It can be interpreted as a line with a slope $\frac{y_1}{x_1}$ and a length. The *length of the vector* is defined as $\|\vec{p}\| = \sqrt{x_1^2 + y_1^2}$.

We can arrange the vector as a row (as opposed to a column) by taking the *transpose* of the vector, $\vec{p}^T$. That is,

$$\vec{p}^T = [x_1 \quad y_1] \tag{B.11}$$

or in other words:

$$\begin{bmatrix} x_1 \\ y_1 \end{bmatrix}^T = [x_1 \quad y_1], \qquad [x_1 \quad y_1]^T = \begin{bmatrix} x_1 \\ y_1 \end{bmatrix} \tag{B.12}$$

Say we have two vectors: $\vec{p_1}^T = [5 \quad 5]$ and $\vec{p_2}^T = [2 \quad 0]$. We can then calculate the sum of $\vec{p_1}$ and $\vec{p_2}$ as

Fig. B.2 (**a**) Adding two vectors. (**b**) Subtracting two vectors

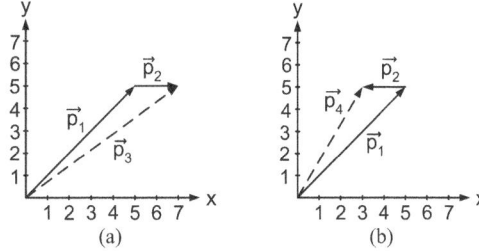

Fig. B.3 The angle between two vectors

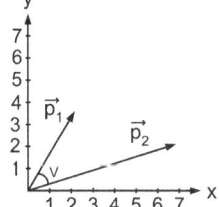

$$\vec{p_3} = \vec{p_1} + \vec{p_2} = \begin{bmatrix} 5 \\ 5 \end{bmatrix} + \begin{bmatrix} 2 \\ 0 \end{bmatrix} = \begin{bmatrix} 5+2 \\ 5+0 \end{bmatrix} = \begin{bmatrix} 7 \\ 5 \end{bmatrix} \tag{B.13}$$

In the same way we can calculate the difference of $\vec{p_1}$ and $\vec{p_2}$ as

$$\vec{p_4} = \vec{p_1} - \vec{p_2} = \begin{bmatrix} 5 \\ 5 \end{bmatrix} - \begin{bmatrix} 2 \\ 0 \end{bmatrix} = \begin{bmatrix} 5-2 \\ 5-0 \end{bmatrix} = \begin{bmatrix} 3 \\ 5 \end{bmatrix} \tag{B.14}$$

These operations can also be interpreted geometrically as illustrated in Fig. B.2.

Two vectors cannot be multiplied but we can calculate the *dot product* between them. Say we define $\vec{p_1} = [a \quad b]^T$ and $\vec{p_2} = [c \quad d]^T$. The dot product between them is then defined as

$$\vec{p_1} \bullet \vec{p_2} = ac + bd \tag{B.15}$$

The dot product can also be interpreted geometrically as

$$\vec{p_1} \bullet \vec{p_2} = \|\vec{p_1}\| \cdot \|\vec{p_2}\| \cdot \cos V \tag{B.16}$$

where $\|\vec{p_1}\|$ is the length of vector $\vec{p_1}$, $\|\vec{p_2}\|$ is the length of vector $\vec{p_2}$, and V is the angle between the vectors, see Fig. B.3. Note that it is always the smallest of the two possible angles that is calculated using Eq. B.16, i.e., $0° \leq V \leq 180°$. The biggest angle is found as $V_{\text{big}} = 360° - V$.

B.6   Matrix

When we have multiple vectors we can represent them as one entity denoted a *matrix*. For example, $\vec{p_1} = [a \quad b]^T$ and $\vec{p_2} = [c \quad d]^T$ can be represented as

$$\mathbf{P} = \begin{bmatrix} a & c \\ b & d \end{bmatrix} \tag{B.17}$$

A matrix is often denoted by an uppercase letter in boldface, but other representations can also be used. To avoid confusion a textbook involving vectors and matrices therefore often contains a preface stating how vectors and matrices are defined.

We say a matrix has a vertical and horizontal dimension, e.g., $\mathbf{P}$ has dimension 2×2. Note that the dimensions need not be equal. Similar to a vector a matrix can also be transposed by making the columns into rows:

$$\mathbf{P}^T = \begin{bmatrix} a & b \\ c & d \end{bmatrix} \tag{B.18}$$

Matrices can be added and subtracted similar to vectors, but they need to have the same dimensions:

$$\begin{bmatrix} a & c \\ b & d \end{bmatrix} + \begin{bmatrix} e & g \\ f & h \end{bmatrix} = \begin{bmatrix} a+e & c+g \\ b+f & d+h \end{bmatrix} \tag{B.19}$$

$$\begin{bmatrix} a & c \\ b & d \end{bmatrix} - \begin{bmatrix} e & g \\ f & h \end{bmatrix} = \begin{bmatrix} a-e & c-g \\ b-f & d-h \end{bmatrix} \tag{B.20}$$

Matrices can be multiplied in the following way:

$$\begin{bmatrix} a & c \\ b & d \end{bmatrix} \cdot \begin{bmatrix} e & g \\ f & h \end{bmatrix} = \begin{bmatrix} ae+cf & ag+ch \\ be+df & bg+dh \end{bmatrix} \tag{B.21}$$

The entry in row one and column one of the output matrix $(ae + cf)$ is found as the dot product between row one of the left matrix and column one of the right matrix. This principle is then repeated for each entry in the output matrix. This implies that the number of columns in the left matrix has to be equal to the number of rows in the right matrix. On the other hand this also implies that the number of rows in the left matrix and the number of columns in the right matrix need not be the same. For example, a matrix can be multiplied by a vector. The dimensions of the output matrix are equal to the number of rows in the left matrix and the number of columns in the right matrix. Below, some examples are shown:

$$\mathbf{A} \cdot \mathbf{B} = \mathbf{C} \tag{B.22}$$

$$(3 \times 2) \cdot (2 \times 7) = (3 \times 7)$$

$$(12 \times 3) \cdot (3 \times 1) = (12 \times 1)$$

A matrix of particular interest is the *identity matrix*, which in the 2D case looks like this:

$$\mathbf{I} = \begin{bmatrix} 1 & 0 \\ 0 & 1 \end{bmatrix} \tag{B.23}$$

If the product of two matrices equals the identity matrix, $\mathbf{A} \cdot \mathbf{B} = \mathbf{I}$, then we say they are each other's *inverse*. This is denoted as $\mathbf{A}^{-1} = \mathbf{B}$ and $\mathbf{B}^{-1} = \mathbf{A}$, or in other words $\mathbf{A} \cdot \mathbf{A}^{-1} = \mathbf{A}^{-1} \cdot \mathbf{A} = \mathbf{I}$. For a 2×2 matrix the inverse is calculated as

$$\begin{bmatrix} a & c \\ b & d \end{bmatrix}^{-1} = \frac{1}{ad - bc} \cdot \begin{bmatrix} d & -c \\ -b & a \end{bmatrix} \tag{B.24}$$

Calculating the inverse for matrices of higher dimensions can be quite complicated. For further information see a textbook on linear algebra.

B.7 Applying Linear Algebra

Say you want to find the equation of a straight line $y = \alpha x + \beta$. You know that the line passes through the point $P_1(x, y) = (2, 3)$, so we have $3 = 2\alpha + \beta$. Obviously this is not enough information to find α and β, or in other words we have one equation and two unknowns α and β. So in order to solve the problem we need to know the coordinates of one more point on the line or in other words we need two equations to find two unknowns. Say that we then have another point on the line, $P_2(x, y) = (1, 1)$, yielding $1 = \alpha + \beta$, we can solve the problem in the following manner. From the last equation we can see that $\alpha = 1 - \beta$. If we insert this into the first equation we get $3 = 2(1 - \beta) + \beta \Leftrightarrow \beta = -1$ and from this follows that $\alpha = 2$. So the equation for the line is $y = 2x - 1$. This principle can be used to solve simple problems where we have a few equations and a few unknowns. But imagine we have 10 equations with 10 unknowns; that would require quite an effort (and most likely we would make mistakes along the way). Instead we can use linear algebra and get the computer to help us.

Using linear algebra to solve these kinds of problem is carried out by arranging the equations into the form: $\vec{a} = \mathbf{B} \cdot \vec{c}$, where $\vec{a}$ and $\mathbf{B}$ are known and $\vec{c}$ contains the unknowns. The solution is then found by multiplying by the inverse of $\mathbf{B}$:

$$\vec{a} = \mathbf{B} \cdot \vec{c} \quad \Leftrightarrow \tag{B.25}$$
$$\mathbf{B}^{-1}\vec{a} = \mathbf{B}^{-1}\mathbf{B} \cdot \vec{c} \quad \Leftrightarrow \tag{B.26}$$
$$\mathbf{B}^{-1}\vec{a} = \mathbf{I} \cdot \vec{c} \quad \Leftrightarrow \tag{B.27}$$
$$\mathbf{B}^{-1}\vec{a} = \vec{c} \tag{B.28}$$

For the example with the two lines we have

$$\begin{matrix} 3 = 2\alpha + \beta \\ 1 = \alpha + \beta \end{matrix} \quad \Rightarrow \quad \begin{bmatrix} 3 \\ 1 \end{bmatrix} = \begin{bmatrix} 2 & 1 \\ 1 & 1 \end{bmatrix} \cdot \begin{bmatrix} \alpha \\ \beta \end{bmatrix} \tag{B.29}$$

$$\vec{a} = \begin{bmatrix} 3 \\ 1 \end{bmatrix}, \quad \mathbf{B} = \begin{bmatrix} 2 & 1 \\ 1 & 1 \end{bmatrix}, \quad \vec{c} = \begin{bmatrix} \alpha \\ \beta \end{bmatrix}, \quad \mathbf{B}^{-1} = \begin{bmatrix} 1 & -1 \\ -1 & 2 \end{bmatrix}$$

Using Eq. B.28 we obtain the solution $\vec{c} = [2 \quad -1]^T$.

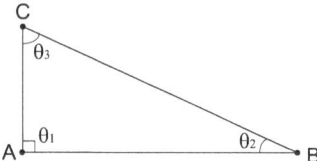

For this particular problem it might seem to be faster to do it by hand, as above, instead of using Eq. B.28. This might also be true for such a simple problem, but in general using Eq. B.28 is definitely more efficient. Recall that you just have to define the matrix and vectors, then the computer solves them for you—independent of the number of equations and unknowns.

When implementing linear algebra in software, it is highly recommended to apply a built-in library as opposed to implementing the solution from scratch. This is especially true for linear systems with more than three dimensions, since these require iterative solutions.

B.8   Right-Angled Triangle

In Fig. B.4 a right-angled triangle is shown. A right-angled triangle is defined as $\theta_1 = 90°$ and $\theta_3 = 90° - \theta_2$. The three points A, B and C define the corners of the triangle. The relationship between the lengths of the three edges is defined using Pythagoras' theorem:

$$\|\overrightarrow{AB}\|^2 + \|\overrightarrow{AC}\|^2 = \|\overrightarrow{BC}\|^2 \tag{B.30}$$

From trigonometry we have

$$\sin(\theta_2) = \frac{\|\overrightarrow{AC}\|}{\|\overrightarrow{BC}\|}, \qquad \cos(\theta_2) = \frac{\|\overrightarrow{AB}\|}{\|\overrightarrow{BC}\|}, \qquad \tan(\theta_2) = \frac{\|\overrightarrow{AC}\|}{\|\overrightarrow{AB}\|} \tag{B.31}$$

B.9   Similar Triangles

In Fig. B.5 two triangles are present. The outer triangle defined by the three points ABC and the inner triangle defined by the three points DBE. If the two triangles have the same angles, i.e., $\theta_1 = \theta_4$, $\theta_3 = \theta_5$, and $\theta_2 = \theta_2$, then the triangles are said to be *equiangular* or *similar*.

If we look at the outer triangle then we know from trigonometry that

$$\frac{\|\overrightarrow{BC}\|}{\sin(\theta_1)} = \frac{\|\overrightarrow{CA}\|}{\sin(\theta_2)} = \frac{\|\overrightarrow{AB}\|}{\sin(\theta_3)} \tag{B.32}$$

Fig. B.5 Two similar
triangles, i.e., triangles with
the same angles

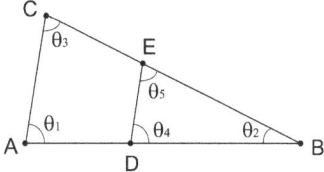

For the inner triangle we have

$$\frac{\|\overrightarrow{BE}\|}{\sin(\theta_4)} = \frac{\|\overrightarrow{ED}\|}{\sin(\theta_2)} = \frac{\|\overrightarrow{DB}\|}{\sin(\theta_5)} \tag{B.33}$$

Combining the two equations we get the following relationships between the two triangles:

$$\frac{\sin(\theta_1)}{\sin(\theta_2)} = \frac{\sin(\theta_4)}{\sin(\theta_2)} = \frac{\|\overrightarrow{BC}\|}{\|\overrightarrow{CA}\|} = \frac{\|\overrightarrow{BE}\|}{\|\overrightarrow{ED}\|} \tag{B.34}$$

$$\frac{\sin(\theta_1)}{\sin(\theta_3)} = \frac{\sin(\theta_4)}{\sin(\theta_5)} = \frac{\|\overrightarrow{BC}\|}{\|\overrightarrow{AB}\|} = \frac{\|\overrightarrow{BE}\|}{\|\overrightarrow{DB}\|} \tag{B.35}$$

$$\frac{\sin(\theta_2)}{\sin(\theta_3)} = \frac{\sin(\theta_2)}{\sin(\theta_5)} = \frac{\|\overrightarrow{CA}\|}{\|\overrightarrow{AB}\|} = \frac{\|\overrightarrow{ED}\|}{\|\overrightarrow{DB}\|} \tag{B.36}$$

$$\frac{\|\overrightarrow{BC}\|}{\|\overrightarrow{AB}\|} = \frac{\|\overrightarrow{BE}\|}{\|\overrightarrow{DB}\|} \quad \Leftrightarrow \quad \frac{\|\overrightarrow{DB}\|}{\|\overrightarrow{AB}\|} = \frac{\|\overrightarrow{BE}\|}{\|\overrightarrow{BC}\|} \tag{B.37}$$

$$\frac{\|\overrightarrow{DB}\|}{\|\overrightarrow{AB}\|} = \frac{\|\overrightarrow{BE}\|}{\|\overrightarrow{BC}\|} \quad \Leftrightarrow \quad \frac{\|\overrightarrow{DB}\|}{\|\overrightarrow{AD}\| + \|\overrightarrow{DB}\|} = \frac{\|\overrightarrow{BE}\|}{\|\overrightarrow{BE}\| + \|\overrightarrow{EC}\|} \quad \Leftrightarrow$$

$$\frac{\|\overrightarrow{DB}\|}{\|\overrightarrow{AD}\|} + 1 = 1 + \frac{\|\overrightarrow{BE}\|}{\|\overrightarrow{EC}\|} \quad \Leftrightarrow \quad \frac{\|\overrightarrow{DB}\|}{\|\overrightarrow{AD}\|} = \frac{\|\overrightarrow{BE}\|}{\|\overrightarrow{EC}\|} \tag{B.38}$$

$$\frac{\|\overrightarrow{BC}\|}{\|\overrightarrow{AB}\|} = \frac{\|\overrightarrow{BE}\|}{\|\overrightarrow{DB}\|} \quad \Leftrightarrow \quad \frac{\|\overrightarrow{BC}\|}{\|\overrightarrow{AB}\|} = \frac{\|\overrightarrow{EC}\|}{\|\overrightarrow{AD}\|} \quad \Leftrightarrow \quad \frac{\|\overrightarrow{AD}\|}{\|\overrightarrow{AB}\|} = \frac{\|\overrightarrow{EC}\|}{\|\overrightarrow{BC}\|}$$

$$\tag{B.39}$$

Learning Parameters in Video and Image Processing Systems

Virtually all video and image processing systems require a number of parameters to be defined. For example a threshold value to convert a gray-scale image into a binary image, the size of a filter kernel, the minimum and maximum allowed values of a feature, etc. Defining suitable values for these parameters is a crucial task every designer/programmer is faced with. This appendix provides a guideline for aiding the designer.

C.1   Training

In general, on-line video-based systems and off-line image-based systems differ a lot. When you have to process a single image off-line you can try different parameters in your algorithms until you achieve the desired output. When you are processing on-line video data, however, you do not know exactly what the images to process look like and your parameters can therefore not be tuned to a particular image. So, what can then be done?

The answer is that we *train* our system and hereby *learn* suitable values for the parameters. By training we mean that we capture images off-line in situations similar to the situation the system is required to be operating in. These captured *training images* are then analyzed and the parameters derived. Let us look at an example.

Say your task is to segment a human hand in a video sequence. You decide to solve the problem through the use of HSI colors. That is, you assume that the reddish skin-color is unique in the image and by thresholding the Hue and Saturation values you can find skin-pixels and hence the hand. The algorithm will be similar to 4.14. The question is now, how do you define the four threshold values: $T_{\text{Sat}_{\min}}$, $T_{\text{Sat}_{\max}}$, $T_{\text{Hue}_{\min}}$ and $T_{\text{Hue}_{\max}}$?

These four threshold values represent the different values a skin-pixel can be. So, if we capture 100 *representative* training images of a hand and look at the Hue and Saturation values, then we can get some input to the choice of threshold values. One could simply find the minimum and maximum values of Hue and Saturation and use these as the threshold values. This will give a perfect segmentation of all training pixels. However, this is likely to also result in some non-skin pixels being segmented. In Fig. C.1(a) a fictive histogram of all the 100 Hue values from the training images are shown. It is evident that the minimum and maximum values are

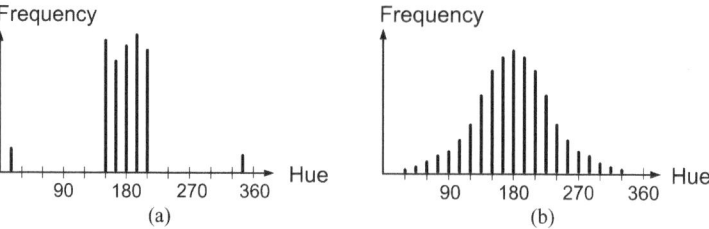

Fig. C.1 (**a**) Histogram of 100 training images. (**b**) Gaussian-shaped histogram

so extreme that virtually every single pixel in the input image will satisfy the condition of a skin pixel. All these non-skin pixels being segmented as skin pixel are denoted *False Positives*. If we want to make sure that only real skin pixels are segmented, then we probably need to have $T_{\text{Hue}_{\min}}$ and $T_{\text{Hue}_{\max}}$ very close to each other. This will of course result in too few real skin pixels being segmented. These errors are denoted *False Negatives*. So, regardless of how we define the thresholds we will, in general, make incorrect segmentation. As a designer you need to balance the false positives and false negatives when you choose the thresholds. *And* understand the consequences of the two error types—are they equally important?

Looking at the histogram once more we might want to define the threshold values around 140 and 220, respectively, since this is where the majority of the values are.

A more general approach is to use statistics, specifically, the mean and variance. The mean is the average value of Hue and is calculated by summing all Hue values and normalizing with the number of pixels, N, used in the training:

$$\text{Hue Mean} = \frac{1}{N} \sum_{i=1}^{N} \text{Hue}_i \tag{C.1}$$

where Hue_i is the Hue value of the ith training pixel.

The variance measures the variation of the Hue values around the mean value. That is, how close/far from the mean the Hue values are in general. The histogram in Fig. C.1(b) has a larger variance than the one in Fig. C.1(a). The variance is calculated as

$$\text{Hue Variance} = \frac{1}{N} \sum_{i=1}^{N} (\text{Hue}_i - \text{Hue Mean})^2 \tag{C.2}$$

The variation is often represented as the *standard deviation* instead of the variance. The standard deviation is simply the square root of the variance: Standard Deviation = $\sqrt{\text{Variance}}$.

Since we now have two values (mean and standard deviation) which represent the data in the histogram we can define the threshold values in more general terms as

Table C.1 The percentage of samples within the interval $[T_{min}, T_{max}]$, given that the data are Gaussian distributed

α	Number of samples
1	68.26%
2	95.44%
3	99.73%
4	99.99%

$$T_{min} = \text{Mean} - \alpha \cdot \text{Standard Deviation} \tag{C.3}$$

$$T_{max} = \text{Mean} + \alpha \cdot \text{Standard Deviation} \tag{C.4}$$

where α is a constant defined by the designer. To get a better feeling of α let us look at the histogram in Fig. C.1(b). Such a bell-shape is said to be Gaussian or Normal and is characterized by most samples (training pixels) being located around one value (the mean) and a symmetrically decreasing number of samples further away from the mean. Many natural phenomena actually have such a shape and therefore this shape is of great importance in many fields—including video and image processing. For the Gaussian shape Table C.1 is true.

This means that if the histogram of your training data is Gaussian and you set $\alpha = 1$, then you know that 68.26% of your training pixels have a value between T_{min} and T_{max}, etc. Even though your training samples are not completely Gaussian, you can still use the table to get a feel for how much of you training data are within the threshold values.

C.2 Initialization

When you train your system make sure to include training samples from as many diverse situations as you expect the system to operate in. For example, if you train your system on a rainy day where not much sunlight is present and then expect the system to operate on a sunny day then, you will probably be disappointed.

Often it is not realistic to train the system to handle all different situations without including too many false positives. A system can therefore include an *initialization phase* prior to operation (sometimes also referred to as calibration). The initialization is a small program which is run before the "real" program is started. With the example from above, the initialization program will ask the user to place his hand in a number of different locations in front of the camera. The captured images are (semi) automatically analyzed (Hue and Saturation values are extracted) and the threshold values are defined. These are then input to the system when it commences either manually or through a file.

One might argue that initialization is not desirable from a user's perspective since it requires an extra effort, but often it is a small price to pay for achieving a much more robust and hence successful system performance.

Conversion Between RGB and HSI

In this appendix the conversions from the RGB color representation to the HSI color representation, and reverse, are derived. That is, we seek a conversion from $[R, G, B]$ to $[H, S, I]$, and one from $[H, S, I]$ to $[R, G, B]$. When deriving the conversions we use a particular point, denoted $P_{RGB} = (P_R, P_G, P_B)$. The rgb version of this point is denoted $P = (P_r, P_g, P_b)$.

D.1 Conversion from RGB to HSI

We recall from Sect. 3.3.1 that HSI is short for *hue, saturation* and *intensity*, and is defined as in Fig. 3.11. For the actual derivation it is, however, easier to define hue and saturation in terms of rgb values as opposed to rg values.

In Chap. 3 it was explained that the rgb values span the triangle in Fig. D.1. This triangle is defined by the three corners $R' = (1, 0, 0)$, $G' = (0, 1, 0)$, and $B' = (0, 0, 1)$. The point $W = (1/3, 1/3, 1/3)$ is the colorless point in the center of the triangle. Saturation is defined as the ratio $\|\overrightarrow{WP}\|/\|\overrightarrow{WP'}\|$ and hue is defined as the angle, θ, between the two vectors: $\overrightarrow{WR'}$ and $\overrightarrow{WP}$.

If we define the points $Q = (1/3, 1/3, P_b)$ and $T = (1/3, 1/3, 0)$ then we have two equiangular triangles WPQ and $WP'T$, see Fig. D.2. Following the law of similar triangles, see Appendix B, we can redefine saturation as

$$S = \frac{\|\overrightarrow{WP}\|}{\|\overrightarrow{WP'}\|} = \frac{\|\overrightarrow{WQ}\|}{\|\overrightarrow{WT}\|} = \frac{\|\overrightarrow{WT}\| - \|\overrightarrow{QT}\|}{\|\overrightarrow{WT}\|} = 1 - \frac{\|\overrightarrow{QT}\|}{\|\overrightarrow{WT}\|} \qquad \text{(D.1)}$$

From the definition of Q, T, and W we have $\|\overrightarrow{WT}\| = 1/3$ and

$$\|\overrightarrow{QT}\| = \sqrt{(1/3 - 1/3)^2 + (1/3 - 1/3)^2 + (0 - P_b)^2} = P_b \qquad \text{(D.2)}$$

Substituting this into Eq. D.1 we get

$$S = 1 - 3 \cdot P_b \qquad \text{(D.3)}$$

Recall that $P_b = \frac{P_B}{P_R + P_G + P_B}$ and notice that $P_B = \min\{P_R, P_G, P_B\}$ when P is located in the triangle $WR'G'$. From this follows that

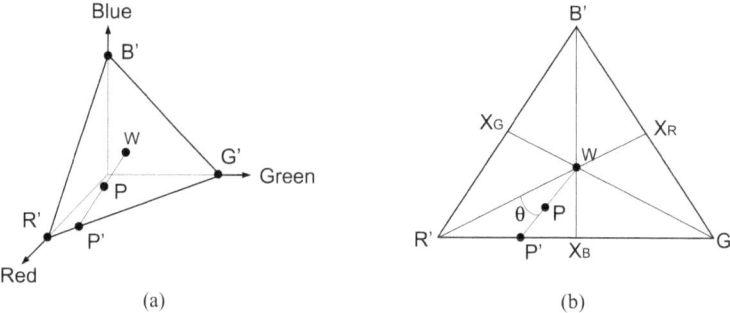

Fig. D.1 (**a**) The rgb triangle inside the RGB color cube. (**b**) The rgb triangle

Fig. D.2 The location of different points used to define saturation

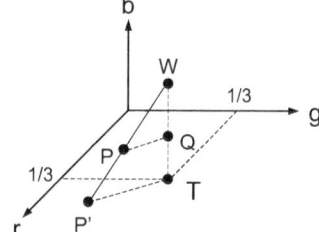

$$S = 1 - 3 \cdot \frac{\min\{P_R, P_G, P_B\}}{P_R + P_G + P_B} \tag{D.4}$$

Similar arguments hold for the other two triangles $WG'B'$ and $WB'R'$ and Eq. D.4 is therefore the general expression for saturation in the HSI representation.

Hue is defined as the angle, θ, between the two vectors $\overrightarrow{WR'}$ and $\overrightarrow{WP}$, see Fig. 3.11. Referring to Eq. B.16 we can express the angle between the vectors as

$$\theta = \cos^{-1}\left(\frac{\overrightarrow{WR'} \bullet \overrightarrow{WP}}{\|\overrightarrow{WR'}\| \cdot \|\overrightarrow{WP}\|}\right) \tag{D.5}$$

Inserting the actual points yields

$$\overrightarrow{WR'} = \vec{R'} - \vec{W} = \begin{bmatrix} 1 \\ 0 \\ 0 \end{bmatrix} - \begin{bmatrix} 1/3 \\ 1/3 \\ 1/3 \end{bmatrix} = \begin{bmatrix} 2/3 \\ -1/3 \\ -1/3 \end{bmatrix} \tag{D.6}$$

$$\|\overrightarrow{WR'}\| = \sqrt{(2/3)^2 + (-1/3)^2 + (-1/3)^2} = \sqrt{6/9} = \sqrt{2/3} \tag{D.7}$$

$$\overrightarrow{WP} = \vec{P} - \vec{W} = \begin{bmatrix} P_r \\ P_g \\ P_b \end{bmatrix} - \begin{bmatrix} 1/3 \\ 1/3 \\ 1/3 \end{bmatrix} = \begin{bmatrix} P_r - 1/3 \\ P_g - 1/3 \\ P_b - 1/3 \end{bmatrix} \tag{D.8}$$

$$\|\overrightarrow{WP}\| = \sqrt{(P_r - 1/3)^2 + (P_g - 1/3)^2 + (P_b - 1/3)^2} \quad \Leftrightarrow$$

$$\|\overrightarrow{WP}\| = \sqrt{P_r^2 + P_g^2 + P_b^2 - 2/3(P_r + P_g + P_b) + 3/9} \quad \Leftrightarrow$$

$$\|\overrightarrow{WP}\| = \sqrt{P_r^2 + P_g^2 + P_b^2 - 1/3} \tag{D.9}$$

where the last reduction is possible since $P_r + P_g + P_b = 1$. Inserting the above expressions into Eq. D.5 yields

$$\theta = \cos^{-1}\left(\frac{\begin{bmatrix} 2/3 \\ -1/3 \\ -1/3 \end{bmatrix} \bullet \begin{bmatrix} P_r - 1/3 \\ P_g - 1/3 \\ P_b - 1/3 \end{bmatrix}}{\sqrt{2/3} \cdot \sqrt{P_r^2 + P_g^2 + P_b^2 - 1/3}}\right) \quad \Leftrightarrow$$

$$\theta = \cos^{-1}\left(\frac{(2P_r/3 - 2/9) + (-P_g/3 + 1/9) + (-P_b/3 + 1/9)}{\sqrt{\frac{9 \cdot 2}{9 \cdot 3}} \cdot \sqrt{P_r^2 + P_g^2 + P_b^2 - 1/3}}\right) \quad \Leftrightarrow$$

$$\theta = \cos^{-1}\left(\frac{2P_r - P_g - P_b}{\sqrt{6P_r^2 + 6P_g^2 + 6P_b^2 - 2}}\right) \tag{D.10}$$

The final step is now to replace (P_r, P_g, P_b) with (P_R, P_G, P_B). Recall that $P_r = P_R/J$, $P_g = P_G/J$, $P_b = P_B/J$, where $J = P_R + P_G + P_B$. Inserting yields

$$\theta = \cos^{-1}\left(\frac{1/J \cdot (2P_R - P_G - P_B)}{\sqrt{1/J^2(6P_R^2 + 6P_G^2 + 6P_B^2) - 2}}\right) \quad \Leftrightarrow$$

$$\theta = \cos^{-1}\left(\frac{2P_R - P_G - P_B}{\sqrt{6P_R^2 + 6P_G^2 + 6P_B^2 - 2J^2}}\right) \quad \Leftrightarrow$$

$$\theta = \cos^{-1}\left(1/2 \cdot \frac{2P_R - P_G - P_B}{\sqrt{P_R^2 + P_G^2 + P_B^2 - P_R \cdot P_G - P_R \cdot P_B - P_G \cdot P_B}}\right) \quad \Leftrightarrow$$

$$\theta = \cos^{-1}\left(1/2 \cdot \frac{(P_R - P_G) + (P_R - P_B)}{\sqrt{(P_R - P_G)(P_R - P_G) + (P_R - P_B)(P_G - P_B)}}\right) \tag{D.11}$$

Note that the last expression is often applied in order to optimize the conversion from an implementation point of view. Since Eq. D.5 is only valid in the range $\theta \in [0°, 180°]$ the final expression for hue is given below, see Appendix B for details.

$$H = \begin{cases} \theta, & \text{if } P_G \geq P_B; \\ 360° - \theta, & \text{otherwise} \end{cases} \tag{D.12}$$

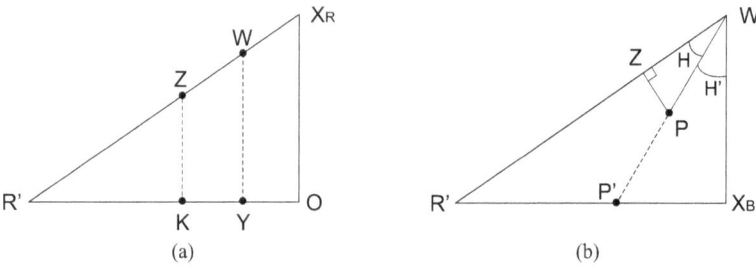

Fig. D.3 Triangles used to derive the conversion from HSI to RGB. Note that (**b**) is one of the triangles in Fig. D.1(b), i.e., $H + H' = 60°$. Note also that the two triangles have the same hypotenuse (except for the length) and that the triangles are perpendicular

D.2   Conversion from HSI to RGB

The conversion from HSI to RGB depends on in which of the following triangles the point is located: $WR'G'$, $WG'B'$, or $WB'R'$. Let us start with the situation where $0° \leq H \leq 120°$, i.e., the triangle $WR'G'$.

We first convert from HSI to rgb and then from rgb to RGB. In the triangle $WR'G'$ we know from Eq. D.3 that $P_b = (1 - S)/3$. Furthermore, we know that $P_r + P_g + P_b = 1$ and hence only need to find one of the unknowns. To this end we define the triangle in Fig. D.3(a). The base of the triangle is the line spanned by $(0, 0, 0)$, denoted O, and R'. The hypotenuse of the triangle is the line spanned by R' and the middle point of the line spanned by B' and G'. This point is denoted X_R, see Fig. D.1. Note that the line spanned by R' and X_R passes through the gray point W. The point Z is the intersection between the line spanned by R' and X_R, and the plane containing P and perpendicular to the red-axis (the line spanned by R' and O), see Fig. D.3. This plane is denoted Γ_1.

From the law of similar triangles follows that

$$\frac{\|\overrightarrow{R'X_R}\|}{\|\overrightarrow{R'O}\|} = \frac{\|\overrightarrow{R'Z}\|}{\|\overrightarrow{R'K}\|} \tag{D.13}$$

We know that $\|\overrightarrow{R'O}\| = 1$ and that $\|\overrightarrow{KO}\| = P_r$. From this follows that $\|\overrightarrow{R'K}\| = 1 - P_r$. We can see that $\|\overrightarrow{R'Z}\| = \|\overrightarrow{R'X_R}\| - (\|\overrightarrow{ZW}\| + \|\overrightarrow{WX_R}\|)$ and can therefore rewrite Eq. D.13 to

$$\|\overrightarrow{R'X_R}\| - P_r \cdot \|\overrightarrow{R'X_R}\| = \|\overrightarrow{R'X_R}\| - \|\overrightarrow{ZW}\| - \|\overrightarrow{WX_R}\| \quad \Leftrightarrow \tag{D.14}$$

$$P_r = \frac{\|\overrightarrow{ZW}\| + \|\overrightarrow{WX_R}\|}{\|\overrightarrow{R'X_R}\|} = \frac{\|\overrightarrow{ZW}\|}{\|\overrightarrow{R'X_R}\|} + \frac{\|\overrightarrow{WX_R}\|}{\|\overrightarrow{R'X_R}\|} \tag{D.15}$$

Using the law of similar triangles: $\|\overrightarrow{WX_R}\|/\|\overrightarrow{R'X_R}\| = \|\overrightarrow{YO}\|/\|\overrightarrow{R'O}\| = \|\overrightarrow{YO}\| = 1/3$. The first term is a bit more tricky to rewrite and we need to introduce yet another triangle to this end. First have a look at Fig. D.3(a) and recall that Γ_1 is a plane perpendicular to the red axis, which contains the points: P, K and Z. We now define another plane, denoted Γ_2, which contains the points: R', Z, W, X_R, and which is perpendicular to the triangle $R'X_R O$. This plane contains all possible values of rgb, and hence also P. Since P belongs to both planes, P must be part of the line defined by the intersection of the two planes. This line contains Z and is perpendicular to the triangle $R'X_R O$. That is, if you place your fingertip on Z in Fig. D.3(a) and lift it vertically, then you are moving along this line and will eventually reach P. Having this in mind we now define the triangle $R'WX_B$, where X_B is the middle point of the line spanned by R' and G', see Fig. D.3(b). Note that this figure is also part of Fig. D.1(b).

From Fig. D.3(b) follows that

$$\cos(H) = \frac{\|\overrightarrow{ZW}\|}{\|\overrightarrow{WP}\|} \quad \Leftrightarrow \quad \|\overrightarrow{ZW}\| = \|\overrightarrow{WP}\| \cdot \cos(H) \tag{D.16}$$

From the definition of saturation we have $\|\overrightarrow{WP}\| = S \cdot \|\overrightarrow{WP'}\|$. Realizing that $H' = 60° - H$ we can express $\|\overrightarrow{WP'}\|$ as

$$\|\overrightarrow{WP'}\| = \frac{\|\overrightarrow{WX_B}\|}{\cos(60° - H)} \tag{D.17}$$

Inserting Eqs. D.16 and D.17 into Eq. D.15 yields

$$P_r = \frac{1}{\|\overrightarrow{R'X_R}\|} \cdot \frac{S \cdot \|\overrightarrow{WX_B}\| \cdot \cos(H)}{\cos(60° - H)} + \frac{1}{3} \tag{D.18}$$

Since $\|\overrightarrow{WX_B}\| = \|\overrightarrow{WX_R}\|$ and $\|\overrightarrow{WX_R}\|/\|\overrightarrow{R'X_R}\| = 1/3$ we can reduce Eq. D.18 to

$$P_r = \frac{1}{3}\left(1 + \frac{S \cdot \cos(H)}{\cos(60° - H)}\right) \tag{D.19}$$

After having calculated P_b and P_r we can find the last coordinate as $P_g = 1 - P_b - P_r$. The final step is to convert from rgb to RGB. We know that $P_r = P_R/(P_R + P_G + P_B)$, $P_g = P_G/(P_R + P_G + P_B)$, $P_b = P_B/(P_R + P_G + P_B)$ and that $I = (P_R + P_G + P_B)/3$. From this follows that $P_R = 3I\,P_r$, $P_G = 3I\,P_g$, and $P_B = 3I\,P_b$. Substituting into Eqs. D.3 and D.19 yields the following expressions which are valid when $0° \leq H \leq 120°$:

$$P_B = I - I \cdot S \tag{D.20}$$

$$P_R = I \cdot \left(1 + \frac{S \cdot \cos(H)}{\cos(60° - H)}\right) \tag{D.21}$$

$$P_G = 3I - P_R - P_B \tag{D.22}$$

Similar expressions can be derived for the remaining hue values. The only difference is that the geometry in Fig. D.3(b) is only valid when $0° \leq H \leq 120°$. The hue value is therefore normalized, denoted H_n, to this interval before being applied. The final conversion from HSI to RGB therefore becomes

$$H_n = \begin{cases} 0, & \text{if } 0° \leq H \leq 120°; \\ H - 120°, & \text{if } 120° < H \leq 240°; \\ H - 240°, & \text{if } 240° < H < 360° \end{cases} \tag{D.23}$$

$$P_R = \begin{cases} I \cdot \left(1 + \frac{S \cdot \cos(H_n)}{\cos(60° - H_n)}\right), & \text{if } 0° \leq H \leq 120°; \\ I - I \cdot S, & \text{if } 120° < H \leq 240°; \\ 3I - P_G - P_B, & \text{if } 240° < H < 360° \end{cases} \tag{D.24}$$

$$P_G = \begin{cases} 3I - P_R - P_B, & \text{if } 0° \leq H \leq 120°; \\ I \cdot \left(1 + \frac{S \cdot \cos(H_n)}{\cos(60° - H_n)}\right), & \text{if } 120° < H \leq 240°; \\ I - I \cdot S, & \text{if } 240° < H < 360° \end{cases} \tag{D.25}$$

$$P_B = \begin{cases} I - I \cdot S, & \text{if } 0° \leq H \leq 120°; \\ 3I - P_R - P_G, & \text{if } 120° < H \leq 240°; \\ I \cdot \left(1 + \frac{S \cdot \cos(H_n)}{\cos(60° - H_n)}\right), & \text{if } 240° < H < 360° \end{cases} \tag{D.26}$$

Conversion Between RGB and HSV

In this appendix the conversions from the RGB color representation to the HSV color representation, and reverse, are derived. That is, we seek a conversion from $[R, G, B]$ to $[H, S, V]$, and one from $[H, S, V]$ to $[R, G, B]$.

E.1 Conversion from RGB to HSV

We recall from Sect. 3.3.2 that HSV is short for *hue*, *saturation* and *value*, and that *value* is defined as

$$V = \max\{R, G, B\} \tag{E.1}$$

We start by defining a sub-cube of dimension (V, V, V) inside the RGB color cube, see Fig. E.1(a). Since V is equal to the maximum RGB value the RGB point to be converted is located on one of the sides of this sub-cube. Imagine now that we define a plane perpendicular to the gray-vector and project the corners of the sub-cube onto this plane. This corresponds to placing your eye at $[255, 255, 255]$ and looking at $[0, 0, 0]$. The result will be the hexagon illustrated in Fig. E.1(b). Each corner of the hexagon will point toward one of the corners of the RGB color cube and are therefore denoted R', Y, G', C, B', and M, corresponding to red, yellow, green, cyan, blue, and magenta, respectively.[1] In the center of the hexagon we will have black and white at the same point, denoted W. The RGB point to be converted is also projected onto the plane and denoted P.

The six corners of the hexagon have the same distance to W. From this follows that the distances between adjacent corners are equal to each other and to the distance from a corner to W. Since all lengths in the hexagon are equal we can scale the hexagon as we please. We choose to scale the hexagon so that all sides have the length V, which should be interpreted in the following way.

If we assume $\max\{R, G, B\} = R$ we know that the RGB point is located on the side of the sub-cube defined as $R = V$. This corresponds to one of the two sextants MWR or RWY. In these two sextants the "position" of P is given as (G, B), see

---

[1]The primes are introduced in order to distinguish the color values (R, G, B) from the R, G, and B corners of the hexagon.

T.B. Moeslund, *Introduction to Video and Image Processing*,
Undergraduate Topics in Computer Science,
DOI 10.1007/978-1-4471-2503-7, © Springer-Verlag London Limited 2012

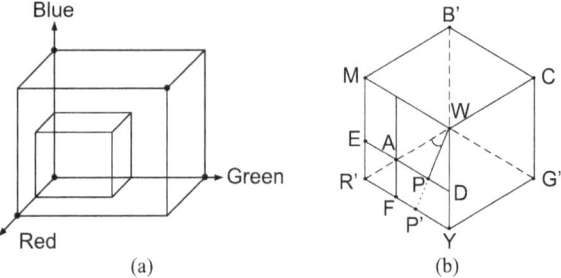

Fig. E.1 (a) The sub-cube inside the RGB color cube. (b) The hexagon defined when looking at the sub-cube from the point $(255, 255, 255)$ and toward the point $(0, 0, 0)$. The corners of the hexagon correspond to the corners of the sub-cube. The *dashed lines* indicate the lines not visible if the sub-cube is solid

Fig. E.1(b), meaning that we can derive hue and saturation in the two sextants from Fig. E.1(b) and then directly express hue and saturation in terms of the RGB values. Similar arguments can be made for the remaining sextants.

E.1.1   HSV: Saturation

Looking at Fig. E.1(b) saturation is defined as the ratio between the distance from the W to P and the distance from W to P', where P' is the intersection between the vectors spanned by W and P, and R and Y. That is, saturation is given as

$$S = \frac{\|\overrightarrow{WP}\|}{\|\overrightarrow{WP'}\|} \tag{E.2}$$

Since the triangles WPD and $WP'Y$ are similar, see Appendix B, we have

$$S = \frac{\|\overrightarrow{WP}\|}{\|\overrightarrow{WP'}\|} = \frac{\|\overrightarrow{WD}\|}{\|\overrightarrow{WY}\|} \tag{E.3}$$

From this follows that

$$S = \frac{\|\overrightarrow{WD}\|}{\|\overrightarrow{WY}\|} = \frac{\|\overrightarrow{WY}\| - \|\overrightarrow{DY}\|}{\|\overrightarrow{WY}\|} \tag{E.4}$$

We know from the definition of the sub-cube that $\|\overrightarrow{WY}\| = V$ and can see in Fig. E.1(b) that $\|\overrightarrow{DY}\| = B$. This yields $S = (V - B)/V$. We can see that $B = \min\{R, G, B\}$ in the sextant where P is located and can therefore express saturation as

$$S = \frac{V - \min\{R, G, B\}}{V} \tag{E.5}$$

where $S \in [0, 1]$. Similar reasoning for the other five sextants in the hexagon shows that Eq. E.5 is indeed a general equation that holds for the entire hexagon.

E.1.2   HSV: Hue

In Fig. E.1(b) hue is illustrated as the angle between $\overrightarrow{WR}$ and $\overrightarrow{WP}$. Hue is, however, *not* calculated as an angle but rather as the following ratio:

$$H = \frac{\|\overrightarrow{AP}\|}{\|\overrightarrow{AD}\|} \tag{E.6}$$

where A, P, and D are defined in Fig. E.1(b). This definition is only valid when P is located in the sextant shown in Fig. E.1(b), i.e., then $R = V$ and $G \geq B$. In this sextant hue will be a value in the interval $[0, 1]$ where hue $= 0$ corresponds to red and hue $= 1$ corresponds to yellow. The calculated hue value is normally multiplied with $60°$ in order to obtain a hue value in the range of $[0°, 360°[$ when considering all sextants.[2] Below we show how hue is calculated in the sextant RWY.

Looking at Fig. E.1(b) we can see that $\|\overrightarrow{AP}\| = \|\overrightarrow{EP}\| - \|\overrightarrow{EA}\|$, $\|\overrightarrow{EA}\| = \|\overrightarrow{AF}\|$ and that $\|\overrightarrow{AD}\| = \|\overrightarrow{WD}\|$. From this follows that

$$H = \frac{\|\overrightarrow{AP}\|}{\|\overrightarrow{AD}\|} = \frac{\|\overrightarrow{EP}\| - \|\overrightarrow{AF}\|}{\|\overrightarrow{WD}\|} \tag{E.7}$$

Above we saw that $\|\overrightarrow{WD}\| = V - \min\{R, G, B\}$ and stated that the "position" of P in this sextant is given as (G, B). Combining this with Eq. E.7 and converting the ratio into degrees we have

$$H_{\text{deg}} = \frac{G - B}{V - \min\{R, G, B\}} \cdot 60° \tag{E.8}$$

A similar geometric reasoning can be carried out for the sextant MWR where $R = V$ and $B > G$ resulting in:

$$H_{\text{deg}} = \left(\frac{R - B}{V - \min\{R, G, B\}} + 5 \right) \cdot 60° \tag{E.9}$$

Moving on to the sextant YWG where $G = V$ and $R > B$ we can derive that

---

[2]Note that the range is defined as $[0°, 360°[$ as opposed to $[0°, 360°]$. The reason for this is that $360° = 0°$, hence $360°$ is not included in the interval, but $359.99999°$ etc. is.

$$H_{\text{deg}} = \left(\frac{V - R}{V - \min\{R, G, B\}} + 1 \right) \cdot 60° \qquad (\text{E.10})$$

For reasons that will be clear when we look at the next sextant, we rewrite Eq. E.10 in the following way:

$$H_{\text{deg}} = \left(\frac{V - R}{V - \min\{R, G, B\}} + 1 + 1 - 1 \right) \cdot 60° \quad \Leftrightarrow$$

$$H_{\text{deg}} = \left(\frac{V - R}{V - \min\{R, G, B\}} + 2 - \frac{V - \min\{R, G, B\}}{V - \min\{R, G, B\}} \right) \cdot 60° \quad \Leftrightarrow$$

$$H_{\text{deg}} = \left(\frac{B - R}{V - \min\{R, G, B\}} + 2 \right) \cdot 60° \qquad (\text{E.11})$$

For the sextant GWC where $G = V$ and $B \geq R$ we can derive that

$$H_{\text{deg}} = \left(\frac{B - R}{V - \min\{R, G, B\}} + 2 \right) \cdot 60° \qquad (\text{E.12})$$

We can see that Eqs. E.11 and E.12 are the same, which means that we only need one equation when $G = V$. The same holds for the last two sextants and the final equation for hue therefore becomes

$$H_{\text{deg}} = \begin{cases} \frac{G-B}{V-\min\{R,G,B\}} \cdot 60°, & \text{if } V = R \text{ and } G \geq B; \\ \left(\frac{B-R}{V-\min\{R,G,B\}} + 2\right) \cdot 60°, & \text{if } G = V; \\ \left(\frac{R-G}{V-\min\{R,G,B\}} + 4\right) \cdot 60°, & \text{if } B = V; \\ \left(\frac{R-B}{V-\min\{R,G,B\}} + 5\right) \cdot 60°, & \text{if } V = R \text{ and } G < B \end{cases} \qquad (\text{E.13})$$

where $H_{\text{deg}} \in [0, 360°[$. Note that hue is sometimes defined as a number in the interval $[0, 1[$. This is obtained by dividing by 6 instead of multiplying by 60. Sometimes the interval $[0, 2\pi[$ is used. This is obtained by dividing by 3 and multiplying by π instead of multiplying by 60.

Note that hue is undefined when no color is present, i.e., $R = G = B$. One could define it to be 0 (or some other value), but a better approach is often to define it as the hue value of the previous pixel. For a gray-scale image this will not make sense, but then again, no point in converting a gray-scale image into an HSV image in the first place! Note also that saturation is undefined in Eq. E.5 when $(R = G = B = 0)$. We therefore make the following definition: $S \equiv 0$ when $(R = G = B = 0)$.

E.2   Conversion from HSV to RGB

The conversion from HSV to RGB depends on in which sextant the point is located. We can assess that by dividing the hue value by 60 and taking the closets integer equal to or just below. This directly provides and index K in the range: $0 \leq K \leq 5$, stating in which sextant the point is.

When $K = 0$ we are in the sextant RWY and find R, G, and B in the following way. First we realize that $R = V$ in this sextant. Next we use the fact that $B = \min\{R, G, B\}$ in this sextant. Inserting this into Eq. E.5 we get $B = V \cdot (1 - S)$. G is found using the following equation derived above:

$$H = \frac{G - B}{V - \min\{R, G, B\}} \tag{E.14}$$

Substituting we have

$$H = \frac{G - V \cdot (1 - S)}{V - V \cdot (1 - S)} \quad \Leftrightarrow$$
$$G = H \cdot V - H \cdot V \cdot (1 - S) + V \cdot (1 - S) \quad \Leftrightarrow$$
$$G = V \cdot (H - H + H \cdot S + 1 - S) \quad \Leftrightarrow$$
$$G = V \cdot \left(1 - S \cdot (1 - H)\right) \tag{E.15}$$

When $K = 1$ the point is located in the sextant YWG. In this sextant we know from above that $G = V$ and $B = \min\{R, G, B\}$. R is found using the following equation, derived above:

$$H = \frac{V - R}{V - \min\{R, G, B\}} \tag{E.16}$$

Substituting we have

$$H = \frac{V - R}{V - V \cdot (1 - S)} \quad \Leftrightarrow \tag{E.17}$$
$$R = V - H \cdot V + H \cdot V \cdot (1 - S) \quad \Leftrightarrow \tag{E.18}$$
$$R = V \cdot (1 - S \cdot H) \tag{E.19}$$

For the remaining four sextants we end up with similar results. The last thing remaining before we can put it all together and derive a general conversion from HSV to RGB is a method to map from H_{deg} to H. This is done as follows:

$$H' = \frac{H_{\mathrm{deg}}}{60°} \tag{E.20}$$
$$K = \lfloor H' \rfloor \tag{E.21}$$
$$H = H' - K \tag{E.22}$$

where $\lfloor x \rfloor$ means the floor of x, see Appendix B. The final conversion is now given as

$$X = V \cdot (1 - S) \tag{E.23}$$

$$Y = V \cdot (1 - S \cdot H) \tag{E.24}$$

$$Z = V \cdot \big(1 - S \cdot (1 - H)\big) \tag{E.25}$$

$$(R, G, B) = \begin{cases} (V, Z, X), & \text{if } K = 0; \\ (Y, V, X), & \text{if } K = 1; \\ (X, V, Z), & \text{if } K = 2; \\ (X, Y, V), & \text{if } K = 3; \\ (Z, X, V), & \text{if } K = 4; \\ (V, X, Y), & \text{if } K = 5 \end{cases} \tag{E.26}$$

In this appendix the conversions from the RGB color space to the YUV/YC$_b$C$_r$ (and similar) color spaces, and reverse, are derived. That is, we seek a conversion from $[R, G, B]$ to $[Y, X_1, X_2]$, and one from $[Y, X_1, X_2]$ to $[R, G, B]$.

In Sect. 3.3.3 it was stated that the luminance, Y, contains intensity information while X_1 and X_2 code the color information as *weighted difference signals* with respect to Y. That is:

$$Y = W_R \cdot R + W_G \cdot G + W_B \cdot B \quad Y \in [0, 255] \tag{F.1}$$

$$X_1 = \frac{W_{X1}}{1 - W_B} \cdot (B - Y) \quad X_1 \in [-W_{X1} \cdot 255, W_{X1} \cdot 255] \tag{F.2}$$

$$X_2 = \frac{W_{X2}}{1 - W_R} \cdot (R - Y) \quad X_2 \in [-W_{X2} \cdot 255, W_{X2} \cdot 255] \tag{F.3}$$

F.1 The Output of a Colorless Signal

When a colorless signal is present, i.e., $R = G = B$, we have

$$X_1 = W_{X1} \cdot \frac{B - Y}{1 - W_B} = W_{X1} \cdot \frac{B - W_R \cdot R - W_G \cdot G - W_B \cdot B}{1 - W_B} \quad \Rightarrow$$

$$X_1 = W_{X1} \cdot \frac{B - W_R \cdot B - W_G \cdot B - W_B \cdot B}{1 - W_B} \quad \Leftrightarrow$$

$$X_1 = W_{X1} \cdot \frac{B(1 - W_R - W_G - W_B)}{1 - W_B} = 0 \tag{F.4}$$

$$X_2 = W_{X2} \cdot \frac{R - Y}{1 - W_R} = W_{X2} \cdot \frac{R - W_R \cdot R - W_G \cdot G - W_B \cdot B}{1 - W_R} \quad \Rightarrow$$

$$X_2 = W_{X2} \cdot \frac{R - W_R \cdot R - W_G \cdot R - W_B \cdot R}{1 - W_R} \quad \Leftrightarrow$$

$$X_2 = W_{X2} \cdot \frac{R(1 - W_R - W_G - W_B)}{1 - W_R} = 0 \tag{F.5}$$

since $W_R + W_G + W_B = 1$.

T.B. Moeslund, *Introduction to Video and Image Processing*,
Undergraduate Topics in Computer Science,
DOI 10.1007/978-1-4471-2503-7, © Springer-Verlag London Limited 2012

F.2   The Range of X_1 and X_2

The minimum value for X_1 will be when $(R, G, B) = (255, 255, 0)$. We will then have

$$X_1 = W_{X1} \cdot \frac{B - W_R \cdot R - W_G \cdot G - W_B \cdot B}{1 - W_B} \quad \Rightarrow$$

$$X_1 = W_{X1} \cdot \frac{-W_R \cdot 255 - W_G \cdot 255}{1 - W_B} \quad \Rightarrow$$

$$X_1 = W_{X1} \cdot \frac{-255 \cdot (W_R + W_G)}{1 - W_B} \quad \Rightarrow$$

$$X_1 = W_{X1} \cdot \frac{-255(1 - W_B)}{1 - W_B} = -255 \cdot W_{X1} \tag{F.6}$$

since $W_R + W_G + W_B = 1$. The maximum value for X_1 will be when $(R, G, B) = (0, 0, 255)$. We will then have

$$X_1 = W_{X1} \cdot \frac{B - W_R \cdot R - W_G \cdot G - W_B \cdot B}{1 - W_B} \quad \Rightarrow$$

$$X_1 = W_{X1} \cdot \frac{255 - W_B \cdot 255}{1 - W_B} \quad \Rightarrow$$

$$X_1 = W_{X1} \cdot \frac{255(1 - W_B)}{1 - W_B} = 255 \cdot W_{X1} \tag{F.7}$$

So the range for X_1 is $[-W_{X1} \cdot 255, W_{X1} \cdot 255]$. Note that a similar argument exists for X_2.

F.3   YUV

The actual conversion from RGB to YUV is found by inserting the following weight factors into Eqs. F.1, F.2, and F.3: $W_R = 0.299$, $W_G = 0.587$, $W_B = 0.114$, $W_{X1} = 0.436$, and $W_{X2} = 0.615$. To simplify matter Eqs. F.2 and F.3 are first rewritten as

$$X_1 = \frac{W_{X1}}{1 - W_B} \cdot (B - Y) \quad \Rightarrow$$

$$X_1 = W_{X1} \cdot \frac{B - W_R \cdot R - W_G \cdot G - W_B \cdot B}{1 - W_B} \quad \Leftrightarrow$$

$$X_1 = \frac{-W_{X1} \cdot W_R}{1 - W_B} \cdot R + \frac{-W_{X1} \cdot W_G}{1 - W_B} \cdot G + W_{X1} \cdot B \tag{F.8}$$

$$X_2 = \frac{W_{X2}}{1 - W_R} \cdot (R - Y) \quad \Rightarrow$$

$$X_2 = W_{X1} \cdot \frac{R - W_R \cdot R - W_G \cdot G - W_B \cdot B}{1 - W_R} \quad \Leftrightarrow$$

$$X_2 = W_{X2} \cdot R + \frac{-W_{X2} \cdot W_G}{1 - W_R} \cdot G + \frac{-W_{X2} \cdot W_B}{1 - W_R} \cdot B \qquad (F.9)$$

Inserting we get the following conversion from RGB to YUV:

$$\begin{bmatrix} Y \\ U \\ V \end{bmatrix} = \begin{bmatrix} 0.299 & 0.587 & 0.114 \\ -0.147 & -0.289 & 0.436 \\ 0.615 & -0.515 & -0.100 \end{bmatrix} \cdot \begin{bmatrix} R \\ G \\ B \end{bmatrix} \qquad \begin{matrix} Y \in [0, 255] \\ U \in [-111, 111] \\ V \in [-157, 157] \end{matrix}$$

$$(F.10)$$

The conversion from YUV to RGB is found by rearranging Eqs. F.1, F.2, and F.3 and inserting the weight factors as above. The equations for R and B follow trivially by rearranging Eqs. F.2 and F.3, respectively:

$$R = Y + X_2 \cdot \frac{1 - W_R}{W_{X2}} \qquad (F.11)$$

$$B = Y + X_1 \cdot \frac{1 - W_B}{W_{X1}} \qquad (F.12)$$

The equation for G is derived by inserting Eqs. F.11 and F.12 into F.1 and rearranging:

$$Y = W_R \cdot \left(Y + X_2 \cdot \frac{1 - W_R}{W_{X2}}\right) + W_G \cdot G + W_B \cdot \left(Y + X_1 \cdot \frac{1 - W_B}{W_{X1}}\right) \quad \Leftrightarrow$$

$$G = \frac{Y \cdot (1 - W_R - W_B)}{W_G} - \frac{X_1 \cdot W_B \cdot \frac{1-W_B}{W_{X1}}}{W_G} - \frac{X_2 \cdot W_R \cdot \frac{1-W_R}{W_{X2}}}{W_G} \quad \Leftrightarrow$$

$$G = Y - X_1 \cdot \frac{W_B \cdot (1 - W_B)}{W_{X1} \cdot W_G} - X_2 \cdot \frac{W_R \cdot (1 - W_R)}{W_{X2} \cdot W_G} \qquad (F.13)$$

Inserting the weights for YUV yields the following conversion from YUV to RGB:

$$\begin{bmatrix} R \\ G \\ B \end{bmatrix} = \begin{bmatrix} 1.000 & 0.000 & 1.140 \\ 1.000 & -0.395 & -0.581 \\ 1.000 & 2.032 & 0.000 \end{bmatrix} \cdot \begin{bmatrix} Y \\ U \\ V \end{bmatrix} \qquad \begin{matrix} R \in [0, 255] \\ G \in [0, 255] \\ B \in [0, 255] \end{matrix} \qquad (F.14)$$

F.4 YC_bC_r

The conversion from RGB to YC_bC_r is found by inserting the following weights into Eqs. F.1, F.8, and F.9: $W_R = 0.299$, $W_G = 0.587$, $W_B = 0.114$, $W_{X1} = 0.5$, and $W_{X2} = 0.5$

$$\begin{bmatrix} Y \\ C_b \\ C_r \end{bmatrix} = \begin{bmatrix} 0.299 & 0.587 & 0.114 \\ -0.169 & -0.331 & 0.500 \\ 0.500 & -0.419 & -0.081 \end{bmatrix} \cdot \begin{bmatrix} R \\ G \\ B \end{bmatrix} + \begin{bmatrix} 0 \\ 128 \\ 128 \end{bmatrix} \qquad \begin{matrix} Y \in [0, 255] \\ C_b \in [0, 255] \\ C_r \in [0, 255] \end{matrix}$$

$$(F.15)$$

The conversion from YC$_b$C$_r$ to RGB is found by inserting the same weights into Eqs. F.11, F.12, and F.13:

$$
\begin{bmatrix} R \\ G \\ B \end{bmatrix} = \begin{bmatrix} 1.000 & 0.000 & 1.403 \\ 1.000 & -0.344 & -0.714 \\ 1.000 & 1.773 & 0.000 \end{bmatrix} \cdot \begin{bmatrix} Y \\ C_b - 128 \\ C_r - 128 \end{bmatrix} \quad \begin{matrix} R \in [0, 255] \\ G \in [0, 255] \\ B \in [0, 255] \end{matrix}
$$

$$(F.16)$$

Note that 128 is added/subtracted in order to bring the values into the range [0, 255].

References

1. http://fcam.garage.maemo.org/
2. Barrow, H.G., Tenenbaum, J.M., Bolles, R.C., Wolf, H.C.: Parametric correspondence and chamfer matching: two new techniques for image matching. In: 5th International Joint Conference on Artificial Intelligence (1977)
3. Boisen, U., Hansen, A.J., Knudsen, L., Pedersen, S.L.: iFloor—an interactive floor in an educational environment. Technical report, Department of Media Technology, Aalborg University, Denmark (2009)
4. Bowmaker, J.K., Dartnall, H.J.A.: Visual pigments of rods and cones in a human retina. J. Physiol. **298**, 501–511 (1980)
5. Canny, J.: A computational approach to edge detection. IEEE Trans. Pattern Anal. Mach. Intell. **8**(6), 679–698 (1986)
6. Casado, I.H., Holte, M.B., Moeslund, T.B., Gonzalez, J.: Detection and removal of chromatic moving shadows in surveillance scenarios. In: International Conference on Computer Vision, Kyoto, Japan, October 2009
7. Dougherty, E.R., Lotufo, R.A.: Hands-on Morphological Image Processing. Tutorial Texts in Optical Engineering, vol. TT59, SPIE Press, Bellingham (2003).
8. Duda, R.O., Hart, P.E., Stork, D.G.: Pattern Classification, 2nd edn. Wiley Interscience, New York (2001).
9. Elgammal, A.: Figure-ground segmentation—pixel-based. In: Moeslund, T.B., Hilton, A., Kruger, V., Sigal, L. (eds.) Visual Analysis of Humans—Looking at People. Springer, Berlin (2011). 978-0-85729-996-3
10. Gonzalez, R.C., Woods, R.E.: Digital Image Processing, 3rd edn. Prentice Hall, New York (2008).
11. Isard, M., Blake, A.: CONDENSATION—conditional density propagation for visual tracking. Int. J. Comput. Vis. **29**(1), 5–28 (1998)
12. Kim, K., Chalidabhongse, T.H., Harwood, D., Davis, L.: Real-time foreground-background segmentation using codebook model. Real-Time Imaging **11**(3), 167–256 (2005)
13. Lowe, D.G.: Distinctive image features from scale-invariant keypoints. Int. J. Comput. Vis. **60**(2), 91–110 (2004)
14. Otsu, N.: A threshold selection method from gray-level histograms. IEEE Trans. Syst. Man Cybern. **9**(1), 62–66 (1979)
15. Prati, A., Mikic, I., Trivedi, M.M., Cucchiara, R.: Detecting moving shadows: algorithms and evaluation. IEEE Trans. Pattern Anal. Mach. Intell. **25**(7), 918–923 (2003)
16. Shi, J., Tomasi, C.: Good features to track. In: IEEE Conference on Computer Vision and Pattern Recognition, Seattle, Washington, USA, June 1994
17. Shi, Y.Q., Sun, H.: Image and Video Compression for Multimedia for Engineering: Fundamentals, Algorithms, and Standards. CRC Press, Boca Raton (2000).
18. Stauffer, C., Grimson, W.E.L.: Adaptive background mixture models for real-time tracking. In: IEEE Conference on Computer Vision and Pattern Recognition, Ft. Collins, CO, USA, June 1999
19. Welch, G., Bishop, G.: An introduction to the Kalman filter. Technical Report TR 95-041, Department of Computer Science, University of North Carolina at Chapel Hill (2006)

20. Zhao, Q., Tao, H.: Object tracking using color correlogram. In: IEEE International Workshop on Visual Surveillance and Performance Evaluation of Tracking and Surveillance, Breckenridge, Colorado, USA, January 2005

Index

A

Absolute value, 191
    Programming, 191
Achromatic color, **26**, 40
Acquisition
    Image, **7**, 171, 180
    Video, 117
Additive colors, 27
Alpha blending, **65**, 166
Alpha-channel, 66
Analog-to-digital converter, 15, 17
Aperture, **14**, 19
Artificial intelligence, 114
Automatic gain control, 15

B

Background subtraction, **120**, 126
Backward mapping, **146**, 161, 162
Bayer pattern, 28
Binary image, 55
Binary Large Object, *see* BLOB
Binary numbers, 187
Binary to decimal, 188
Bit, 187
BLOB, **103**, 175, 182, 184, 185
    Analysis, 4, **103**
    Classification, **110**, 113
    Extraction, **103**
    Feature, *see* Feature
Blooming, 19
Border problem, **74**, 79, 94
Brightness, 25, 40, **43**, 60
Butterfly effect, 176
Byte, 187

C

Calibration, 173, **203**
Camera calibration, 152
Chamfer matching, 88
Chroma-keying, 68
Chromaticity, 136

Chromaticity plane, 32
Classification, 127, 182, *see also* BLOB
    classification
    Box classifier, 110
    Decision region, 110
    Mahalanobis distance classifier, 113
    Statistical classifier, 112
    Weighted Euclidean distance, 112
Closing, 58, **97**, 122, 182
Color channels, 48, 50
Color conversion
    HSI to RGB, 37, 208
    HSV to RGB, 38, 214
    RGB to gray-scale, **30**, 39, 181
    RGB to HSI, 36, 205
    RGB to HSV, 37, 211
    RGB to rgI, 33
        Programming, 33
    RGB to YCbCr, 40, 219
    RGB to YUV, 39, 219
    rgI to RGB, 33
        Programming, 33
    YCbCr to RGB, 40, 220
    YUV to RGB, 40, 219
Color correlogram, 137
Color image, 25
Color representation
    HSI, **36**, 69, 201
    HSV, 37
    Normalized RGB, 32
    RGB, **27**, 158, 181
    rgI, 33
    YCbCr, **38**, 118
    YUV, 38
Color thresholding, **57**, 68, 201
Compression, 117
    Bandwidth, 119
    Blocking artifacts, 119
    Entropy coding, 118
Computer vision, 2
Condensation algorithm, 137

T.B. Moeslund, *Introduction to Video and Image Processing*,
Undergraduate Topics in Computer Science,
DOI 10.1007/978-1-4471-2503-7, © Springer-Verlag London Limited 2012